CHRISTINA ROSSETTI

VICTORIAN LITERATURE AND CULTURE SERIES

Jerome J. McGann and Herbert Tucker, Editors

CHRISTINA ROSSETTI

The Patience of Style

Constance W. Hassett

UNIVERSITY OF VIRGINIA PRESS

CHARLOTTESVILLE AND LONDON

University of Virginia Press

© 2005 by the Rector and Visitors of the University of Virginia

All rights reserved

Printed in the United States of America on acid-free paper

First published 2005

9 8 7 6 5 4 3 2 1

LIBRARY OF CONGRESS CATALOGING-IN-PUBLICATION DATA

Hassett, Constance W., 1943 –

   Christina Rossetti : the patience of style / Constance W. Hassett.

     p.   cm. — (Victorian literature and culture series)

   Includes bibliographical references and index.

   ISBN 0-8139-2339-5 (Cloth : alk. paper)

    1. Rossetti, Christina Georgina, 1830 –1894 — Criticism and interpretation.

2. Women and literature — England — History — 19th century.   I. Title.

II. Series.

PR5238.H375   2005

821'.8 — dc22

                                      2004022676

For Jim, of course

Contents

Acknowledgments

Christina Rossetti: The Patience of Style has accumulated so many debts to friends and colleagues it would take Rossetti's own skill to acknowledge each one properly. I take refuge in an unadorned litany, hoping that those who admire, write about, teach, and even perform Rossetti's poetry, those who have inspired, discussed, and critiqued *The Patience of Style,* will accept these brief thanks and believe that my deepest gratitude for their encouragement is "certain tho' unsaid": Frank Boyle, Margaret Carr, Elizabeth Danson, Mary Erler, Christopher Gogwilt, Kathryn M. Heleniak, John Mahoney, John Maynard, Philip Sicker, Thelma Pearson Walter, Carolyn Williams, Jocelyn Wogan-Brown.

Specific thanks must go to Cathie Brettschneider, Humanities Editor, at University of Virginia Press for her strong interest in Christina Rossetti and her expeditiousness, to the anonymous parties in-house and out for their meticulously generous reading of the manuscript, and to Jerome J. McGann and Herbert Tucker, editors of the Victorian Literature and Culture Series, for their cordial welcome to a manuscript long in the making. I am grateful, too, to Colleen R. Clark for her lynx-eyed assistance with the manuscript, to Martin White for his expertise in preparing the index, and to Mark Mones for his charm and patience in seeing the book through production.

The dedication page acknowledges the poet James Richardson, author most recently of *Interglacial: New and Selected Poems and Aphorisms,* sometime Victorian scholar, and my spouse.

This book was begun and eventually completed during sabbatical leaves from Fordham University. I would like to thank the Faculty Research Council for unencumbered time.

Rossetti's poetry is from Rebecca W. Crump's edition; materials from the third volume are reprinted by permission of Louisiana State University Press from *The Complete Poems of Christina Rossetti: A Variorum Edition,* vol. 3, edited by Rebecca W. Crump, © 1990 by Louisiana State University Press.

Selected extracts from the poetry of Letitia Landon are reprinted from *Letitia Elizabeth Landon: Selected Writings,* edited by Jerome McGann and Daniel Riess, Broadview Press, © 1997 by Jerome McGann and Daniel Riess.

Abbreviations

References to the works listed below are made within the text. Typically, these references include, in addition to the abbreviated title, the volume number (if any) and page number from which the specific quotation or reference is drawn. For longer poems or for those discussed extensively in the text, the full page range for the poem is given at first citation only, followed by line numbers for specific quotations; subsequent citations to the poem include line numbers only. For the sonnet sequences, such as *Monna Innominata* and *Later Life,* only the title abbreviation and the number of the sonnet or division are included, although in some instances line numbers are cited as well.

Examples:

LDGR, 1:1 = *Letters of Dante Gabriel Rossetti,* vol. 1, p. 1
CP, 1:11–26; 115, 173–174 = *Complete Poems,* vol. 1, pp. 11–26, lines 115 and 173–74
MI 4 = *Monna Innominata,* sonnet 4
C 72; 10 = *Canzoniere,* poem 72, line 10

AT	Alfred Tennyson, *Tennyson: A Selected Edition,* ed. Christopher Ricks. London: Longman, 1989.
EBB	Elizabeth Barrett Browning, *The Poetical Works of Elizabeth Barrett Browning,* with intro. by Ruth M. Adams. Boston: Houghton Mifflin, 1974.
C	*Petrarch: The Canzoniere; or, Rerum vulgarium fragmenta,* trans. Mark Musa. Bloomington: Indiana Univ. Press, 1996.

CGRFL *The Family Letters of Christina Georgina Rossetti,* ed. William Michael Rossetti. London: Brown, 1908.

CP Christina Rossetti, *The Complete Poems of Christina Rossetti: A Variorum Edition,* ed. Rebecca W. Crump, 3 vols. Baton Rouge: Louisiana State Univ. Press, 1979–90.

FD Christina G. Rossetti, *The Face of the Deep: A Devotional Commentary on the Apocalypse.* London: Society for Promoting Christian Knowledge, 1892.

Hemans *Felicia Hemans: Selected Poems, Letters, Reception Materials,* ed. Susan J. Wolfson. Princeton, N.J.: Princeton Univ. Press, 2000.

HL *The House of Life,* in *The Pre-Raphaelites and Their Circle,* ed. Cecil Y. Lang, 2nd ed. Chicago: Univ. of Chicago Press, 1975, 79–129.

Keats John Keats, *Complete Poems and Selected Letters of John Keats,* with intro. by Edward Hirsch. New York: Modern Library, 2001.

Landon *Letitia Elizabeth Landon: Selected Writings,* ed. Jerome McGann and Daniel Riess. Peterborough, Ontario: Broadview, 1997.

L *The Letters of Christina Rossetti,* ed. Antony H. Harrison, 4 vols. Charlottesville: Univ. Press of Virginia, 1997–2004.

LL *Later Life,* in *The Complete Poems of Christina Rossetti: A Variorum Edition,* ed. Rebecca W. Crump, vol. 2. Baton Rouge: Louisiana State Univ. Press, 1986, 138–50.

LDGR *Letters of Dante Gabriel Rossetti,* ed. Oswald Doughty and John Robert Wahl, 4 vols. Oxford: Clarendon, 1965–67.

MI *Monna Innominata,* in *The Complete Poems of Christina Rossetti: A Variorum Edition,* ed. Rebecca W. Crump, vol. 2. Baton Rouge: Louisiana State Univ. Press, 1986, 86–93.

NRNT *Nursery Rhymes and Nursery Tales of England,* ed. James Orchard Halliwell, 5th ed. London, 1855.

P Christina Rossetti, *Selected Prose of Christina Rossetti,* ed. David S. Kent and P. G. Stanwood. New York: St. Martin's, 1998.

PW Christina Rossetti, *Christina Georgina Rossetti: The Poetical Works,* ed. William Michael Rossetti. 1906; New York: Olms, 1970.

PWH *The Poetical Works of Mrs. Felicia Hemans,* ed. William Michael Rossetti. Boston, 1856.

SP   *Sonnets from the Portuguese,* in *A Variorum Edition of Elizabeth*
            Barrett Browning's "Sonnets from the Portuguese," ed. Miroslava
            Wein Dow. Troy, N. Y.: Whitston, 1980.

CHRISTINA ROSSETTI

Introduction

THE PHRASE "patience of style" takes deliberate advantage of the ambiguity of "of," letting it assert, first of all, that Rossetti's poetic style *is* patient. By "patience" I mean something like the quality that readers have also called "reticence" or "reserve" because it marshals such tendencies of theme and form as muteness, understatement, gently restrained rhythm, and rhymed stanzaic shape. The style is patient with itself, trusting its own subtleties of manner to achieve resonance and allowing inexplicitness to do its evocative work: poems plead their inability to say what they know—"I cannot tell you how it was"—while details converge around some mystery (*CP,* 1:51). Gay banter protects an unguessed secret, or sullenness yields ever-so-minimally to a muttering of words of consent, "I do not deprecate" (*CP,* 1:153−54; 1:68). One might almost say that silence itself is Rossetti's medium, for she never forgets either the pressure of wordless inner turmoil or its opposite, the flattened diffidence that, with patience, turns quietly articulate. The most characteristic moments in her poetry resonate with what goes unsaid, or, if I may borrow a line from Philip Larkin, who counted himself an admirer of hers, they sound "like something almost being said," where the "almost" is most Rossettian.[1]

Second, while style itself is the topic, so too is Rossetti's own patience *with* style, with the varieties and possibilities "of" style. Rossetti listens attentively all her life to the poetry of others, is always in conversation with work she admires, work less muted than hers and therefore a stimulus to her own reserve. While still in her teens she becomes fascinated by the obstacles to romance in the "ancient" ballads collected by Bishop Percy; in her twenties she is stirred by the fervent melancholy of her immediate precursor Letitia Landon; and later she is challenged by the lyric tradition's great founder, borrowing lines from Petrarch's *Canzoniere* to preface each sonnet in her own sequence about an impossible love. Some of her finest poems scrutinize their own style as well, often by changing texture or folding in another kind of poetry altogether. A narrative may stop for the sake of a lyric, implying that another genre provides access to a desired insight, or a reticent song may incorporate a song that is sensuous, expansive, and self-revealing. Rossetti's poems often seem to be in patient conversation with themselves, considering their aesthetic options.

Rossetti's attention to her own and others' work was meticulous, and her early admirers, however impressionistic their appreciation of her skill, were inclined to call her poems "perfect." These contemporary fans, occasionally cited in the following pages for their loyal discernment, stayed the course with her, memorizing, singing, illustrating, and anthologizing poems from *Goblin Market* (particularly "A Birthday," about which more in a moment), *The Prince's Progress,* and *A Pageant.* Their whole-hearted fondness extended to the *Sing-Song* volume of nursery rhymes for children, and made her last collection, the devotional *Verses* (1893), a best-seller, with four printings in the first year of its publication. But one of these admirers, her friend Edmund Gosse, offered praise that has since been turned against her. While rightly approving some of her earliest work, he claimed that "at the age of twenty her style as a poet was completely formed." His mild exaggeration has become aligned with a corollary notion that Rossetti's style did not evolve and, worse still, that she persisted monotonously on "when all her inspiration had fled or flagged." Sandra Gilbert has allowed herself to "wonder what kind of verse Rossetti would have written if she had not defined her own artistic pride as wicked 'vanity.'"[2]

Rossetti, to put the matter another way, is supposed to have lacked ambition. One of the aims of the present study is to correct this serious misimpression by taking a close look at her full career. Every reader knows that at the outset Rossetti writes of the danger lurking in a goblin-infested glen, but few seem aware that at the very end she confronts the terrifying woes envisioned by John of Patmos. I hope, in the final chapter, to interest the reader in Rossetti's resistant reading of the Apocalypse, in the way she attempts, for example, to mitigate the devastation attendant on the opening of the seventh seal with a tender elegy on the pallor of the "morning that is scarcely morn" (*CP,* 2:252). The late, devotional poems show that Rossetti stayed a poet by staying interested in the perils of the human condition, including those threatened in a hectoring canonical text. It is perhaps not an exaggeration to say that the patience of her ambition led Rossetti from Bishop Percy through Petrarch to John the apocalyptist.

Third, the subtitle glances at the patience Rossetti asks of her reader. Fortunately, for my purposes, the literary criticism of recent years, even in the wake of older formalisms, offers compelling examples of how to proceed. In every literary period, there are scholars who resist the temptation to "skim along the plain" (as Pope once put it) of an impatient argument, and willingly accommodate the text at whatever pace it requires—whether to examine the impact of a medial caesura or the visibility of a pun. I cite here a few most relevant to my project.

I turn gratefully, for example, to Heather Dubrow's discussion of a "seemingly unremarkable" poem by Thomas Watson in the opening pages of *Echoes of Desire,* her splendid study of English Petrarchism. Confident in her choice, Dubrow lavishes rewarding care on a poem that has never been a canonical favorite: indeed, "In all this world I thinke none lov's but I," a dialogue between Echo and Author, was not among the excerpts from *Hecatompathia* in Hyder E. Rollins and Herschel Baker's vast compendium *The Renaissance in England* (1954); and Watson himself has been excised entirely from the massive early modern section of the *Longman Anthology of British Literature* (2003). But in three deft pages, while showing how Watson's Echo "finesses" each of the male Author's questions, Dubrow demonstrates that the "ostensibly powerless" female voice challenges "the authority of Petrarchan love poetry." Dubrow, in other words, opens up the broader question of Watson's engagement with the tradition (his repetitions) by examining the precise form of his speakers' "closely-matched and often indeterminate" struggle. What is perhaps most illuminating in Dubrow's method is that she attends not simply to the poem's tone and imagery but to its momentum. I will have much to say later about Rossetti's own dialogue with Petrarchism. What I wish to emphasize here is Dubrow's implicit but crucial point about the relevance of style: if we wish to understand a poem as a response to an issue, we must treat it not only as a statement but as an action; what it says is inseparable from how it moves.[3]

Equally relevant, and historically nearer, is Lawrence Lipking's monumental study *Abandoned Women and Poetic Tradition,* with its tour de force chapter on Sappho's eighteenth-century reputation and seven versions of the Second Ode. Lipking's refined readings describe the emotional curve and the corresponding aesthetic motive in each, whether it be the impulse to balance a line (Smollet provides symmetrical negatives in "Unheard I mourn, unknown I sigh"), to invent a detail (Robinson supplies a "neglected" lyre), or to match the original rhythm (Foscolo "restores the Sapphic measure"). Among Lipking's most stunning successes is his recovery of the Ambrose Philips translation—touted by Joseph Addison in the *Spectator*—which set off a two-century-long craze that eventually reached the teenaged Christina Rossetti and the mature Swinburne. Undaunted by the necessary admission that this once-popular poem sounds "namby-pamby to modern ears," Lipking engages so sensitively with the text that its passionate tones become as fresh to him as they assuredly were to Philips, thereby persuading us that this "gentle translation," with its "crucial placement" of "highly suggestive" verbs, does indeed preserve the "sexual rhythm" of the Sapphic original. Lipking's gorgeous precision retrieves these poems from the blur of period style. His implicit promise is that perceived uniformity is a difficulty a patient ear for style can solve. Rossetti is a greater poet than any Lipking considers, and her "period" is less lost to us than Philips's. She defined herself, in any case, subtly in opposition to it: we are in no danger of losing her to "the Victorians." But patient reading may rescue the poems of Rossetti from the blur of "Rossetti."[4]

And lastly, there is Stephen Booth's genial testament in *Precious Nonsense* to the appeal of the nursery rhyme "Little Boy Blue" and his dazzling riff on the "monumentally clumsy" refrain of "Home on the Range":

> Oh give me a home where the buffalo roam,
> Where the deer and the antelope play;
> Where seldom is heard a discouraging word
> And the skies are not cloudy all day.

Booth's toying with the mute pun of "heard" and "herd," or, as he puts it, "the pertinence of the sound of the word 'heard'" in a stanza about "buffalo, deer, and antelope," is too hilariously subtle for reprise here except to note that it admirably confirms his book's basic tenet: the seemingly effortless and casual "process of perceiving" any poem "is vastly more eventful than its paraphrasable substance implies." This is something to keep in mind with Rossetti's *Sing-Song* nursery rhymes, but also and especially with those humbly transparent major lyrics that seem to defy commentary. Inspired by the precedent of these three critics (and others too numerous for inclusion here), an admirer of Rossetti comes to believe that even a poem like the apparently simple and monologically lyrical "A Birthday" requires and will repay close scrutiny. The challenge, here, is to break the appreciative silence or bored condescension that has been awarded to a "universal favorite" and to do so by patiently considering what its style and momentum invite us so "effortlessly" to enjoy.[5]

All who are moved to comment on "A Birthday" attest to its ebullience, to the "ringing melody" that, in the words of one Victorian booster, expresses the "healthy happiness . . . of a joyful young heart." As for the poem's reception, the record is clear: its appearance in the April issue of *Macmillan's Magazine* (1861) helped launch Rossetti's career. "Uphill" had already appeared in February and earned the publisher congratulations "on having got a poet at last," which he conveyed to Dante Gabriel Rossetti, who eagerly passed the news to his sister (*LDGR,* 2:389–90). "An Apple-Gathering" would appear in August, followed soon by Macmillan's decision to bring out *Goblin Market and Other Poems* (1862). Another kind of response is documented by Lorraine Janzen Kooistra, whose beautiful (in all senses) study *Christina Rossetti and Illustration* confirms the poem's appeal to the artists in the Pre-Raphaelite circle: Arthur Hughes's *The Dove* is based on Rossetti's poem, an inspiration he acknowledged at exhibition time by having it inscribed "at full length" on the frame. The highlight of the poem's reception history comes in Virginia Woolf's essay "I Am Christina Rossetti," written for the centenary of Rossetti's birth. Quoting the poem from memory, Woolf predicts that it will be sung by "remote posterity." Woolf, it should be noted, is referring to actual singing, for the poem became a performance piece as soon as it appeared, a form of tribute that frankly pleased its author: "How delightful, my song at Traventi's concert; nicely set too, as Maria reports" (*L,* 1:277).[6]

And indeed, "remote posterity" remains impressed with "A Birthday." The poem's ardent conclusion, "the birthday of my life / Is come, my love is come to me," has tempted many to suppose, perhaps inevitably, that an actual lover inspired it. Early on, Lona Mosk Packer "identified" him as William Bell Scott. Thinking along slightly modified lines, Jan Marsh suspects some slighter amorousness, some "unexpected intimation of romance," and she nominates the painter John Brett. Others, knowing how readily Rossetti's poetry folds the sacred into the profane, assume that the lyric marks a privately significant day in its author's spiritual life. For these readers, an experience of the divine is what occasions the "birthday," and the poem is said to be "a love lyric to Christ the Saviour." Recently, Alison Chapman has offered a forceful protest against biographical and "lyric-confessional" readings. In *The Afterlife of Christina Rossetti,* she traces the assumption that Rossetti "directly transcribes personal experience" to William Michael Rossetti, whose notes to the 1904 edition of *The Poetical Works* are so often "at pains to give the poetry a relation to an actual event." Chapman observes, however, that William allows at least for the possibility that "A Birthday" may be, in his words, "a mere piece of poetic composition, not testifying to any corresponding emotion of its author at the time," though he himself is "hardly prepared to think that." And so, Chapman's salutary effort to clear the biographical air returns us to the poem.[7]

Consider the first stanza:

> My heart is like a singing bird
>   Whose nest is in a watered shoot;
> My heart is like an apple tree
>   Whose boughs are bent with thickset fruit;
> My heart is like a rainbow shell
>   That paddles in a halcyon sea;
> My heart is gladder than all these
>   Because my love is come to me.   (*CP,* 1:36)

Much can be said about this string of similes, beyond noting that conspicuous anaphora is a convention of religious litanies and that it lends a gently reverent quality to the speaker's listing of what are, in fact, elements from the natural world. We might attend to each, noting first of all that the "singing bird / Whose nest is in a watered shoot" could have been taken right out of the English countryside in spring, the word "shoot" referring to new growth, while the phrase "watered shoot" suggests a nesting place beside a stream or even a waterfall. A quick check in Thomas Bewick's *A History of British Birds* confirms that the sedge warbler "frequents the sides of rivers and boggy places, where reeds and sedges grow, and builds there," and that it "sings night and day, during the breeding time." Another likely candidate is the ring ouzel, a bird whose melody is mimed in one of Tennyson's English Idyls: "The mellow ouzel fluted in the elm." The point here is that Rossetti's image quite naturally connotes youthful newness, an unexotic if not quite specifically English freshness. So pleasing an image probably beguiles most readers into ignoring the slight improbability of locating the nest in "a" shoot; anyone who notices the precariousness of this nesting arrangement might conclude that Rossetti's quaintly singular noun is determined (ineptly?) by the need to rhyme with "fruit." (This rhyme pair will come up again in the discussion of stanza 2.) The second image, the "apple tree / Whose boughs are bent with thickset fruit," is as visually gratifying as it is acoustically mouth-filling. The mind's eye summons up the Keatsian "season" of "mellow fruitfulness" that will "bend with apples the moss'd cottage-trees" (*Keats*, 249). So the discrete similes turn out, on close reading, to be related: the springtime promise of the first is realized in the mid-to-late-summer ripeness of the second. The third item, the "rainbow shell / That paddles in a halcyon sea," opens up literally new territory. On her annual seaside holiday, Rossetti enjoyed gathering whatever shells were "quaint with curve, or spot, or spike" (*CP*, 1 : 191). Her odd notion that a marine crea-ture "paddles" is probably a genuine mistake, if not a whimsical semantic transfer from the shell collector who may properly be said, according to the *Oxford English Dictionary*, to paddle or wade in shallow water for "play or pleasure." In either case, the word's artlessness anticipates the quality of its pleasing half-rhyme with the "gladder" heart. The "halcyon sea" conjures up the geographically more distant Sicilian coast where, accord-ing to ancient legend, the "halcyon" or kingfisher calmed the waters of the winter solstice. The heart's joy is thus deepened by association with holi-days and "halcyon days," days that are calm, happy, golden, even affluent.[8]

It turns out, then, that Rossetti's lyric similes sweep from near to far: from the native land bird's watery nesting place to the sea beyond Gibral-tar and the halcyon's mythical habitat. And of course, as Ovid tells it, the halcyon takes its name from the loving woman—the widowed Alcyone—whose metamorphosis turned anguish into peace. This little world's worth of allusion has been gathered for the sake of a blithe announcement—"my love is come to me"—and the reader comes away with the impression of both the stanza's and the speaker's sweet naiveté.

As it happens, however, extreme simplicity is not likely to sustain in-terest for more than a few lines. Enough is enough, and at the brink of the second stanza, the experienced reader may be excused for faintly dreading more of the same. The arrangement of similes like beads on a string and the determinedly perfect rhymes have already come perilously close to sounding like a beginning poet's faux pas—and that, I submit, is part of this poem's charm. The lyric speaker is in the throes of an entirely new kind of joy; unpracticed in its telling, she has yet to find an idiom adequate to the fervor that sets her "heart" aglow. Rossetti, after all, is shrewder than her speaker and has set the stage for the surprise of the second stanza:

> Raise me a dais of silk and down;
>   Hang it with vair and purple dyes;
> Carve it in doves and pomegranates,
>   And peacocks with a hundred eyes;
> Work it in gold and silver grapes,
>   In leaves and silver fleurs-de-lys;
> Because the birthday of my life
>   Is come, my love is come to me.

The speaker now breaks into a new and fully exultant style. Unconstrained by the first stanza's formal patterns, she grandly extends one image through most of the second while indulging in apostrophe, that most demanding of rhetorical modes, and issuing egotistical commands. Her phantom addressee, an artisan of rare skill (and perhaps a figure for the poet herself) is instructed to "raise" an attention-focusing "dais," to adorn it with opulent textiles, and to incise, emboss, and embroider it with rich colors. The details are medieval (the "dais" was that portion of the hall reserved for aristocrats, and "vair" a luxury fur), biblical (the legendary Solomon had a "pomegranate" orchard), and regal (Persia's fabled golden throne was flanked by jeweled "peacock" tails, and "fleurs-de-lys" were emblems of the French monarchy). The details come in bountiful multiples: unlike the first stanza's discrete listing of bird (and shoot) and tree and shell, the second counts "a hundred eyes" and a host of "doves" and "peacocks." The hint of affluence in the first stanza's "halcyon" is subtly confirmed when the feathers that protect a bird's body and nest reappear in the decorative texture of "silk and down."

Such pomp provides the objective correlative to the self-centered gloriousness of new love. As everyone knows, and as Catherine Belsey's *Desire: Love Stories in Western Culture* reminds us, reciprocated passion is primarily about ME, the utter change in ME, the thrilling importance of ME. It is this profound transformation in status that Rossetti's poem reports and also mimes by its own momentum. The first stanza's simple surface provides the ground, so to speak, for her speaker's exhilarated leap into imperious and even imperial self-celebration in the second. Even the rhymes participate in the newly hyperbolic glee; instead of the predictable match of "sea" and "me," Rossetti now enlists her pronoun in an utterly extravagant, regally bilingual partnership with "fleurs-de-lys." If proof were needed that Rossetti "could" have found substantively flawless rhymes for her opening stanza, the bravura acoustics of the second make the case. Even the supplemental chiming of "pom<u>gr</u>anate<u>s</u>" and "<u>gr</u>ape<u>s</u>" contributes to the impression of jubilant excess.[9]

It would be hard to deny that "A Birthday" is about as lyrical as a lyric poem can get, yet what we are seeing is that it is far from monological. It has two subtly different voices in its two stanzas, and their contrast implies at least a mutual commentary, and perhaps a story and an ambition. The first stanza, fresher and more disconnected, playfully seeks equivalents for an emotion it seems surprised by. The second, more commanding and coherent, more "poetic" perhaps, or even more Romantic, extends the *instant* of feeling into something that can be contemplated, possessed, given a texture or narrative of feeling—the germ of a love story. That Rossetti shades this transition toward the imperial, the self-involved, and what Hopkins sometimes called the Parnassian, implies that her ambition, or at least her instinct, in this poem is something like a critique of ambition.[10]

It is worth mentioning that "A Birthday" attracted the compliment of a superlative parody, that is to say, an imitation that admires Rossetti's original by carefully filling its "prescribed" form with inappropriately silly subject matter, viz., pawned garments, male carousing, and elements of domestic farce. Whoever the anonymous author may be, he is a good critic, for not only does he match Rossetti's syntax and pun on her rhymes (her "halcyon sea" becomes his "upper C" and her fabric "dyes" becomes his synonym for perishing), he expertly preserves her second stanza's acoustic extravagance by outlandishly topping it.

"An Unexpected Pleasure"
(After Christina G. Rossetti)

My heart is like one asked to dine
    Whose evening dress is up the spout;
My heart is like a man would be
    Whose raging tooth is half pulled out.

My heart is like a howling swell
   Who boggles on his upper C;
My heart is madder than all these—
   My wife's mamma has come to tea.

Raise me a bump upon my crown,
   Bang it till green in purple dies;
Feed me on bombs and fulminates,
   And turncocks of a medium size.
Work me a suit in crimson apes
   And sky-blue beetles on the spree;
Because the mother of my wife
   Has come—and means to stay with me.   (*PW,* 481)

Rossetti, who included her own parodies in *Maude,* must have been delighted to hear her "pomegranates" and "fleurs-de-lys" so inventively matched with chemical "fulminates" and coleopteran creatures "on the spree." Much could be said about how "An Unexpected Pleasure" manipulates the Victorian gender code or substitutes analogy for simile, but here we need only attend to the speaker's precise identification of the party causing his outburst and realize how much *more* of a narrative or of future discord the arrival of "the mother of [his] wife" compels us to imagine. In comparison, Rossetti's conclusion—"the birthday of my life / Is come, my love is come to me"—is a model of decorous evasion. The lovely insistence of its twice-repeated verb redirects attention from the beloved to the transport of ecstasy that is the poem itself. Chary of details about this joy-bringing individual, the poem keeps the speaker's uninhibited self-delight in full view. In the throes of fulfilled desire, she declares this "the birthday of my life" and gives credence to the belief that simple rapture provides "the foundation of a lifetime of happiness." No wonder Michael Schmidt, in his magisterial *Lives of the Poets,* describes "A Birthday" as "almost cloying" even as he celebrates its having "become embedded deep in the tradition." It strenuously precludes any awareness of the complexity of desiring the desired, admitting not a trace of timidity, resistance, or doubt, not the faintest intimation of bittersweetness. This later knowledge comes, of course, in other poems, for Rossetti understands as well as any modern theorist that desire is fissured, ambivalent, or balked, "always," in Belsey's words, "caught up with prohibition and loss," and so always qualified by its extension into narrative or drama.[11]

The pages that follow attempt to show that Rossetti returns again and again to the promise of happiness embedded in these final lines. The most famous instance is the very next year's masterpiece, "Goblin Market," in which exhilaration turns toxic and passionate yearning becomes so nearly fatal that Rossetti devises a brilliantly controversial ending in order to whisk her heroines off to a pastoral Eden. Only in this never-never-land can she imagine them passing beyond "forms of wanting that cannot be borne to those that," in Jeff Nunokawa's lovely phrase, "can be sustained with élan, even pleasure." There is no such relief for others, however, only lurid dreams for the novice of "The Convent Threshold"; in retreat from her interdicted lover, she is humiliated and literally stifled by her own self-alienating desire (*CP,* 1:61–65). Even the *Sing-Song* nursery rhymes gently probe the mysteries of attraction—a diamond will "catch the world's desire" but the darkly humble flint "holds fire"—while the devotional poems compare the soul's yearning to "a fire of pale desire in incompleteness" and imagine the saint as "wishless in the sanctuary" (*CP,* 2:43, 273, 283). Desire in its many varieties and gradations was regarded by Rossetti as absolutely central to poetry. It is more than a theme, however; the finest Rossettian poem itself stirs desire—desire for the poem, for its completion on the page and the satisfying incompleteness of its lingering in the mind. And it does this not simply by its tone, imagery, or "qualities of content" but, as poet-critic Robert Hass explains, by its overall shape, the momentum that is "the poem's process." I share Hass's equation of the "form of a poem" with "the shape of its understanding" and believe, with him, that "the presence of that shaping constitutes the presence of poetry." Rossetti, for her part, was ceaselessly patient, inventive, and surprising; and for my part, I hope to share my pleasure in discovering how intensely Rossetti lived "in the presence of poetry." [12]

For readers who would like an overview of the chapters to come, the following information is happily provided, though with necessary apologies that, in so brief a space, the account must be more suggestive than discursive.

Chapter 1, "Questions of Desire in *Goblin Market and Other Poems,*" opens by exploring Rossetti's deep interest in the paradoxes of desire and then takes up the bittersweet two-mindedness that energizes her most admired lyrics. The chapter's midsection, "Counterdiscourse," examines some apparently atypical poems, those with sparring antagonists, and

offers a fresh account of the so-called "sister-ballads" that have disconcerted scholars. Here, as in "Goblin Market," Rossetti is seen to probe
the compulsive illogic of desire and, as she creates verbal clashes, to disclose the proximity of contention and inarticulateness. The final portion
of the chapter considers the striking and, for a woman poet, most crucial
feature of Rossetti's art, "The Silences of Poetry." Taking the "Goblin
Market" heroines' agonized and exhilarated wordlessness as indicative
of Rossetti's poetics in general, this section demonstrates that even as
Rossetti exercises the lyric's generic privilege, its fiction of intimate musing, she works resistantly against it, providing somber, taunting, and
giddy displays of muteness. Structured like desire, contradictory in the
pursuit of what it does and does not want to say, Rossettian reticence is
a continuing motive for new poems and new forms.

Chapter 2, "Influence and Restraint: Victorian Women Poets and the
Rossettis," examines Rossettian intertextualities. Beginning with the signally eminent Felicia Hemans, whose importance was mediated, in part,
by William Rossetti's admiring 1856 edition of her *Works,* this chapter also
considers the nearer influence of Letitia Elizabeth Landon (L.E.L.),
whose style in *The Venetian Bracelet* and *The Golden Violet* made her something of a poet's poet to Christina Rossetti, and directs attention to the latter's monologue, "L.E.L.," with its endorsing epigraph from Elizabeth
Barrett Browning and welcome emendations by Dante Gabriel Rossetti.
Taking up the broader issue of joint artistic efforts, "Listening to Herself"
examines the Pre-Raphaelite poets' habit of soliciting revisions and finds
in their collegial practice an alternative to the hierarchical model invoked
by critics who mistrust Gabriel's involvement with *The Prince's Progress
and Other Poems* (1866). His suggestions, the changes and cuts gladly made
by Christina, and the siblings' occasional agreement to disagree are as-
sessed with an eye to aesthetic merit and their implications for Christina's
perceived place among women writers. Gabriel's belated objection to
"The Lowest Room," his notorious complaint that it echoes Barrett
Browning's "falsetto muscularity," and Christina's brief self-defense are
examined for what they reveal of her poetics, viz., the strict aesthetic
economy that is the "primary impulse" of her best work. Her fascination
with the unsaid and with the restrained flow of words is taken up in the
chapter's final section, "'Your Secret Ways': Rossettian Understatement."

Chapter 3, "The Nonsense and Wisdom of *Sing-Song: A Nursery Rhyme
Book,*" looks at Rossetti's collection of 121 original poems for children.

Divided into four sections, this chapter observes, first of all, that Rossetti's mixing of paradoxes, puns, and strange metaphors delights its audience with what theorists like to call the "wildness and shimmering contingency" of language. Then, building on Lucy Rollin's documentation in *Cradle and All* of the traditional nursery rhyme's anthropomorphic investment in birds, the section "On Mayhem and Wisdom" draws attention to the rampant ebullience of Rossetti's many wrens and robins and to the wise skepticism of her paired and contradictory adages. Contrary to the didactic impulse prompting much nineteenth-century poetry for children (witness Jane Taylor's *Rhymes for the Nursery*), Rossetti's volume makes a game of thinking and knowing. The third section, "To Speke of the Wo That Is in Childhood," takes up the fraught issue of lullabies and elegies to argue, with some assistance from Marina Warner and Adam Phillips, that Rossetti's treatment of children's grief is both honest and kind, resisting the (impossible) task of explaining death while acknowledging the severe bewilderment of loss. Lastly, the chapter returns to Rossetti's love of nonsense, noting that she revels in the proximity of logical syntax and surreally disconnected images and that her inventiveness when it comes to special effects with rhythm, rhyme patterning, and stanza shape invites children to play as the author plays with the constitutive elements of her craft.

Chapter 4, "Ambitious Triangles: Rossetti and the Sonnet Tradition," examines Rossetti's great, revisionary sonnet sequences, *Monna Innominata* and *Later Life*. Rossetti's essays on Dante and Petrarch and the prose preface to *Monna Innominata* provide an introduction to the triangular reach of her ambition, a configuration defined by the tradition's magisterial fourteenth-century founders; their "Great" nineteenth-century heir, Elizabeth Barrett Browning; and Christina Rossetti herself. The core of the chapter is devoted to the *Monna Innominata* sonnets, reading them within the frame of their epigraphs from *La divina commedia* and the *Canzoniere* as well as the context of Barrett Browning's *Sonnets from the Portuguese* and Dante Gabriel Rossetti's *The House of Life*. The aim is to identify Rossettian departures from the available myths of love (e.g., her privileging of amnesia over memory, her rejection of tropes of measure, her revision of the immortality topos), the distinctiveness of the selves, feelings, and moments she values, and the ways of a poetics that rejects prevailing assumptions about the sonnet's "arduous fullness." Because Rossetti's second sequence, *Later Life,* has been largely ignored by critics, the final portion of the chapter, subtitled "A Sonnet Sequence for the Aftertimes," takes a close look at these restlessly beautiful poems and finds that the Victorian anthologist Elizabeth Sharp chose well when she reprinted sonnets 6 and 26 with a handful of Rossetti's "essentially characteristic poems" in an anthology titled *Women's Voices*.

Taking Christina Rossetti's response to the untimely death of Dante Gabriel Rossetti as a traumatic point of reference, chapter 5, "Rossetti's Finale: *The Face of the Deep* (1892) and *Verses* (1893)," provides an account of the urgency, spiritual honesty, and consummate skill of the best of the late-life poems. Identifying her strategies of invocation, lamentation, and consolation, the chapter traces Rossetti's overriding concern with wordlessness (a version of the threat facing every poet in the late stages of a career) and her wide range of tones, varying from the masochistic to the beguilingly kind-hearted and the humorously self-satirical. The weaknesses of the weaker poems also come under scrutiny, including the impatience that sometimes produces forced momentum and overdetermined closure. The second half of this chapter offers a comprehensive analysis of *The Face of the Deep,* Rossetti's audacious 500-page commentary on the Apocalypse. Entitled "Brazenness," this section examines Rossetti's recoil from the violence of John's prophecy, her method of close biblical glossing, her avoidance of historical or millenarian interpretation, and, most important, the success of her poetry at reining in the terrifying implications of the canonical text. Finally, the chapter considers Rossetti's decision to liberate her poems by republishing them in the collected *Verses* of 1893 and proposes a reassessment of this neglected volume's contribution to her poetic achievement.

Questions of Desire in *Goblin Market and Other Poems*

FOR THE PAST several decades, studies of Christina Rossetti have customarily admitted she was neglected during much of the twentieth century, and then have hastened to add that a Rossetti revival has been going on for some time. It had already been under way fifteen years when Jerome McGann, writing in 1980, described "the remarkable scholarly effort to recover our contacts" with Rossetti and other "lost" Victorian poets. It was fourteen years later when Antony Harrison, noting eleven more books and eighty articles, celebrated the "extraordinary resurgence" of "Rossetti's reputation" in his introduction to a special issue of *Victorian Poetry.* And when Mary Arseneau presented the "emergent Christina Rossetti" in a recent volume of essays by many hands, she wisely declined to count the ways in which this great poet's life and art have been studied. Christina Rossetti has become what Lorraine Janzen Kooistra calls "Victorian studies' hottest property." [1]

The same might well be said of "Goblin Market," the title poem of her first book and the first piece in the collected works of 1875, the posthumous volume of 1904, and the variorum edition of *The Complete Poems.* From the very beginning, admirers have touted its appeal to widely diverse audiences. Alexander Macmillan, who was about to become the publisher of *Goblin Market and Other Poems,* read it to a group of working men and reported exultantly that their initial bewilderment soon turned to loud applause. Mrs. Charles Eliot Norton, one of Rossetti's first reviewers, compared it with *Rime of the Ancient Mariner* and recommended it to adults and children equally. Within a few years, the poem was performed as an elocution piece fitted, the poet wryly reported, "sandwich-wise between 2 specimens of Shakespeare," and not long afterward it was set to music as a cantata (*L,* 1:294). Before publishing his score, the fortunate composer managed to meet Rossetti and pleased her "very decidedly" with a private recital on her own pianoforte (*L,* 2:225). Eclipsed in the twentieth century, but never entirely forgotten, the poem maintained a low-level visibility in school readers and in twenty-two illustrated editions—which Kooistra lavishly documents—and slowly gained admittance into scholarly anthologies, at first with a trace of hesitation about including a specimen of "children's literature" and then with a sly hint from Cecil Y. Lang in *The Pre-Raphaelites and Their Circle* that it *not* be read "merely for the 'story.'" Eventually, the poem attracted commentators; poet-critic Sandra Gilbert, for example, proposed reading it as an allegory of its own aesthetics. Now a canonical "masterpiece" of the Victorian period, "Goblin Market" is celebrated with exuberant readings in ever-new contexts ranging from the symptomology of anorexia to the history of penitentiaries for fallen women, and from the crop freeze and fruit shortage of 1859 to the jingling advertisements in the new Victorian marketplace. At the same time the poem's popular appeal increases. First published with woodcuts by Dante Gabriel Rossetti, it has been beautifully and, of course, erotically illustrated by Kinuko Craft for the "Ribald Classics" feature of *Playboy* magazine (1973) and again, for fantasy enthusiasts, by John Bolton in a 1984 issue of *Pacific Comics.* Recently adapted by Peggy Harmon with music by Polly Pen, "Goblin Market" is now a theater piece affording audiences as many varieties of entertainment as there are directors. In one production, two sisters in period dress move in a steeply receding set and loom as large as overgrown Alices in Wonderland; in another a dozen pairs of sisters dance intimately, never quite touching, reciting and singing the while.[2]

"Goblin Market" introduces the study of Rossetti's first volume and her work as a whole not only because of its preeminence but, as I hope to show, because it broaches, twice over, the most enduring concern of her long career. The fable presents two encounters with the paradox of desire, with the contradictory excitements that can feel like a thrilling affliction, a fearsome liberation, or both. As each of its heroines undergoes the experience of "baulked desire," she enacts a version of the private two-mindedness that so often sets Rossetti's solitary lovers, dreamers, and ghosts musing about the pursuit of what so bittersweetly pleases and eludes them. The first two portions of this chapter focus, accordingly, on continuities linking "Goblin Market" with a handful of Rossetti's typically yearning lyrics.

Because "Goblin Market" also has affinities with Rossetti's ballads about pairs of women who divide over what attracts one or both, the third section of this chapter, "Counterdiscourse: Rossettian Volubility," considers the effect of embodying in two characters the torments that "Goblin Market" and the lyrics embody in one, and, more arrestingly, the resultant proximity of contention and inarticulateness. And lastly, "'Not One Word': The Silences of Poetry" attends to the omissions in "Goblin Market," noting that for all its narrative amplitude the poem enforces its heroines' recourse to wordlessness and cagily scrutinizes exactly that verbal barrier Rossetti herself must cross with every poem she writes. In returning to "Goblin Market," this time to align it with a handful of manifestly inexplicit poems, the intention is to pursue Rossetti's fascination with silence, with the myriad forms of reticence, and with what I am calling the patience of style.

"Baulked Desire" in "Goblin Market"

Once described by Gabriel Rossetti with a letter writer's offhand ease as "the poem about the two Girls and the Goblins," Christina Rossetti's narrative does indeed tell how the maiden Laura is beguiled into tasting forbidden fruit only to discover its true bitterness and how, when the experience unexpectedly cloys, her sister comes to her aid (*LDGR*, 2:389). Lizzie confronts the goblins, endures their clawing assault, and secures the needed antidote, the juice for a second taste. A fuller summary than Gabriel's would also mention the cautionary tale about the goblin-beguiled Jeanie and take notice of the self-interrupting manner of Christina's storytelling. Songlike litanies arrest the flow and ruffle the implication of already ambiguous episodes as two poems, or rather two kinds of poetry, interweave to form the whole. A good place to begin is with "the two Girls," as "sweet-tooth Laura" regales her sister with a euphoric account of the fruit she has eaten:

> "You cannot think what figs
> My teeth have met in."   (*CP*, 1:11–26; 115, 173–74)

Laura's vividly odd phrasing means simply that she has bitten into lusciously toothsome fruit, but her unexpectedly literal detail—"my teeth have met"—with its hint at the body's discovering (perhaps alienating) itself, anticipates further adventures of the mouth. For the moment, Laura expects to repeat her experience and croons on about the mouth-tingling and velvety sensations that she knows cannot be reproduced in words. She does, however, convey the fervor of her desire for more of this "sugar-sweet" fruit (183) and her elation at the gorging, so unforgettably depicted as infantile-erotic:

> She sucked and sucked and sucked the more
> Fruits which that unknown orchard bore;
> She sucked until her lips were sore.   (134–36)

The intensity of Laura's oral pleasure comes as another slight shock and bears out Adam Phillips's suggestion that the "pitch" of a nursing child's pleasure may be "daunting" to an onlooker. Rossetti conveys the quality of excess by tripling the rhyme and exercising the poet's privilege of going back again and again to the same word, allowing her language to operate in proximity to the inarticulate. As an art, poetry remembers that all words were, once upon a time and for everyone, pleasurable babble; it deals in what the poet Donald Hall has called "mouth-joy," a deeply archaic delight in nonsemantic form and, as here, in an almost claustral excess of recurrence. Rossetti cannot continue at this pitch, but in this display of its own intensity, the passage intimates the extreme difficulty of what the poem eventually asks "the two Girls" to do, that is, to forgo the fruit's mouth-delighting pleasure. Since Laura is not, in fact, a nursing child, her lips become "sore," and the episode already hints at her imminent torment. She is soon to be overwhelmed by the discovery that this joy-bringing fruit is forever inaccessible; and as bitter overbalances sweet, the succulence her "teeth have met in" will set her teeth on edge. By the next nightfall, she will have become a distraught insomniac who weeps as if "her heart would break" and "gnashe[s] her teeth" (268, 267). But that is getting ahead of the story. We should go back to the temptation that initiates Laura's adventure; to the language Rossetti uses, so prescient of what is to come; and to the wonderfully heuristic question she lets the unassuming Laura so innocently ask.[3]

On first seeing the goblin merchants' produce, Laura marvels that the grapes are "so luscious" (61), her innocent word already intimating treachery; for older uses of "luscious" convey the sense of something excessively sweet or cloying. The *Oxford English Dictionary* lists its early occurrences in a sequence with "grosse and unwholesome" and in the description of a "luscious lump" of gooey sugar in the bottom of a cup. Whether or not Rossetti was aware of such usages, she herself always locates the word in ominous contexts such as in "My Dream," where "luscious fat" oozes from a crocodile's jaws (*CP*, 1 : 39), or less repellently in a memento mori piece entitled "Luscious and Sorrowful" (*CP*, 2 : 93). At the first taste of succulent goblin fruit, the incredulous Laura poses an important and explicit question: "How should it *cloy* with length of use?" (133; emphasis added). Since in her case the fruit is withdrawn after only a *single* use, she might seem to have asked the wrong question. The satiety she cannot imagine seems temporally quite different from the deprivation she is about to endure; and yet the plight of the sufferer who can no longer be gratified by what was once fervently wanted is also, ultimately, Laura's. Neither scenario permits full exhilaration, while both expose the ephemerality of joy, thus pointing to desire itself as the source of pain.

Here again, Laura's word choice is unexpectedly apposite. The term *cloy* is derived from *acloien,* which means "to lame," and the Latin *inclavare,* meaning "to drive in a nail," and ultimately from *clavus,* or "nail." Further back, the surmised Indo-European root *klāu,* "possibly, hook, peg," evolves not only into *cloy* but into *close, clause,* and *cloister,* seeming to hint at a psychological link between the cloying and the claustral, whether the excess is fruit or language. To become cloyed has less to do with the time it takes for appetite to be impaired than with the sensation of internal injury: one feels the pain of an interior nail. The question within Laura's question is how to endure cloyed and clawing desire, how to live while one lacks and must continue to lack joy; and it remains unanswered although Laura's misadventure ends well, or rather, *because* it ends well. Even as Rossetti arranges for an exemplary act of heroism and a miracle to release Laura from torment, her suffering raises an issue that remains, so to speak, an open question.

In both her general irresolution and her particular disillusion, Laura stands as a prototype for the many questioners in Rossetti's poetry. Some of them wonder poignantly about the losses and vanishings that befall them as pursuers of love or song—"Youth gone and beauty, what remains of bliss?" (*CP*, 2 : 93)—and their gentle variations on the *ubi sunt* theme offer lovely snatches of the very tunefulness they lament:

> Where are the songs I used to know
> Where are the notes I used to sing?   (*CP*, 2 : 59)

But others ask about the condition of desire itself and the obstructing two-mindedness that yearns simultaneously to pursue what is wanted and to abandon pursuit. They consider the anomalous mixing of ardor with aridity and the ambivalent shrinking before the prospect of a full, new life:

> Sometimes I said: It is an empty name
> I long for; to a name why should I give
> The peace of all the days I have to live?   (*CP*, 1:52)

> Why should we shrink from our full harvest? why
> Prefer to glean with Ruth?   (*CP*, 1:75)

The resonance of such unanswerable questions lingers long after the poem closes and becomes a key effect in Rossetti's poetry. Over the course of a lifetime Rossetti writes thrillingly of risk taking, sad-heartedness, and the intertwining of euphoria and emotional ravage. She tells of the chase that compels a pursuer to "laugh" and "weep" at the same time and of rapturous birdsong that floods the listener with "sorrow and delight" (*CP*, 1:50, 211). Her lyricist's questions about desire, passionateness, and the obstacles to exhilarated fulfillment are unanswerable, and for Rossetti always fresh, strange, and enigmatic. She returns to them again and again.

Within "Goblin Market," the query about cloying provides a cannily exact forewarning of the torment that befalls both these Rossettian sisters. To the betrayed Laura, the absence of goblin fruit is an affliction, a sickening of desire itself. The "passionate yearning" that racks her is variously described as the "heart's sore ache," as a "cankerous care," and climactically as "baulked desire" (261, 300, 267). A late emendation replacing "hope deferred," this last phrase was added at a stage when Gabriel, who suggested among other things the very title "Goblin Market," was looking over the poem (*CP*, 1:235). If he indeed had a hand in it, the phrase is a splendid bit of collaboration, for not only does it echo an earlier lyric in which Christina's speaker is "baulked of much desired," it precisely identifies the central issue of "Goblin Market": something comes between Laura and what she wants (*CP*, 1:88). The fruit she desires is not simply missing, it is withheld. Rossetti's goblins are not just tempters, they are desire, or rather the agents of desire's paradox; they deal in what arouses, exhilarates, and injures appetite, and the sisters experience them differently. Each in her own way is a desirer of the goblins' fruit, and each discovers for herself the convulsive, self-divided nature of her yearnings.[4]

Lizzie knows, instinctively, that if the cloyed Laura is to recover, she must have what the goblins deny her. Cora Kaplan puts the matter succinctly: "Laura is ill with 'baulked desire'" and Lizzie will cure her "by getting her sister more of what she wants." This fetching provides another narrative shock, for as no reader can forget, Lizzie is assaulted by the goblins. In keeping with the harsh logic of magic repetition, underscored by half-rhyme and perhaps pseudo-etymology, Lizzie must be "clawed" in order to secure the fruit that cures Laura's "cloyed" desire. To remove a nail, Lizzie must endure goblin nails. But the attack is not immediate; when Lizzie arrives at the glen, the goblins are initially cordial. Using "sugar-baited words," they invite her to "Bite at our peaches" (234, 355). They regard her, like her sister, as ripe for cloying and begin by flattering her and begging her to "take a seat with us / Honour and eat with us" (368–69). Such cajolery activates one of the ancient meanings of *claw,* which is "to claw by the back" pleasurably, to "stroke down, flatter, fawn upon" and to "humour" (according to the *Oxford English Dictionary*). When this cordial stroking has no effect, the goblins "Scratch their pates" and then close in; "snarling" and making free use of their nails, they claw, tear, and scratch at her (390, 393):

> Lashing their tails
> They trod and hustled her,
> Elbowed and jostled her,
> Clawed with their nails,
> Barking, mewing, hissing, mocking,
> Tore her gown and soiled her stocking,
> Twitched her hair out by the roots,
>
> . . . .
>
> Coaxed and fought her,
> Bullied and besought her,
> Scratched her, pinched her black as ink.   (398–404, 425–27)

In an attempt to force-feed her, the goblins hold back her hands and try squeezing their "fruits" into "her mouth" (406–7). As they struggle tooth and nail, Lizzie does not bite; her teeth will not meet as Laura's did in these embittering fruits. She clamps her mouth resolutely shut, and, as the expression goes, "sets" her "teeth" against "danger, opposition, or difficulty" (*Oxford English Dictionary*). Her jaw clenched tight, Lizzie refuses to "open lip from lip" and is smeared with the juices that will cure Laura (431).[5]

A handful of Victorian readers were not at all sure they liked "Goblin Market," among them John Ruskin, who saw Rossetti's poem in manuscript and argued against publication. In a now-infamous letter to Gabriel, Ruskin complains about Christina's rhythm: "I sate up till late last night reading [the] poems. They are full of beauty and power. But no publisher—I am deeply grieved to know this—would take them, so full are they of quaintnesses and offences. Irregular measure (introduced to my great regret, in its chief wilfulness, by Coleridge) is the calamity of modern poetry. . . . Your sister should exercise herself in the severest commonplace of metre until she can write as the public like. Then if she puts in her observation and passion all will become precious. But she must have the Form first." The Coleridgean "calamity" is the license to use strong-stress rhythm or, as Coleridge says in the preface to "Christabel," to count "the accents, not the syllables," in the lines. Technically, "Goblin Market" achieves its extraordinary "wilfulness" by mixing two-beat half-lines among three- and four-beat ballad measures, sometimes combining these into five-beat pentameters. The overall effect is a brilliantly nervous and ever-shifting tempo that adjusts constantly to the sisters' tension, distress, and exultation.[6]

No critic has ever taken Ruskin's complaint at face value, and U. C. Knoepflmacher states the consensus best when he suggests that "Rossetti's failure to observe proprieties that went beyond versification must have weighed heavily on Ruskin's mind. The unspecified 'quaintnesses and offences' which, according to him, Victorian publishers would find unacceptable, surely hint at immoderations that go beyond meter." Perhaps Ruskin might have been able to hear the poem better had he been less troubled by its transgressions. There is no question that "Goblin Market" offends against the code of maidenly decorum and challenges the equation of bodily indulgence with irrevocable harm. Not only does "Goblin Market" resist unambiguous endorsement of the wisdom of avoiding "the haunts of goblin men," it insists on Laura's recovery in a rapturous scene that begins its many offenses with a nearly blasphemous sacramental invitation (146). The juice-covered Lizzie invites her sister to taste the antidote:

"Hug me, kiss me, suck my juices
    Squeezed from goblin fruits for you,

Goblin pulp and goblin dew.
Eat me, drink me, love me."   (468–71)

What follows is an uninhibited consummation scene in which Laura is transported with pleasure and pain:

She clung about her sister,
Kissed and kissed and kissed her:
Tears once again
Refreshed her shrunken eyes,
Dropping like rain
After long sultry drouth;
Shaking with aguish fear, and pain,
She kissed and kissed her with a hungry mouth.   (485–92)

That the saving intervention takes the form of same-sex closeness hardly needs stressing, though we might note that the scene has become a favorite with illustrators, who, as Kooistra has shown, re-envision it in ways ranging from frankly erotic to naively chaste, while even these last include discreet allusion to physical suffering. Interestingly, when Rossetti's printer read of Laura's "aguish fear," he assumed the poet intended "anguish," and so it appears in the page proof (*CP,* 1:236); but Rossetti penciled in the word she had written and wanted. The transfer of goblin juice is both lovelike and assaultlike; it causes symptoms of feverish sweat and pain. Rossetti seizes on the ancient metaphor of erotic death to depict Laura's transformation as a nearly killing seizure.[7]

As the scene continues, the once sugar-sweet fruit becomes pure bitterness. It now brings Laura, with her curiosity, her questions, and what might be called her "insistent body," to a gorging consummation:

Her lips began to scorch,
That juice was wormwood to her tongue,
She loathed the feast:
Writhing as one possessed she leaped and sung,
Rent all her robe, and wrung
Her hands in lamentable haste,
And beat her breast.

. . . .

She gorged on bitterness without a name.   (493–99, 510)

Characterized by an ecstasy of loathing that vents itself in a robe-rending enactment of what goblin nails have done to Lizzie and by an unnameable thrill of self-indulgence, Laura's experience of the antidote is absolutely contradictory. Rossetti insists on the full force of the paradox and contrives matters so that, as Isobel Armstrong trenchantly puts it, "the condition of Laura's freedom seems to be an *assent* to being overwhelmed by the power of the fruit. . . . Her freedom is in proportion to, and depends upon, her resistance to it." The magic is brilliantly conceived: desire's disease, the balked condition of wanting and not wanting to want, is resolved by a final, extraordinary paroxysm of conflicted appetite. The intemperateness of Rossetti's scene well might give a squeamish reader pause. Eric Robertson, the Victorian editor of *English Poetesses,* concluded his "Goblin Market" entry with the demurral, "I do not think this is a pleasant story."[8]

Other, milder "offenses" are given throughout "Goblin Market" and they are very conspicuous, for Rossetti's poem—as a poem—seems to be of two minds about how to present its tale. This is a matter not of indecision but of conflicting certainties. The poem's own mixed desire, its wish to reprove and to cherish the victim of desire, emerges as a mixing of genres, a long and implicit dialogue about its own style. More simply, Rossetti's unwillingness to condemn Laura's initial lack of restraint is corroborated by the poem's own straining against generic discipline with what look like self-indulgent displays of imagery. Prominent among its moral/formal "quaintnesses" are the columns of similes launched with the word "like." These mark off highly visible spaces where the momentum of the goblin narrative is suspended while pockets of lyric resist, intensify, and complicate the tale being told. From the very outset, they provide aberrant nuances that prevent a Ruskin or a Robertson from finding the proper meanings he expects. When Laura, for example, first attends to the goblin cry, Rossetti includes a brief song of innocence, a sweet little litany that withholds censure and already anticipates her final renewal of innocence. As Laura stretches "her gleaming neck" to see the goblins, she is said to be

> Like a rush-imbedded swan,
> Like a lily from the beck,
> Like a moonlit poplar branch,

Like a vessel at the launch
When its last restraint is gone.   (81, 82−86)

Even as the passage tells of shedding "restraint," the lines themselves are
smoothly and almost contentedly patterned: four are syntactically parallel; each is precisely seven syllables long and rhymes with a nearby partner. Each offers the appealing sight of a curving line or arc associated with
the feminine. With the image of the "vessel at the launch," there is a
lovely surge as the thought is launched into the open sea and the white
space of the page. But it is a morally unexpected thought: sailing ships are
supposed to raise anchor, their sails are meant to fill with wind, and the
poetic line that speaks of launching must flow into the next to complete
its meaning. Is Laura then supposed to abandon her inhibitions? The expected warning against the shedding of restraint is itself restrained by the
propitiousness of the visual images and the soothing lyric rhythm. Or to
put the matter another way, this crowd of images celebrates the heroine's
breaking free. The lyric strand of "Goblin Market" wants Laura, in literally other words, to *have* the experience the narrative strand warns against.

Later, when Laura returns home having eaten goblin fruit, Rossetti
fends off ready-made judgments about moral contamination with yet another lyric passage, a fondly tender celebration of the sisters' innocent
similitude. Texturally marked off from the narrative and its damaging
implications, this gathering of similes again implies that another genre—
and another way of reading Laura's deed—may provide access to a better truth about what has happened:

Golden head by golden head,
Like two pigeons in one nest
Folded in each other's wings,
They lay down in their curtained bed:
Like two blossoms on one stem,
Like two flakes of new-fall'n snow,
Like two wands of ivory
Tipped with gold for awful kings.   (184−91)

The code word "fallen" is present, but folded harmlessly into the phrase
"new-fall'n snow." In singing the sisters' affection ("folded in each
other's" arms), their inviolability ("curtained"), and their lovely identity

as "two" who are the same, the lines describe a welcome closeness and provide, by their own clustering, a nesting refuge. Again there is the unifying rhythm of seven syllables, the only ripple occurring when a pronoun unites the sisters: "They lay down in their curtained bed."

This passage, it is important to note, supplies the line "Golden head by golden head," which Dante Gabriel Rossetti chose for the caption to his title-page illustration, one of the famous pair he did for the poem's first appearance in *Goblin Market and Other Poems*. The other was the frontispiece to the volume, for which he took a line from the temptation scene, the goblins' enticement to " 'Buy from us with a golden curl' " (125). Gabriel's choices are very astute, for as the best authority on these woodcuts puts it, his frontispiece "directs" the reader's attention to the poem "as moral allegory in which the two sisters are differentiated according to a flesh/spirit paradigm," whereas "the title-page vignette replaces sororal difference with feminine sameness." Kooistra, whose interest is in "the historical particularity" of Rossetti's book and its "transmission in the marketplace," is chiefly attentive to the "dialogic" relationship between illustration and text in this signally lovely first edition and to the contradictory readings suggested by the visual representation of the sisters' experience. We might notice, in support of this view, that Gabriel's choices also reflect a poet's awareness of the dialogic relationship *within* his sister's text. The author of such lyrical narratives as "The Blessed Damozel" (a version of which had already appeared in *The Germ*), and one who is keenly attuned to formal imperatives, Gabriel selects one line apiece from the narrative and the lyric sections of "Goblin Market." In effect, he invites readers to notice, as he does, that the poem's generic strands promote divergent meanings.[9]

As Laura's crisis deepens, however, Rossetti allows the soothing rhythm of the litanies to become increasingly disrupted, as if resistant but no longer immune to the turbulent confusions of the narrative. Lyric advocacy becomes hectic and metrically unruly, celebration more agitated. At the violent purgation scene, when it is no longer possible to compare Laura to what is gently graceful or flowerlike or pristine, Rossetti turns to what is athletic and wild and masculine to create a transformation litany that is as appropriate for a battlefield champion as for a maiden:

> Her locks streamed like the torch
> Borne by a racer at full speed,

Or like the mane of horses in their flight,
Or like an eagle when she stems the light
Straight toward the sun,
Or like a caged thing freed,
Or like a flying flag when armies run.   (500–506)

Laura is not running (or racing or flying); but a fierce energy sends the hair streaming out from her head as if, though she's still, time has speeded up and become a wind. The pattern of anaphora and terminal rhyme still holds, though a powerful new momentum propels the five comparisons into five exultantly different syntaxes. The rhythm forces its way through blocks of stressed syllables ("locks streamed," "torch / Borne," "full speed," "light / Straight," "caged thing freed") to break into the high-speed iambics of the final verse, "Or like a flying flag when armies run." A few lines later when Laura finally falls, broken by the passion of this strife, Rossetti amasses richly amplified similes to convey the sublimity and mystery of this excruciating event:

Sense failed in the mortal strife:
Like the watch-tower of a town
Which an earthquake shatters down,
Like a lightning-stricken mast,
Like a wind-uprooted tree
Spun about,
Like a foam-topped waterspout
Cast down headlong in the sea,
She fell at last;
Pleasure past and anguish past,
Is it death or is it life?   (513–23)

In this, the poem's final litany, lyric devices are scattered and disarranged in a remarkable display of chaotic fervor. Anaphora is now only intermittent, hardly visible at the margin, and less a source of order than of mystery. Lines 517–20 may be saying that the uprooted tree spins like a waterspout or that Laura in her not-yet-mentioned fall spins like the one and falls like the other. Such syntax spins the reader around in momentary but real suspense while the sublime congeries of natural forces—earthquake, lightning, wind, waterspout—gathers to make a dazzling comparison with one girl. The passage is undeniably beautiful: Laura may be suffering here, but Rossetti is riding the euphoria of language. Laura's is a consummation to be wished and her poet is rapturous as she works the verbal magic that wrests triumph from calamity. At last the question comes: "Is it death or is it life?" And this time, there is an answer; she has attained new life. There will be no more litanies; their empathetic lyric advocacy has done its work and the whole poem now moves to affirm the recovery of innocence.[10]

Before taking up Rossetti's coda, we should return briefly to Gabriel's description of "Goblin Market" and note that he might have referred to it more accurately as "the poem of the *three* Girls and the Goblins." "Jeanie" turns up repeatedly in the poem, first as a simple cautionary figure in Lizzie's "wise upbraidings" (142):

> "Do you not remember Jeanie,
> How she met them in the moonlight,
> Took their gifts both choice and many,
> Ate their fruits and wore their flowers
>
> . . . .
>
> She pined and pined away;
> Sought them by night and day,
> Found them no more but dwindled and grew grey;
> Then fell with the first snow,
>
> . . . .
>
> You should not loiter so."   (147–50, 154–57, 162)

In revising the genre she knows well enough to echo—her characterization of "one who should have been a bride" (313) coming right out of a Percy ballad about "fair Ellinor"—Rossetti puts Jeanie's tale to unexpected and ironic use. As a fatal version of the seduction-and-abandonment plot, it not only shows what can happen to a goblin victim, it nearly *causes* the death it threatens. Rossetti shapes the "Goblin Market" narrative so that just as Lizzie feels compelled to seek out the goblins, she remembers the scare tale of Jeanie and grows frightened of joining her "in her grave" (312). Suddenly wanting and not wanting to cross the heath, Lizzie delays until her sister is "at Death's door" (321). For the would-be rescuer, as for so many of Rossetti's heroines, love is an urgency that imperils the lover, a hazard that brings the shock of self-division. Lizzie's triumph comes, as does Laura's, when she accepts the burden of this paradox.[11]

Since neither sister's adventure corroborates the lesson of the death-struck Jeanie's tale, Laura's own tale telling proposes an exultant new moral: "There is no friend like a sister" (562). The tidiness of this adage leaves many readers dissatisfied and sends them back into the poem to further explore the gap between Laura's vividly represented experience and its blandly compact summation. In a sense, its value might be said to rest on precisely this failure to reprise "Goblin Market" as a whole. Another way to think about Laura's coda is to notice how little effort is made to minimize the disturbing effect of the question that launched her adventure: "How should it cloy?" The now-nostalgic Laura reimagines the luscious sweetness of her experience in "the haunted glen,"

> The wicked, quaint fruit-merchant men,
> Their fruits like honey to the throat
> But poison in the blood;
> (Men sell not such in any town).   (552–56)

Cured of "baulked desire" and miraculously precipitated into an idyllic (some would say "cloying") condition, Laura savors the recollection of honey-sweet fruit. Her parenthetical lingering to endorse its uncommonness as unavailability ("Men sell not such in any town") awakens a pleasurable yearning, reminiscent perhaps of Keats's impulse in "Ode on Melancholy" to crush "Joy's grape" against the "palate" (*Keats,* 251). This enfolding of temptation into Laura's present happiness is Rossetti's way of giving texture to the innocence that has triumphed over "poison in the blood."

The "Bittersweet" of Lyric

Such mixing of what pains and pleases, such cultivating of refined strains of passion, is one of the hallmarks of Rossetti's poetry. Even in shorter poems, when imagining tranquility or anticipating detachment, she always, somehow, preserves the evidence of what stirs longing in the first place. There is frequently a wistfulness akin to Laura's nostalgia, but tinged with a melancholy that confirms the appeal of the deliberately abandoned or soon-to-be-forgotten. Irony is so gently omnipresent that restraint and fervent self-denial become thoroughly suffused with heartsick want. Occasionally Rossetti's shorter poems interlace lyric with narrative so that, as in "Goblin Market," sweet and bitter tonalities qualify one another, and even in the "pure" love lyrics, ardor is intensified by pain. To consider a handful of these poems, an array of five anthology favorites, is to discover not only that they explore the many degrees of yearning ambiguity but that the transparency of their much-praised "simplicity and directness" is, as the poet C. H. Sisson tells us, the illusory effect of extraordinary craft. The next few pages will attend to the formal aspects of Rossetti's distinctive passionateness—her particular way of troping insensateness, her tight-edged lineation, her quietly stunning use of biblical quotation—but also to some of the broader implications of her style. These five poems show, unmistakably, that Rossetti had discovered the advantage of assuming the mask of ghostliness, the pleasure of aesthetic distance, and the dangerous porousness of the lyric genre.[12]

One of Rossetti's personal favorites, affectionately dubbed "my dreary poem," enriches its gloom by means comparable to Laura's in the "Goblin Market" coda (*L*, 1:18). "Dream-Land" tells of a completed quest to reach a "purple land" and the shelter of "charmèd sleep" (*CP*, 1:27). There is no mention of motive, no goblin treachery or any of the milder betrayals, the "hardness, coldness, slights," intimated in other poems (*CP*, 1:66). She has simply come "from very far" to enter a twilight realm where physical stimuli create little or no impression. And yet, in celebrating this sought-after tranquility, Rossetti allows sensation to creep in:

> She cannot see the grain
> Ripening on hill and plain;
> She cannot feel the rain
>   Upon her hand.   (*CP*, 1:27)

In detailing what is not seen or felt, Rossetti poignantly compounds the soft anguish of Tennyson's Mariana, whose poem sounds the sound she missed: "unlifted was the clinking latch" (*AT*, 4).

This paradoxical tendency to affirm-while-denying is also a habit among Rossetti's living and a source of wistful irony. Her "Song" forbidding mourning, one of the best known of the so-called "death lyrics," seems to lift the obligation to grieve—"When I am dead, my dearest, / Sing no sad songs for me"—and to forgive the addressee in advance of any defection: "And if thou wilt, remember, / And if thou wilt, forget" (*CP*, 1:58). Curiously, however, as the speaker prolongs the surrendering of her desire to be memorialized, she too adduces a list of sensations manqué:

> I shall not see the shadows,
>   I shall not feel the rain;

> I shall not hear the nightingale
> > Sing on, as if in pain.   (*CP,* 1 : 58)

At mention of the nightingale, the interdicted "sad songs" are covertly reintroduced, and the ambiguous phrase "*as if* in pain" may say less about the sadness of the mateless nightingale than about the doubtful sincerity of the addressee's impending grief. And so, in the second and final stanza, the future dreamer who will not see, hear, or feel adds that she will not remember those who survive her:

> And dreaming through the twilight
> > That doth not rise nor set,
> Haply I may remember,
> > And haply may forget.   (*CP,* 1 : 58)

The mood of these lines can be read in any number of ways *except* as straightforward disinterest. It might be that this nongrieving grievance is the future amnesiac's way of practicing immunity from the pain of being forgotten. Certainly the poem surprises by capping its anticipation of insensateness with an insouciantly double "haply." To some ears, the word echoes the sound of *happily* and may carry a trace of gaiety; to others, it perhaps recalls the *happys* in "Ode to a Nightingale" with its numbness that pains. The song, in any case, is energized by the presence of opposite meanings, the one forgiving and the other liberated from the need to forgive.

In "Remember," Rossetti again entwines an expressed desire and its opposite. Its speaker asks three times in quick succession to be remembered; but at the sonnet's turn, and as a kind of afterthought, the possibility of the mourner's inattention comes in for consideration. Just as in the "Song," detachment here is achieved by absolving the living prior to any lapse from grief:

> Yet if you should forget me for a while
> > And afterwards remember, do not grieve.   (*CP,* 1 : 37)

This time, the irony is probably not the speaker's but Rossetti's. Formally, she prolongs the forgiving thought in a way that defers the crucial "afterwards remember" until after the line break. This is one of those small adjustments of tempo that Wordsworth extols as the essence of poetry, the "pleasurable surprise from the metrical arrangement," and it allows the verse itself to mime the belatedness it dreads. For the final quatrain, Rossetti deftly arranges for the speaker to repeat the permission to forget and, at the same time, rearticulate the initial wish to be remembered:

> For if the darkness and corruption leave
> A vestige of the thoughts that once I had,
> Better by far you should forget and smile
> Than that you should remember and be sad.   (*CP,* 1:37)

This long, smoothly gliding hypothetical ("if . . . Better . . . Than") yields a wording that precisely restates her desire: "you should remember and be sad." The gently granted permission to forget is thus suffused with a regretful desire made visible in the palimpsest of the last line. However reconciled to oblivion the speaker may be, Rossetti's syntax refuses, as another poem puts it, to be "forgetful of forgetfulness" (*CP,* 3:82).[13]

This bittersweet two-mindedness is most perfectly actualized in a fourth poem, "At Home," a dramatic lyric whose speaker is a phantom, a present absence, at the scene of her own forgottenness:

> When I was dead, my spirit turned
> To seek the much frequented house:
> I passed the door, and saw my friends
> Feasting beneath green orange boughs;
> From hand to hand they pushed the wine,
> They sucked the pulp of plum and peach;
> They sang, they jested, and they laughed,
> For each was loved of each.   (*CP,* 1:28)

The revenant's crossing of the threshold does not amount to actual entering; she cannot share either the pleasure of sucking the "plum and peach"—the verb slightly unexpected and, like Laura's "sucked," microscopically "daunting"—or the laughter of the living. Such fruits are inaccessible to the enghosted "I" who remains unseen and unheard, shielded within the charmed circle of her soliloquy. Formally, she is heard only by the poem's reader; and her poem is precisely what John Stuart Mill, in a famous formulation, says lyric should be: "feeling confessing itself to itself, in moments of solitude." Mill is distinguishing poetry from eloquence, the latter having a design on its audience while the former is utterly unconscious "of a listener." Such privacy, in his view, makes lyric ideally expressive, a form as subjectively intimate as breath itself; an admired song seems to him "the very soul of melancholy exhaling itself in solitude." A consequence of Mill's idea of solitude, what Northrop Frye specifies as "the assumed concealment of the audience," is that it puts the reader in the position of an eavesdropper. In Mill's phrase, we are "listening, unseen," to outpourings of sincere feeling.[14]

These notions of genre are useful for showing the canniness of Rossetti's dealings in lyric. "At Home" is a soliloquy, but it does something more than adduce the speaker's interiority. Rossetti arranges matters so that the reader overhears the lyric speaker as she overhears others. Installed at the core of "At Home" is precisely the kind of multivoiced drama that the lyric in Mill's definition ordinarily precludes, and by this means Rossetti poignantly stages the ghostly nonguest's ambivalent yearning toward the living:

> I listened to their honest chat:
>   Said one: "Tomorrow we shall be
> Plod plod along the featureless sands
>   And coasting miles and miles of sea."
> Said one: "Before the turn of tide
>   We will achieve the eyrie-seat."
> Said one: "Tomorrow shall be like
>   Today, but much more sweet."
>
> "Tomorrow," said they, strong with hope,
>   And dwelt upon the pleasant way:
> "Tomorrow," cried they one and all,
>   While no one spoke of yesterday.
> Their life stood full at blessed noon;
>   I, only I, had passed away:
> "Tomorrow and today," they cried;
>   I was of yesterday.   (*CP,* 1:28)

This layering of what Herbert Tucker calls the voice of feeling over "the alien voices" of the ghost's history enables the reader to listen with and through the revenant's bittersweetness as longed-for friends actively forget their friend. Attention to their inattention fills the poem's core. Out of this come many ironies, not least of which is that the figures in the social scene are heedless not only of the ghost but of their own inevitable ghostliness. Without severity, but with subdued eagerness in representing the friends' "honest chat," the poem folds this deeper forgetfulness into the overheard plan-making. The strange syntax of "we shall be / Plod plod" registers as onomatopoetic, recording the plash and thud of feet on wet beach. The word's nounlike shape recalls the unhearing "sod" of "Ode to a Nightingale" and anticipates the mild shock lurking in the description of the barren shore (*Keats*, 237). In reality, the ocean shingle is littered with what Rossetti whimsically describes in a letter as "*precious stones, weeds, and monsters*," but in the poem, it is symbolically "featureless" (*L,* 1:137). Like the unseen ghost who watches them, these friends will someday "pass away" into the anonymity of the sands they tread. They, too, will become ghosts of yesterday or yesteryear. The irony accomplished, Rossetti restores the speaker's lyric privacy and allows the social "extern" to withdraw without a trace (*L,* 3:221):

> I shivered comfortless, but cast
>   No chill across the tablecloth;
> I all-forgotten shivered, sad
>   To stay and yet to part how loth:
> I passed from the familiar room,
>   I who from love had passed away,
> Like the remembrance of a guest
>   That tarrieth but a day.   (*CP,* 1:28)

The visitant entirely forgoes the ghostly privilege of disturbing the living and demurely casts "no chill" on the festivities—or rather, on the tablecloth. With extreme delicacy, Rossetti includes a reference to domestic linen by one whose own linen is an unmentioned shroud. This is not a ghost who comes, in the words of Tennyson's "The Lotos-Eaters," with "strange" looks "to trouble joy," but one who exercises the restraint of the returned Enoch Arden as he resolves, on finding his wife remarried, "Not to tell her, never to let her know" (*AT,* 76, 612). The revenant of "At Home" feels a mutely self-divided yearning to leave and to linger; and to convey this gentle two-mindedness, Rossetti exploits her poem's margin: "I all-forgotten shivered, sad / To stay and yet to part how loth." The caesura isolates "sad" on the nearside of the line break; but with the next verse, the syntax reorganizes itself so that "sad" is pulled across the gap, thereby enacting its own drama of reluctant, bittersweet lingering. In the end, the poem trails off with an open vowel and a word-perfect citation of Wisdom 5:15, "As the remembrance of a guest that tarrieth but a day."

"Ghost" and "guest" are a conceptual half-rhyme, connected by a wisp of connotation, that deepens the poem's inference about ephemerality. It makes for resonant closure even as the visitant's inaudibility is preserved.[15]

The advantage to Rossetti or any poet who writes as a specter is that it positions her beyond the reach of real anxieties. For the duration that the writer becomes a ghost, life's terror and dismay are less paralyzing. To face the present as if it were irrevocably past is to force betrayal and even the fear of betrayal into the distance. A journal entry in which Thomas Hardy reports actually playing the revenant might well serve as a gloss on lyric ghostliness: "For my part, if there is any way of getting a melancholy satisfaction out of life it lies in dying, so to speak, before one is out of the flesh; by which I mean putting on the manners of ghosts, wandering in their haunts, and taking their views of surrounding things. To think of life as passing away is a sadness; to think of it as past is at least tolerable. Even when I enter into a room to pay a simple morning call I have unconsciously the habit of regarding the scene as if I were a spectre not solid enough to influence my environment; only fit to behold and say, as another spectre said: 'Peace be unto you!'" To imagine oneself a haunter is to inhabit the present unencumbered by desire and beyond the reach of disappointment. When as a very young writer—not yet fifteen—Rossetti described a feeling of "passionless sadness without dread," she was giving one of many possible names to this sensation of emotional insulation (*CP*, 3:94). Others have called it melancholy and some, courage; but by any name, the distance from life that Rossetti is so quietly excited about is *aesthetic* distance. Variously figured as the remoteness of the twilight zone in "Dream-Land," the between-world of the revenant in "At Home," and the pastoral never-never land at the end of "Goblin Market," this distance is charmed and magically freeing. Often when readers notice that a poem is about art, it is because of a hint about the inadequacy of life in art's palace: Tennyson's Lady of Shalott grows "half sick" of shadowy images and song (*AT*, 23). But what Rossetti calls attention to in her spectral or death-seeking poems is not limitation so much as the basic emotion of poetry, the poet's sense of having emotions without actually having them. Wordsworth once attributed this sensation to "the tendency of metre to divest language . . . of its reality" and to permit a "sort of half consciousness" of those situations and sentiments that have a "proportion of pain connected with them." Rossetti gladly escapes into this soft-edged sadness as a way of recasting life's sharper and more specific anxieties. In this she anticipates the twenty-year-old Yeats's discovery of "sorrow that gives for guerdon liberty." [16]

In at least one instance, my fifth and last example, the fantasy of death's soulful remoteness allows an outpouring of erotic yearning purely for yearning's bittersweet sake. Imagining a love betrayed by time's "finished years" and a lover suspended in the nowhere between this world and eternity, Rossetti writes an ardently unselfconscious appeal for dreams (*CP*, 1:46). The title "Echo" might suggest that the lyric comes in reply to an overheard beloved; but this person is never made present, and the poem never slips into the dramatic mode of "At Home." Instead, a carefully preserved absence of story allows the premised "echo" to become broadly evocative, suggesting not only the wished-for response of the beloved but also the repetitions of the speaker's own longing, and perhaps, too, the poem's own echoes of other poems. Meanwhile, this unheard, unuttered appeal affirms the pleasure of its anguish, using all the lyric devices of rhyme, anaphora, and repetition to convert it to mellifluous sound:

> Come to me in the silence of the night;
>   Come in the speaking silence of a dream;
> Come with soft rounded cheeks and eyes as bright
>   As sunlight on a stream;
>   Come back in tears,
> O memory, hope, love of finished years.
>
> Oh dream how sweet, too sweet, too bitter sweet,
>   Whose wakening should have been in Paradise,
> Where souls brimfull of love abide and meet;
>   Where thirsting longing eyes
>   Watch the slow door
> That opening, letting in, lets out no more.
>
> Yet come to me in dreams, that I may live
>   My very life again tho' cold in death:
> Come back to me in dreams, that I may give
>   Pulse for pulse, breath for breath:
>   Speak low, lean low,
> As long ago, my love, how long ago.   (*CP*, 1:46)

As might be expected, the melic qualities of this poem drew admirers, and Rossetti's pleasure in attracting a composer is conveyed to Gabriel in a happily reverberant announcement that "Echo expectant, awaits her musical echoes" (*L,* 1:222). So delicately cadenced a *cri de coeur* is "susceptible," as the Victorians put it, "of an astonishing range and stress of musical expression," and to this day "Echo" resounds in new settings for women's choruses and a staged version of an Alcott short story.[17]

But if, in the language of one genre theorist, Rossetti's poem gives evidence of lyric's literally "melodic origins," it also admits a glad debt to the lilting pentameters of Tennyson's "Tears, Idle Tears" and that poem's melancholy "no more" (*AT,* 266). Interestingly, the manuscript of "Echo" shows that at an early stage Tennyson is also a trouble to Rossetti's poem insofar as recognizable borrowings accumulate—perhaps without her initial awareness. His poem's "dear" ("Dear as remembered kisses") becomes her "dearer":

> Dearer than daylight on an unknown sea,
>   Or oasis in a far desert place,
> Dearer than hope and life, come back to me,
>   Full of a *tender grace,*
>   Not changed except
> For trace of *weary tears* thou too hast wept.
>   (*CP,* 1:247; emphasis added)

Rossetti's "tender grace" is also "the tender grace of a day that is dead" in Tennyson's "Break, Break, Break," and by a kind of lyric fusion, the "weary tears" recall Rossetti's earlier "Twilight Calm," in which "weary eyelids drop / O'er weary eyes" (*CP,* 1:251); both hearken back to the "The Lotos-Eaters" and the music "that gentlier on the spirit lies, / Than tired eyelids upon tired eyes" (*AT,* 165, 73). Tennyson's haunting of Rossetti's poem is a consequence not only of her admiration but, more important, of the porousness of lyric itself. In her joking reference to "Echo expectant," Rossetti glances at this truth of genre: lyric says what it already hears, and poems listen for and return "musical echoes" of other poems. Thus it happens that when first imagining a speaker completely lost in love and relieved by death of an individual identity, Rossetti abandons particularizing language and succumbs to the general music of featureless soulfulness, i.e., general among lyric writers. Momentarily flooded with possibilities, she assembles a stanza that is too full of features (a sea, an oasis, and a miniature story of tears already wept), too diffuse, and rather confusedly bland. In the event, when Rossetti sets about eliminating the Tennysonian echoes, what she elsewhere calls "inconvenient resemblances," a thrill of ruthlessness prompts her to make additional sweeping deletions (*L,* 1:243). She cuts four of seven stanzas, and in doing so suddenly finds the "lean" and "enigmatic" poem that, as McGann once told us, so often results from her "severe prunings." In draft, "Echo" has a living speaker who wants to dream and to die midfantasy, to "gaze my soul away / And from thy presence pass into my rest" (*CP,* 1:247). The newfound poem does not fumble over the distinction between sleep and death, but puts its speaker securely in the other world and focuses on the indistinctness of desire's sweet pain. As finished, the poem is more Rossettian than Tennysonian, and we might notice, as Susan Conley does, that Rossetti has her own ideas about lineation. Modifying the languorously matched lines of the "Tears, Idle Tears" quintain, Rossetti breaks a pentameter in two and sculpts a sexain that focuses considerable erotic tension at the poem's edges. In stanza 2, for example, Paradise is a place where souls await one another,

> Where thirsting longing eyes
>   Watch the slow door.   (*CP,* 1:46)

With the line break at "eyes," the reader looks literally into a white space and watches for what comes, just as the "eyes" of the dead "watch" for the arrival of the beloved. The intentness of the speaker's longing is present in the reaching intention of the line itself and the straining slowness of the "slow door," mimetic effects that are perhaps best explained by Robert Pinsky's reminder that the poetic line is "a form of attention." As this dream-beseeching song approaches its end, Rossetti brings the momentum to an almost ecstatic halt. The would-be dreamer yearns to exchange "Pulse for pulse, breath for breath," and the line allows a brief intake of breath at the caesura. Then comes the hushed erotic imperative, "Spéak lów, léan lów." Ardor slows the tempo and then yields—gratifyingly—to the return of alternating rhythm, "As long ago, my love, how long ago," and croons alliteratively to a long-voweled close. "Echo" ends with the speaker thinking of the words she will hear and thus will be able to say.[18]

Counterdiscourse: Rossettian Volubility

"Speak low": this loving imperative at the close of "Echo" might almost
be taken as Rossettian self-instruction, a reminder that her style tends
toward the soft-voiced and gentle. In "Goblin Market," the cautious
Lizzie's "upbraidings" are so tenderly nonabrasive that Laura resists with
only the mildest of demurrals, "Nay, hush, my sister" (142, 164). A sibling struggle for the highest stakes could hardly be conducted with less
acrimony. Rossetti's lyric speakers, as we have seen, also prefer modulated
tones when taking leave, testing remembrance, or as their author later
puts it, "softly protesting" the unfaithfulness of others (*CP,* 2:252). The
close twining of conflicted impulses, the suffusing of desire with reluctance or regret, is what gives these poems their appealingly subdued intensity. Their drama is almost too delicate to be thought of as drama; it
happens inwardly and registers as small hesitations of mood and line, as
when a ghost tarries, "sad / To stay" but reluctant "to part" (*CP,* 1:28).

It would be a mistake, however, to think that this "charmèd" unem-
phatic mode is unexamined or inevitable, for in the *Goblin Market* volume, Rossetti scrutinizes her own aesthetic in a handful of very different
poems that experiment with harsh judgments and aggrieved feelings.
The resultant body of poetry is aggressively "loud," which is to say, it
deals with audible fractiousness and is willing, in that other acceptation
of the term *loud,* to explore the gaudier, indelicate emotions, the lurid
fantasies, and the vituperative scenarios that are the result of human com-
pulsion. This next section considers the Rossettian mode that is not quite
lyric, and certainly not hushed or diffident; here in her first book's other
poems, there is drama, even melodrama, aplenty as the principals disrupt
one another's lives and romances. The wry two-mindedness, which in
"Remember" can rescind even while urging detachment, is recast as firm
rejection of a would-be lover. The censure that is never hurled at Laura
appears now in the mutual recrimination of a pair of sisters whose
adamance is a bit startling, possibly off-putting. Gabriel Rossetti was a
little uneasy about the most vigorous of these "other" poems, and a doc-
trinaire gender critic might be too comfortable with them. Rossetti herself seems to regard the more obstreperous clashes as in some way problematic, tonally off-balance; indeed, one of the implicit subjects of the
quarrelsome pieces is their own embarrassment, their volume and volubility. As these poems explore the possibilities of vehemently simplified
emotion, the challenge for the critic is to see how they are discernibly

Rossettian, i.e., cagey, subtle, and moving, and how they work the border of lyric inwardness and silence.

"A Triad" is a signal poem in this regard; a fierce little allegory, it ponders love's deformities. Abandoning the musicality of "Echo" and its dreamy dissolution of the self, Rossetti focuses instead on colors—crimson, yellow, and blue—and sorts the shades of desire that tint and taint would-be lovers. The poem's women are singers, and with a gesture toward her own choices as singer, Rossetti notes that they express themselves in distinguishably ardent, droning, or harsh modes.

> Three sang of love together: one with lips
>   Crimson, with cheeks and bosom in a glow,
> Flushed to the yellow hair and finger tips;
>   And one there sang who soft and smooth as snow
>   Bloomed like a tinted hyacinth at a show;
> And one was blue with famine after love,
>   Who like a harpstring snapped rang harsh and low
> The burden of what those were singing of.
> One shamed herself in love; one temperately
>   Grew gross in soulless love, a sluggish wife;
> One famished died for love. Thus two of three
>   Took death for love and won him after strife;
> One droned in sweetness like a fattened bee:
>   All on the threshold, yet all short of life.   (*CP,* 1:29)

In the early days of the Rossetti revival, this rather caustic sonnet received considerable attention; that Rossetti seems to "rage against the pettiness" of women's "cramped existence" was welcomed; her "critique of wifehood" seemed "of particular interest" both for puncturing the bourgeois "illusion" of marriage and as a corrective to the "redolently feminine" quality of her work. But soon after publication, the unaccommodating harshness, the tone figured in the poem itself as the sound of "a harpstring snapped," strikes Rossetti herself as unacceptable. The "burden" of stigmatizing others as famished, shamed, or vulgarized and castigating them as self-degraded is rather too "low." In 1875, when organizing the collected edition of her first two books, she excludes "A Triad," embarrassed by its obvious unkindness and perhaps regretting the one-sidedness of its presentation.[19]

In her more typical renderings of scorn or feistiness, Rossetti works with multiple voices so that the agitated speaker must also listen to the person scorned. The poems build on the tension between accusation and clever or sometimes exasperated response, presenting their author with interesting formal challenges and becoming inevitably noisier as disapproved parties are allowed their say. When, for example, a woman fends off an overly persistent suitor in "No, Thank You, John," Rossetti contrives by indirect citation to include his voice in the text; the poem is a wrangle over the suitor's rhetoric and the wheedling courtship strategies that have become a "weariness" to listen to (*CP,* 1:50). The opening salvo is a rebuff of a distinctively Rossettian kind; the poet of delicate effects reminds a "bad reader" what she has not said. Her response to John's coerciveness is to defend the absoluteness of her verbal abstentions:

> I never said I loved you, John:
>> Why will you teaze me day by day,
> And wax a weariness to think upon
>> With always "do" and "pray"?   (1–4)

Technically, Rossetti's poem is a monologue; and she might well have invoked the generic "demand for silence" and kept John a mute auditor— as inaudible as the gleaming-eyed sister in Wordsworth's "Tintern Abbey" or the virtually wordless Lucrezia in Browning's "Andrea del Sarto."[20] Instead, she allows bits of the wooer's continuing suit to appear as echoed back talk in the woman's remarks:

> I have no heart?—Perhaps I have not;
>> But then you're mad to take offence
> That I don't give you what I have not got:
>> Use your own common sense.
>
> Let bygones be bygones:
>> Don't call me false, who owed not to be true:
> I'd rather answer "No" to fifty Johns
>> Than answer "Yes" to you.   (13–20)

Heard only in quotation, the suitor's words are, nevertheless, quite revealing. Even in courtship, he shows his anger with the supposedly loved woman. In a style that he might have learned from any number of Petrarchan poets (which is not to exclude the influence of Victorian men), John makes love by making accusations and, still wanting the woman who refuses him, reproaches her for heartlessness and dishonesty. In a probing recent commentary on "the workings of hostility" in traditional love poetry, Heather Dubrow shrewdly warns against the assumption that such anger is "an understandable response to the disdain of the lady," for it may very well be that the lady's disdain has been "constructed precisely to excuse the hostility." Rossetti's witty heroine, in this instance, dismisses the charges for what they are, lame inventions of John's frustration. In the end, his aggressiveness simmers down to a pesky impoliteness that is fun to deflect. Offering to "wink at" *his* "untruth," she offers him friendship, but with a proviso. The "only" that introduces her final stipulation propels the only sentence that crosses a stanza break:

> Let us strike hands as hearty friends;
>   No more, no less; and friendship's good:
> Only don't keep in view ulterior ends,
>   And points not understood
>
> In open treaty. Rise above
>   Quibbles and shuffling off and on:
> Here's friendship for you if you like; but love,—
>   No, thank you, John.   (25–32)

In suspending the thought at "understood," Rossetti presents a gaping opportunity to quibble. John (not to mention the reader) momentarily enters that opening and surveys the vague or implicit "points" that persistence might yet seize on. With a crafty pun on "open," Rossetti then closes down both the sentence and the courtship: what is "not understood / In open treaty" is simply not available for dispute. In the beginning of the poem Rossetti's speaker protests the invasion of her silences ("I never said"); in the end she puts love, literally, out of the question.[21]

Rossetti's formal interest in the relationship between the monologue's speaker and auditor leads her, not surprisingly, to poems where debate is more than implied. But what *is* surprising is that she imagines *women* vehemently opposing one another. Instead of the "open treaty" briefly mentioned in "No, Thank You, John," she depicts the open quarrel that results when a woman comes between lovers. Still more unexpected is the way her two most contentious ballads, "Noble Sisters" and "Maude Clare," allow love's obstructionist to bring accusations against the bereft woman and to put her yearning after an absent or secret lover into question. The antagonism in these poems, which is overt but by no means easy to unravel, deliberately challenges the sympathy conventionally awarded the abandoned woman; though in each case she is plainly wronged, she is also made to appear somehow wrong-hearted. This ambivalence about the integrity or worth of the heroine's love has resulted in baffled, if not vexed, responses to these poems. Some have lamented that the author whose tale of Laura and Lizzie encourages expansive claims about sisterhood—either as "a kind of universal emotional kinship" or "a protecting framework" for "female sexuality"—should expend so much creative energy undermining the "dearly cherished trope of female unity." Others have suspected regretfully that a degree of temperamental captiousness prompts Rossetti to focus so disturbingly on the division between women. Joseph Bristow, for example, amends Rossetti's own adage that "there is no friend like a sister" by adding "no enemy either"; and he summarizes what he views as feminism's distress about these ballads, contending that they show "how conflicted woman-to-woman relations could become" in Rossetti's work.[22]

Scholars have sometimes defended or at least explained what they regard as Rossetti's skepticism about sisterhood by invoking her literary sources, that is to say, the ballads she was reading and the representation of courtship and female enmity to be found there. Bristow says rightly that Rossetti's poems "take on aspects of the medieval ballad to bring into sharp relief rivalry between women in love." Used with care, this can be a helpful approach, for Rossetti is demonstrably familiar with the poems collected by Bishop Percy, Walter Scott, and contemporary Victorian editors. In 1865, for example, she writes to her publisher Alexander Macmillan for "a copy of Mr Allingham's *Ballad Book*"; her knowledge of Allingham's project dates from the mid-1850s when Gabriel and Elizabeth Siddal are preparing sketches for what they expect will be an illustrated collection (*L*, 1:236). As for tracking down specific ballads, some of this work has been ably done by Dolores Rosenblum, who locates Percy's tales of women deceived by fickle lovers and explains that these originals emphasize "faithless love" with a focus on the betrayal of "vows," whereas Rossetti's reconceive treachery as "the betrayal of one woman by another." But Rossetti's interest in ballads begins early on, and what first attracts her attention—even prior to the rivalry topos—is the image of love as a fearsome pursuit. For Rossetti these topoi are functionally equivalent: they give different dramatic shapes to the self-divisions of love.[23]

Specifically, among the unpublished poems from Rossetti's fourteenth year is a piece entitled "Lord Thomas and Fair Margaret." Perhaps because of the attempt at Scottish dialect, the manuscript bears a note in Maria Rossetti's hand indicating that "this is imitated from the ballad of 'Sweet William's Ghost,' in Percy's 'Reliques of Ancient English Poetry'" (*CP*, 3:409). For most of the poem, Rossetti follows her source closely: in Percy's text, a ghostly William asks Margret (*sic*) to return his "faith and troth" and draws her to his grave in the "kirk yard." Rossetti adopts the heroine's name and story but makes an important change at her adventure's end. In Percy's version, when the "constant Margret" reaches the burial ground, she discovers herself abandoned and gently dies:

> O stay, my only true love, stay,
> The constant Margret cried:
> Wan grew her cheeks, she clos'd her een,
> Stretch'd her saft limbs, and died.

In Rossetti's ballad, the heroine pursues the speeding Thomas across "ploughed land and hillocks" to the edge of a stream, whereupon he challenges her to enter the "running" waters:

> 9
> "Oh fair Marg'ret, oh sweet Marg'ret,
>   We now maun parted be,
> If in the last trail thou shalt go through
>   Thy heart should fail in thee."   (*CP*, 3:130)

Voluntary drowning is a different caliber of ordeal from closing one's "een" and passing out of existence; and Rossetti's impulse to make the lover's death harder is profoundly right. Though the young poet hardly knows how to amplify the episode, she supplies a delaying stanza before compelling Margaret to enter the stream and die:

> 10
> On glided the ghost, while the starry host
>   Glittered down on the sleeping stream;
> O'er the waves glided he impalpably,
>   Then vanished like a dream.

11
Fair Margaret still followed him,
    Till she sank amid the wave;
Thus died for each other these lovers true,
    And were joinèd in the grave.   (*CP,* 3 : 130)

As William vanishes "impalpably" (the strangely cumbersome adverb almost belies his evanescence), the still embodied Margaret stands facing "the waves" that promise her death and love. The insight built into the plot as Rossetti places this watery barrier in the heroine's path is that there is always an impediment, always something that comes between lovers. Whether figured as an element of the terrain or the social setting (a body of water or the body of another woman), the obstacle that separates lovers is narrative's way of reflecting on the excitingly sad fact of lovers' absolute separateness. In halting Margaret's narrative at that terrifying stream's edge and suspending the action just when love might "fail" to propel her into the water, Rossetti stages a version of the dilemma that is central to the experience of love and to most love poetry: Margaret wants and yet can hardly want to follow her elusive lover. In lingering to describe the "sleeping stream," the tale itself hesitates to enact her self-obliterating immersion. Obstacles are neither accidental nor merely obstacles: all love poetry, as Anne Carson says in *Eros the Bittersweet,* is premised on the enthralled lover's own resistance to love, the self-protective instinct that fears self-loss in the "now" of love, or injury in the "then" of love.[24]

Indeed, inhibited pursuit is a favorite Rossettian paradigm, as a few examples will quickly show. In "Goblin Market," Lizzie hesitates on the narrative brink of her quest to secure her loved sister's "antidote," constrained, as we have seen, by the recollection of Jeanie. The lyric "Fata Morgana" offers a counterpart for her risky adventure. Intrigued by a "laughing, leaping" phantom, the pursuer is both ardent and sluggish, so that ambivalence feels like running with weights: "Like lead I chase it evermore, / I pant and run" (*CP,* 1 : 49). To give chase is to experience an anomalous mix of exuberance and dismay: "I laugh, it is so brisk and gay; / It is so far before, I weep" (*CP,* 1 : 50). To desist-and-resume intermittently, as in "A Pause of Thought," is to earn caustic self-reproach:

Alas, thou foolish one! alike unfit
    For healthy joy and salutary pain:

> Thou knowest the chase useless, and again
> Turnest to follow it.   (*CP,* 1:52)

To hesitate is to become, in yet another poem, one's own worst enemy, "self stabbing self with keen lack-pity knife" (*CP,* 2:125). To give up altogether, in the manner of the novice who renounces her lover in "The Convent Threshold," is to invite nearly fatal agony (*CP,* 1:61–65).

In this last instance, love is barred, as in many of Scott's *Minstrelsy* ballads, by family rivalry:

> There's blood between us, love, my love,
> There's father's blood, there's brother's blood;
> And blood's a bar I cannot pass.   (1–3)

This obstructive history serves the same purpose as the interdiction that separates Héloïse and Abélard—an analogy suggested in William Rossetti's note to the poem (*PW,* 482)—or the curse that dooms Tennyson's Lady of Shalott. The deaths of kinsmen effect love's incompleteness as surely as the more intimate causes psychoanalysts tell of: a lover is a primally impaired being who cannot, in the very nature of things, love wholly; a beloved is unalterably alien to the already self-alienated lover; desire is internally structured as lacking what is impossibly and irrationally wanted. Bloodshed brings such inadmissible evidence into the poem by narratively forcing the novice's revulsion from her own desire. Afflicted with the want of someone whom shame and self-loathing make her unable to want, she conceives of love as tainted:

> My lily feet are soiled with mud,
> With scarlet mud which tells a tale
> Of hope that was, of guilt that was,
> Of love that shall not yet avail;
> Alas, my heart, if I could bare
> My heart, this selfsame stain is there.   (7–12)

In a passionately amplified replay of Margaret's anxiety at the stream's brink, the novice's fear and yearning intensify simultaneously. Even as she renounces the family enemy whom she must and does hate, he becomes present in her nightmare. In a surreal parody of "Echo," the novice sees herself dead, her bedclothes bloodied, and by this ruse of the unconscious brings the beloved into "the speaking silence" of her dream.

The earlier love poem's exchange of "pulse for pulse, breath for breath" is transformed into an erotically macabre swoon. A torpid leadenness seems to push the dreamer into the swallowing earth, and the space separating her from her lover becomes grotesquely "sodden" (123). Love is loathsome and yet she loves. Torn apart by conflicting emotions, the novice almost literally ages (like another Jeanie or Laura) in the course of the night:

> . . . . When this morning broke,
> My face was pinched, my hair was grey,
> And frozen blood was on the sill
> Where stifling in my struggle I lay.   (133–36)

This blood on the windowsill is a reminder, to be sure, of the bloody feud that separates the lovers, but its more important symbolic function is to verify the novice's inward strife. It is lurid proof, conveyed in part by the stifled rhythm, that she is "stifling in [her] struggle" and not of one mind about loving her beloved.[25]

Thus the novice at "The Convent Threshold" becomes her own enemy; and in this, her experience of balked and mortified erotic attachment, she has an affinity with the unhappy women in "Noble Sisters" and "Maude Clare." Tales such as the novice's (or Fair Margaret's), in providing bloodshed (or a brink) to interfere with the pursuit of love, give an external equivalent for what sister-debates accomplish with two people. Structurally, the obstacle becomes the "other" woman, her presence an alternative cause for the bitterness of love's bittersweetness. She brings, moreover, the advantage of a speaking voice, making it possible for erotic self-division to be narrated as a verbal breach between the lover and her same-sex alter ego. It is Rossetti's aesthetic fascination with genre and varied tones of voice, rather than some mistrust of women, that compels the vigorous feuds in her wrangling ballads. Here, as Sharon Smulders astutely observes, Rossetti "experiments with different formal shapes to contain the varieties of feminine experience." She moves temporarily beyond lyric constraints and beyond the monologue's reliance on scraps of back talk to make ballads-in-dialogue out of her scrapping speakers' rancorous back-and-forth.[26]

"Noble Sisters" opens in a way that is common in *Minstrelsy* ballads, whose heroines often expect a "bony bird" to carry a token of "true love": the courted woman asks with allowable disingenuousness if her sister has noticed a falcon "flying toward my window" (*CP,* 1 : 33; 3).[27] In response, she is told with feigned solicitude that a falcon was seen "swooping" but that it has been driven off (9). Further questions elicit mocking replies that underscore the women's bitterly different attitudes. Awaited letter-bearers are treated as pests and driven off—the hound for "baying," the page for "creaking" the gate (22, 35)—and their dispatch is followed by the climactic dismissal of the suitor himself:

> "Oh patience, sister. Did you see
>   A young man tall and strong,
> Swift-footed to uphold the right
>   And to uproot the wrong,
> Come home across the desolate sea
>   To woo me for his wife?
> And in his heart my heart is locked,
>   And in his life my life."—
>   "I met a nameless man, sister,
>   Who loitered round our door:
>   I said: Her husband loves her much,
>   And yet she loves him more."   (37–48)

The "nameless" suitor's low birth is as great a "bar" as the death of kin in "The Convent Threshold." Goaded by this interfering duplicity, the hitherto meek sister becomes fiercely indignant:

> "Fie, sister, fie, a wicked lie,
>   A lie, a wicked lie,
> I have none other love but him,
>   Nor will have till I die.
> And you have turned him from our door,
>   And stabbed him with a lie.
> I will go seek him thro' the world
>   In sorrow till I die."   (49–56)

It is at this juncture that some readers align themselves with the betrayed woman. Helena Michie, for example, reads "Noble Sisters" and "Maude Clare" as "bitter battles" from which a clear and unambiguous winner emerges; in her view, the initially weaker woman gains "confidence in the course of poetic argument" and passes "from a position of helplessness to power. It is as if these poems were the testing ground . . . the one place where female voices can hear themselves argue, can 'talk' themselves into an assurance of control." More recent commentators have demurred, however, and Smulders, once again, is particularly cogent, noting that Rossetti "is far more impartial" than this power analysis suggests and that the "only certainty lies with the violent breach" at the end of the sisters' debate. In support of this reading, we might add that, within the ballad tradition, a heroine's pledge making is universally ominous. The wily heroine of "The Gay Goss-Hawk" fulfills hers by simulating death and being delivered in a coffin to her waiting lover; and so many fail altogether that William Morris, in his modern-antique "Golden Wings," tells of a questing woman who is "slain outright" as soon as she leaves her castle. In Rossetti's poem, the rashness of such a search exacerbates the quarrel and, in the final line, provokes vehement condemnation:

> "Go seek in sorrow, sister,
>   And find in sorrow too:
> If thus you shame our father's name
>   My curse go forth with you."   (57–60)

Much like the blood on the convent sill, the invocation of the "father's name" is a sign of irreconcilability. There can be no winner of this contest, and further speech will only continue the quarrel's incompleteness. Such an impasse makes for successful closure, however, for the reader (if not the sisters) understands that an inflammatory height has been reached and that cessation is called for, if only of the poem itself. The final stanza, to use one of Barbara Herrnstein Smith's cagey formulations, "allows the reader to be satisfied by the failure of continuation."[28]

What might be described as the Rossettian stalemate, her keeping open the fiery space between quarrelers, intensifies and shapes the erotic conflict in "Maude Clare" (*CP,* 1:44–46). In this instance, Maude Clare's antagonist is not her sister but Nell, whose wedding she interrupts. The next surprise is Nell's defense of her suddenly undermined bridal devotion and what it reveals of the similarity in the rivals' dilemmas. It soon becomes apparent that both women speak from the self-divided position of "baulked desire," each wanting a love she knows cannot bring the fullness that is wanted—or, more accurately, each implacably wanting what is *not* what she wants.

Before examining the women's clash, it should be noted how much cutting Rossetti did in order to achieve the poem's final, contentious form. Originally forty-three stanzas long, "Maude Clare" went through two prunings before emerging as a twelve-stanza episode on the church steps. In eliminating the bulk of her draft, Rossetti patiently sacrifices interesting details (e.g., Maude Clare's queenly self-presentation) and entire episodes (e.g., the couple's exchange of vows and the postnuptial feast, complete with knowing toasts by the male guests). Especially indicative is Rossetti's excising of the young lord's motive for betrayal: "Maude Clare for all she was so fair / Had never an inch of land" (*CP,* 1:245). The baleful influence of real estate on erotic choice is a traditional theme that Rossetti would have come upon in any number of ballads. "Lord Thomas and Fair Ellinor" (the source for Jeanie's description in "Goblin Market") tells of choosing a bride for the sake of "houses and lands." But in the late days of revision, the economics of betrayal are no longer a concern, nor is ordinary common sense. The bride's level-headed objection that her rival ought to have spoken before the wedding is also cut. The issue that fascinates Rossetti is the compulsive illogic of desire, so she keeps only the material that attends to the lovers' inescapable dilemma.[29]

In a single scene (in both senses of that word) the unhappily emboldened Maude Clare presents the newly wedded Thomas with a gift:

> "Here's my half of the golden chain
>   You wore about your neck,
> That day we waded ankle-deep
>   For lilies in the beck:
>
> "Here's my half of the faded leaves
>   We plucked from budding bough,
> With feet amongst the lily leaves,—
>   The lilies are budding now."   (21–28)

Lest there should be any mystery about this display of former intimacy, the next gift is for the bride. With Nell, Maude Clare does what is usually only threatened by blackmailers and extortionists; she makes an unwelcome display of the truth:

> "Take my share of a fickle heart,
>   Mine of a paltry love:
> Take it or leave it as you will,
>   I wash my hands thereof."   (37–40)

By addressing Nell so openly, Maude Clare submits to the logic of dialogue and is compelled to hear the bride's reply. Once again, as in "Noble Sisters," when the obstructing woman—the one whose role in the narrative is to keep the loved male at a distance from his lover—gets to speak, she is formidable. Though a compromised bride, she manages to fend off Maude Clare's scorn:

> "And what you leave," said Nell, "I'll take,
>   And what you spurn, I'll wear;
> For he's my lord for better and worse,
>   And him I love, Maude Clare.
>
> "Yea, tho' you're taller by the head,
>   More wise, and much more fair;
> I'll love him till he loves me best,
>   Me best of all, Maude Clare."   (41–48)

Echoing Maude Clare's "take" and "leave" and adding a phrase from the marriage vow, Nell takes for herself the role of the wronged woman. The confrontation suddenly becomes, borrowing Dubrow's terms, a "closely-matched" and "indeterminate" struggle. Neither the self-exposed Maude nor the self-deluded Nell can exclude the other from the experience of her own desire, and the reader finds it impossible to ignore either woman's pain. Given this empathetic bind, the unsteady Thomas turns out to be an unexpectedly representative figure; he serves in some sense as the voice of the reader's bewilderment. There is a moment, before Nell speaks up, when he briefly attempts to take control of the scene—and fails:

> He faltered in his place:
> "Lady," he said,—"Maude Clare," he said,—
>   "Maude Clare:"—and hid his face.   (30–32)

Reduced to stammering their names, this man in the middle utters fragments that link and separate the two women, but he says nothing to make betrayal intelligible or endurable. Standing between his jilted lover and his bride, he finds himself mutely incapable of addressing the yearnings that torment them all. At the poem's end, the reader is at a comparable impasse. As in "Noble Sisters," the women come to the outspoken finish of their unfinished struggle and the reader accepts the truth of the quarrel's permanent openness. At the same time, there is an awareness that crucial words are missing—words of compassion, grief, possibly forgiveness—consigned forever to the poem's silences. In the very domain of the voluble, the reader becomes aware, as so often in Rossetti's poetry, of a pressing inarticulateness, of something that has not been or cannot be put into words.[30]

"Not One Word": The Silences of Poetry

The wrangling of "Noble Sisters" and "Maude Clare" prompts the realization that Rossetti distrusts her quarrelers' fluency; their too-ready flow of words achieves little more than an overwrought inarticulateness. As clashing antagonists, they say emphatically more than the inaudible ghosts or half-articulate speakers who populate the lyrics; but in these instances, more is less. Though Rossetti masters volubility, she remains committed to quieter expression and with a subtle resourcefulness plays innumerable variations on inexplicitness per se. Throughout *Goblin Market* and the later volumes, her reticent speakers openly lament having neither "will nor wish to say" what is needful; they tell of turning "in silence to the wall" and admit being nearly mute: "My words were slow, my tears were few" (*CP,* 1:30, 154, 65). The instinct that cautions Rossetti against the spontaneous overflow of language returns her again and again to the possibilities of silence. For her, the withholding of speech is constitutive. So manifestly does her poetry prefer low tones, shy avoidance, and quiet watchfulness, so readily do her speakers allow things to "stay unsaid" almost as if they *know*—contrary to the lyric convention—someone is listening to them, that the style might well be described as explicitly inexplicit (*CP,* 1:167). In their display of reticence, as Armstrong points out, Rossetti's poems "come to be *about* reserve"; shaped by a deep rivalry between evasiveness and aesthetic control, they "struggle to express and not to express, to resist and not to resist" the appeal of words.[31]

To take up the paradox of Rossettian silence requires a return, in this final section, to "Goblin Market," where the sisters, one cloyed by "luscious" goblin fruit, the other clawed by its vendors, are subjected to one further torment: they are rendered wordless. This effect is prominent enough, and in Lizzie's case startling enough, to invite the teasing out of its implications for Rossetti's style. It has been suggested more than once, of course, that the poem might concern authorship, either as admonition against "the risks and gratifications of art" or the opposite, a commentary urging women to "claim their place" in the "garden of English poetry," with both readings taking their cue from the maleness of goblin men's offerings. But McGann's suggestion that Lizzie's *response* to the goblins provides "a stylistic metaphor standing for Rossetti's poetry" seems to me particularly cogent. It directs attention to Lizzie's "inward laughter," which, as an unheard sound, is a singularly appropriate emblem of the artist's exhilarated struggle with wordlessness. In pursuing Rossetti's interest in the strains of silence, this chapter will close with four splendid poems, each enacting its own form of reticence and each achieving the impression of access denied, yet all the while suggesting the desirability of what is so assiduously guarded.[32]

"Goblin Market" twice allows goblin treachery to drive the sisters mute. When Laura realizes that the fruit merchants' "sugar-baited words" have become inaudible, her shocked response is an answering silence: "She said not one word in her heart's sore ache" (234, 261). Her muteness is the clash of remembered ecstasy and wrenching deprivation. When a little later Lizzie's closed mouth serves as a physical barrier against the fruit's toxicity, Rossetti again insists that her heroine utters "not a word" (430). Amid the chaos of the goblin assault, Lizzie's wordlessness conveys not only her terror but her literally unspeakable euphoria. At this juncture, the narrative—which must continue its stream of words or Rossetti has no poem—becomes remarkably oblique. Instead of access to what the tight-lipped Lizzie is thinking, there is the jubilant assurance that "she laughed in heart to feel the drip / Of juice that syrupped all her face" (433–34). The reader is to ponder a nonverbal feeling (the "feel" of juice) and a completely internal sound. This inarticulate human noise, inaudible and ineffable, is the accompaniment to Lizzie's sprint for home: "Windy-paced" she runs and runs, "quite out of breath with haste / And inward laughter" (461, 462–63).

Silent laughter is a wonderfully unexpected image, since poetry is, after all, a hearable art. And it is nicely startling that Rossetti should think of her chosen medium as, in some sense, a laughing matter. To be sure, she has some support in this insight, for more than one author has spoken of the intensity of the writing process as an involvement that approaches rapture. Louise Glück, for example, tells us that "the poet engaged in the act of writing feels giddy exhilaration." This sense of elation, she adds, is independent of the pain, love-sorrow, weariness, fear, or grief that is the poet's subject: "The poet, writing, is simultaneously soaked" in her "materials" and liberated by them.[33] "Inward laughter" suggests freedom, detachment, but also privacy—and Rossetti makes refined use of it. Along with the poet's "exhilaration" there comes the inevitable anxiety of the creative process, and "Goblin Market" lays out this ambiguity as phases in Lizzie's narrative. Her first mute laugh "in heart" is defensive as she protects herself from abuse. Her vulnerability, should she laugh *out loud,* corresponds to Rossetti's own risk should she recklessly open herself to readers. Aesthetic self-exposure can bring the pain of rough handling by those who would put words (or fruit) in one's mouth. When laughter is mentioned the second time, the issue shifts from the necessity of muteness—Lizzie has by now escaped being force-fed—to the *inevitability* of inwardness. The word-enraptured poet laughs, but laughter is a sound that eludes transcription; it can be alluded to and surrounded with meaning, but never fully represented. Shelley once compared artistic inspiration to a coal-not-yet-faded, and his metaphor carries the conviction that the exultant, creative self dies or fades or becomes silent precisely as the poem comes into being. Countless artists have registered their agreement with Shelley's notion, and Lizzie's laughter shows that Rossetti concurs. The artist who is euphoric in the midst of creation, whose "heart," to use one of Rossetti's most familiar analogies, "is like a singing bird," and who is miraculously songful when writing her poem, gets only a portion of that music into language; the rest is unheard (*CP,* 1:36). This silence is not a source of grievance for Rossetti; on the contrary, it is something she savors, pondering it under the guise of laughter, muteness, and sometimes both simultaneously.

A further and quietly brilliant instance of Rossetti's fascination with the unspoken comes at the conclusion of "'A Bruised Reed Shall He Not Break.'" Drawing on the time-honored connection between spiritual affliction and sullenness, Rossetti imagines God coaxing a sufferer who clings to dejection's prerogative and remains resolutely incommunicative. Ever so patiently, the deity offers to bless "the germs and small beginnings" of goodness and asks only that the addressee "choose My love" (*CP,* 1:67). Unfortunately, such wooing elicits hapless one-liners: "Alas, I cannot will," "I cannot wish, alas!" (*CP,* 1:67). Refrainlike in their sameness, these lame rejoinders bespeak the paralysis of failed desire. Only when the divine suitor refers to his own torture does he elicit a few parsed syllables that indicate a willingness to accept grace:

> What, neither choose nor wish to choose? and yet
>   I still must strive to win thee and constrain:
>   For thee I hung upon the cross in pain,
>   How then can I forget?
> If thou as yet dost neither love, nor hate,
>   Nor choose, nor wish,—resign thyself, be still
>   Till I infuse love, hatred, longing, will.—
>   I do not deprecate.   (*CP*, 1:67)

The final response, "I do not deprecate," gives the merest and most-delayed indication of change. The phrasing shifts only negligibly from "cannot" to "do not" but it sets up, after all, the last word's quiet semantic surprise: "deprecate" negates the negative, and the statement proves to be, as W. David Shaw nicely puts it, "an affirmation in disguise." The respondent does not avert God's effort, does not *not* accept what is offered. The sound, too, contributes to the laconic effect, as the collected d's and t's attest that acceptance is spoken in the teeth, literally, of reluctance. Here as always, Rossetti is acutely aware that what is said in words is a thing apart from the speaker's wordless inner turmoil. God (and God only) knows what goes on in the sufferer's heart, but the final word is squeezed out and it is sufficient.[34]

Sometimes, a poem confesses that feeling exceeds lyric formulation, admits it own inarticulateness, and proceeds as it must. "May," for example, opens by pleading an inability to specify what it is about:

> I cannot tell you how it was;
> But this I know: it came to pass
> Upon a bright and breezy day
> When May was young; ah pleasant May!   (*CP*, 1:51)

What starts out as an echo of biblical phrasing, "it came to pass," and seems on the brink of an allusion to, say, God's temptation of Abraham, promptly eludes solemnity at the line break. With the enjambment at "pass," the unidentified event becomes a breezier matter, and it seems that the reader is being encouraged to guess at the riddle of what has

passed. The next stanza even supplies hints about the avoided subject, lo-
calizing its arrival within May's boundaries:

> As yet the poppies were not born
> Between the blades of tender corn;
> The last eggs had not hatched as yet,
> Nor any bird foregone its mate.   (*CP*, 1 : 51)

The displaced precision of this image, with its yet-to-be-born poppies
among discrete blades of grain, creates an impression of accuracy that
works to heighten the poem's basic reserve. Inclusions signal exclusions,
and the pressure of something left out is gently intensified. "It" becomes
a felt absence, something missing from a scene that is itself about ab-
sences. Just as in the "Dream-Land" stanzas reporting the sleeper's non-
sensations, these lines attend to what has not been born, not hatched,
and, ominously, not "yet" abandoned. Though the reader naturally envisions the scene—that is one of the key effects of the poem's
reticence—what is offered to view is underdeveloped as a picture; and
this, too, is typical of Rossetti's poetry. What is seen is often something
evanescent and half-hidden: ripples that "flow" and "vanish," a "leaf-
nested primrose," violets buried in a "double shade" of "withering"
leaves (*CP*, 3 : 53; 1 : 48; 1 : 194). Such details have the quality of sightings,
rather than sights, and are the result of accustomed and yet highly discreet watchfulness. The attention paid in a Rossettian poem is eminently
tactful. A brief comparison will make this last point clearer.

When a spring poem takes note of "chill-veined snowdrops" (*CP*,
1 : 48), the appealingly exact phrase exhibits none of the invasiveness
that propels Tennyson's notice of the "lines of green that streak the
white / Of the first snowdrop's inner leaves" (*AT*, 289). Rossetti shuns the
hypersensitivity of the Tennysonian manner that imagines the folding
up of individual petals: "Now sleeps the crimson petal, now the white"
(*AT*, 318). The opulence of this imaginative singling out of petals that
do not, after all, close up one by one, is the hallmark of what Arthur
Hallam named the "poetry of sensation." This near preciosity of manner,
something that Tennyson learned from Keats, does not call attention
so much to the lilies as to "the impression made by the world upon . . .
delicate senses." There can be no doubt of the delicacy of Rossetti's
senses, but there is every indication that she prefers not to call attention

to it. Her most precise details are pressed into the service of evasion, converging around some reticence in the lyric, some mystery not easily comprehended.[35]

When "May" comes to an end, the lines are still reluctant to specify the loss they regret:

> I cannot tell you what it was;
> But this I know: it did but pass.
> It passed away with sunny May,
> With all sweet things it passed away,
> And left me old, and cold, and grey.   (*CP,* 1 : 51)

Lingeringly, the adjectives accumulate, "old, and cold, and grey," so that the wish to give evidence of a grief no single word can describe and the reluctance even to speak of it are felt in the rhythm. By so thoroughly circumventing its apparent subject, "May" seems to make only modest claims for the importance of the event it barely records, and yet it creates the sense of an impressively large and ineluctable emotion. In effect, what might be called Rossetti's decorum of omission serves to block interpretation and ultimately to protect her theme. No particular loss, but rather the enigma of loss, remains the poem's undiminished concern.

Rossetti's open secret is that reticence sustains her as a poet. Structured like desire, contradictory in the pursuit of what it does and does not want to say, it does not "cloy with length of use" and is a continuing motive for new tonalities and forms. Two of Rossetti's most successful poems consider a kind of reticence that masquerades as its opposite. Using interrogatives that seem artlessly to-the-point—"must I knock?" "You want to hear it?"—her questioners manage to perplex the issues they raise and keep interest alive long after their poems have closed. The best known is probably "Up-hill," Rossetti's first poem to appear in *Macmillan's Magazine,* and so popular with autograph seekers, musicians, and anthologists that she once professed delight at being "asked for something that is mine, instead of for *Uphill* [*sic*]" (*L,* 1 : 222). While the "crystal ingenuous openness" of its style no doubt led some of these admirers to mistake it for a simple allegory, Gabriel and his friends were aware of its elusiveness; as he reported cheerfully, "Every one seems to have been struck (on own hooks) by *Up-hill*" (*LDGR,* 2 : 394). Presented

as a brisk dialogue with prompt replies, the poem seems sufficiently cat-
echetical to preclude bafflement:

> Does the road wind up-hill all the way?
> > Yes, to the very end.
> Will the day's journey take the whole long day?
> > From morn to night, my friend.   (*CP,* 1:65; 1–4)

Once the alternating pattern is established, however, the rote quality of
these exchanges becomes mildly puzzling: the compulsory end stops become slightly tiresome and force the overly prominent rhymes to go flat.
"Poetry," it has been said, "is involved, more than prose, in persistently
stopping and starting—and yet it must not be a thing of stops and starts."
By this account, "Up-hill" is precisely what a poem should *not* be. That
the questioning continues without gathering the momentum appropriate to urgent probing or wild surmise is Rossetti's sure indication that
something is amiss:

> But is there for the night a resting-place?
> > A roof for when the slow dark hours begin.
> May not the darkness hide it from my face?
> > You cannot miss that inn.
>
> Shall I meet other wayfarers at night?
> > Those who have gone before.   (5–10)

Though told that one "cannot miss that inn," the questioner rather wit-
lessly misses the point. The fault, it should be noted, is not in the reply;
for readers find "that inn" to be hauntingly evocative, and at least one
poet, A. E. Housman, borrowed it for an elegy that touchingly sends a
soldier to "idle / At the inn of night for aye." Rossetti's questioner, however, instead of sensing the advent of death or dreading the blight of body
and perhaps soul, simply starts another, manifestly obtuse, question. The
interrogative form itself has become the wordy medium of constricted,
defended thinking and an emblem of incomprehension:

> Then must I knock, or call when just in sight?
> > They will not keep you standing at that door.
>
> Shall I find comfort, travel-sore and weak?
> > Of labour you shall find the sum.

> Will there be beds for me and all who seek?
> Yea, beds for all who come.   (11–16)

Having exhausted his battery of queries about "the *ascensus,*" that is to say, "the journey or ordeal upward through experience to knowledge," the questionmonger still dodges the looming epiphany. This failure seems unaccountable. The riddling responses are not opaque enough to block comprehension, and even the mild wittiness of "They will not keep you standing" offers little challenge. One might justifiably complain that the hints about "the very end," "night," and "beds for all" are insufficiently ambiguous and demand too little interpretive effort. And yet the surge of realization is missing and the meaning of the uphill trek remains open to question. Another way to say this is that "Up-hill" is *deliberately* not a very good riddle because the focus of its interest is on the barriers erected by repression. The mystery it ponders is the way one can balk at the knowledge one has nearly always known and escape the implications of answers one seems explicitly to seek.[36]

Rossetti's interest in enigmatic exchanges and verbal evasion provides the structure in another, much-admired poem. The final example in this chapter, "Winter: My Secret," considers the wonderfully paradoxical possibilities of flagrant concealment and garrulous reticence. With a manner that fluctuates between coaxing and baffling, between "help and hindrance," the speaker presents a secret—the title in the *Goblin Market* volume was simply "My Secret" (*CP,* 1:247)—as if sharing it were a game conducted within the bounds of permissible teasing:

> I tell my secret? No indeed, not I:
> Perhaps some day, who knows?
> But not today; it froze, and blows, and snows,
> And you're too curious: fie!
> You want to hear it? well:
> Only, my secret's mine, and I won't tell.   (*CP,* 1:47; 1–6)

Having been brought into this exchange by means of ascribed characteristics and responses ("you're too curious"), the one-who-would-guess is promptly forced into a contradictory hypothesis:

> Or, after all, perhaps there's none:
> Suppose there is no secret after all,
> But only just my fun.   (7–9)

Rhetorically astute commentators have noted that the mere profession of
a secret premises a self that can have, tell, or withhold it; secrecy is "a
sign" of the speaker's "individuality." This suggestion can be corroborated by the experienced reader–riddlee's detection of the solution cryptically embedded in the claims that "my secret's mine" and it's "just my
fun." The individual self, signified by the pronoun "I" and its possessives,
is as conspicuous as the inaudibly audible girl's name in the children's
nursery rhyme:

> There was a girl in our town,
> Silk an' satin was her gown,
> Silk an' satin, gold an' velvet,
> Guess her name, three times I've told it.   (Anne)

Even for the reader who was not raised on riddles, the speaker's hint that
the secret reduces to "just my fun" is too gleefully self-delighting to be
accepted as a straightforward denial. It is a covert declaration that a talent for nonsense is integral to the secret-keeper's identity.[37]

"Nonsense," as it happens, was the poem's title in manuscript; and
"precious nonsense," as Stephen Booth brilliantly attests, is the stuff of
poetry (*CP*, 1:247). In this teasing monologue, the speaker's frivolity
serves as yet another intimation of the poet's elation, of the inward laughter that is a consequence of her "immersion in her materials," in rhythm,
riddling, and the play of words. Herein lies the genuine evasiveness of this
evasive poem; it is Rossetti herself who is so unabashedly delighted with
the elements of language. Early on, for example, her speaker says of the
weather that "today it froze, and blows, and snows," as if "to fro" were
an extant infinitive with "froze" its present tense (2). This line is a whimsical example of Rossetti's delight in what Booth calls "nonimporting pattern," the basic device of "repetition with variation" by which a poem
"gets the feel of coherence." It is also an instance of serious triviality, for
by indulging in the pleasure of an irresistible rhyme, it signals a linguistic
insight into wordlessness. There are irregular verbs (*freeze, froze, frozen*)
and other realities of language that come between a speaker and her
meanings. The elusiveness of "it" is especially conspicuous here as well.
Usually it refers to the "secret" ("You want to hear it?"), though here it
tells of the weather ("it snows"), which is to say the winter, a duality
Rossetti happily points to in the 1875 edition with her revised title's
funny linkage: "Winter: My Secret." In a weird way, the poem, which is

between the "winter" and the "secret," the reader and the writer, is like the colon. That Rossetti overrides limitations with a neologism, ungrammaticality, or other caginess calls attention, humorously, to the general fact that what can be said in words is necessarily remote from the speaker's wordless apprehension. In this sense, every poet deals in recondite "secrets" that never make it into the poem; the chosen medium, language itself, locates the poet at the giddy threshold of an impossible revelation.[38]

And so Rossetti's monologist continues her game from behind a closed door:

> I cannot ope to every one who taps,
> And let the draughts come whistling thro' my hall;
> Come bounding and surrounding me,
> Come buffeting, astounding me,
> Nipping and clipping thro' my wraps and all.   (13–17)

Animated and hostile, these "draughts" recall the goblins who come "leaping, / Puffing and blowing" as they surround the beleaguered Lizzie and point to the other, protective explanation for the poet's leaving things unsaid (332–33). The implication is that the opening of this door will be no more likely than Lizzie's opening of "lip from lip" (431). But then, Rossetti's garrulous secret-keeper proves to be of two minds about concealment. Imagining that not every season is so harshly inclement, she raises the tantalizing possibility of new weather and riskless disclosure. At first, reticence is protected by a nearly whimsical mistrust of the pleasing but still variable season:

> Spring's an expansive time: yet I don't trust
> March with its peck of dust,
> Nor April with its rainbow-crowned brief showers,
> Nor even May, whose flowers
> One frost may wither thro' the sunless hours.   (23–27)

Even as she resists vernal/verbal expansiveness, the logic of the calendar brings the prospect of summer's gorgeous out-of-doors. With a tentative "perhaps," and a distant echo of Keats, the speaker warms to the possibility of languid drowsiness, golden ripening, and perfect atmosphere, openly yearning for the conditions of a transparently soulful lyricism:

> Perhaps some languid summer day,
> When drowsy birds sing less and less,

And golden fruit is ripening to excess,
If there's not too much sun nor too much cloud,
And the warm wind is neither still nor loud,
Perhaps my secret I may say,
Or you may guess.   (28–34)

Regrettably, as Armstrong points out, this proposed season is "a time of impossible plenitude and equilibrium." Even as it is articulated, the lyric wish is abandoned. The conditions of the ideal day are refined and over-specified: it is "not too . . . nor too . . . neither . . . nor" and therefore *not* at all likely. But in a final bit of reticence, the poem remains guarded about refusing unguardedness, and closure comes with the jauntily eva-sive suggestion that on some perfect (and perfectly nonexistent) occasion "perhaps my secret . . . you may guess." Ending with a fantasy that holds the probabilities of disclosure and nondisclosure in ambiguous suspen-sion, Rossetti has the fun of her poem while emphatically maintaining her distance.[39]

"Winter: My Secret" may, for this reason, stand as a singularly repre-sentative piece. Rossetti implies something of the sort when, in a letter to Gabriel, she defends herself against his disparagement of the outspo-ken "muscularity" of her style. This nearly implausible complaint against Christina has much to do with Gabriel's perception of her indebtedness to other women poets and is a story for the next chapter. Here it is only necessary to notice the way she brings "Winter: My Secret" into her ar-gument. Provisionally accepting the hypothesis that her work tends to-ward the abrasive, she isolates three poems for comment. The "indiscre-tion" of "No, Thank you, John," is surely to be tolerated, since "John" is a fictional character. "The Queen of Hearts" is another that "surely cannot give deep umbrage," especially in comparison to "Winter: My Secret." Halfway into her explanation, Rossetti sees she's left the latter poem vulnerable to attack and so she promptly attaches a personal plea: "I hardly think ['The Queen'] as open to comment as 'My Secret,' but this last is *such a favorite* with me that please don't retort 'Nor do I—'" (*L,* 2:74; emphasis added). At the time she writes this letter, Rossetti has just brought out her collected edition, the "nice fattish volume" of 1875 (*L,* 2:38). Of all the poems she might appeal to at this point in her ca-reer, she chooses the one with a speaker whose high-volume reticence insists on telling us that there's something she isn't telling. This "favorite" manages to be simultaneously flagrant and reserved, to withhold a secret even as it enfolds the hope of a poetry that is sensuous, expansive, and self-revealing. It enacts, in other words, the paradox of her own authorial desire, the impulse to write of what is lyrically private, countered by the sure knowledge that words do and do not reveal the poet's "inward laughter."

Influence and Restraint

Victorian Women Poets and the Rossettis

WHEN FELICIA HEMANS died in Dublin in 1835, she was one of the most famous poets of the age, and in some venues the highest paid, though she is hardly known today. The outpouring of formal grief at her death included an elegy by Letitia Landon, the considerably younger contemporary whose talent had already attracted the attention of the mighty *Westminster Review*. Neither writer is now remembered except among scholars, who, given the general interest in recovering lost poets and the near coincidence of the women's careers, almost inevitably mention them in tandem, sometimes in the same sentence. They have become a pair of names identified by a single poem or book title; and in these distant summaries, they can seem nearly indistinguishable. That they share certain topics, among them the pursuit of art, the blighting effect of fame, and the failure of love, has caused them to blur. That their names chime—Felicia Hemans, Letitia Landon—makes for inevitable slips of the tongue, as with Laura and Lizzie (who hasn't done that, says McGann!). In the mid-nineteenth century, however, they are distinct to the Rossettis: to Gabriel who collects Landon's books, to William who edits Hemans's work, and to Christina who admires, imitates, and resists the freshness and originality of both women as she herself becomes a very well remembered poet. Her response is a complicated story, two stories, in fact, with different trajectories. Rossetti values Hemans as a woman of genius whose celebrations of women as artists, mothers, and public heroines inspire her own more nuanced treatment in *The Prince's Progress and Other Poems*. But "The Lowest Room," a long narrative plainly indebted to Hemans, prompts harsh criticism from Gabriel and, as we shall see, a strangely delayed literary quarrel. Landon proves a less problematic influence. Her style in *The Venetian Bracelet* and *The Golden Violet* makes her something of a mentor to Rossetti, who offers her the unique compliment of a named monologue, "L.E.L.," complete with an endorsing epigraph from Elizabeth Barrett Browning and welcome emendations by Gabriel. Tracing the influence of these women serves, ultimately, to crystallize our perception of Rossetti's poetics, that strict aesthetic economy which is the "primary impulse" (Gabriel's phrase) of her best work.[1]

Felicia Hemans: Hail and Farewell

When William Michael Rossetti, as an aspiring man of letters, sets about his 1856 volume of *The Poetical Works of Mrs. Felicia Hemans,* he does so with a confidence befitting the editor of an established and enduring author. His "Prefatory Notice" celebrates Hemans's "genius" as a fact "conceded by all lovers of poetry" (*PWH,* 3). That her work enjoyed an "entirely unexampled" popularity during her lifetime seems to him a clear portent of the future; her fame will burn like the "flame" that is "kindled from the ashes of the great" (*PWH,* 5, 3). Hemans's extraordinary productivity—nineteen books published between 1808 and 1835— and the aura attaching to her lifelong dedication had already given rise to the legend that she dictated her last poem, "Sabbath Sonnet," "amid fever and delirium" as she lay dying. William respects the gravity of Hemans's poetic aim: "it was none other than to be the worthy interpreter of worthy truth." Admitting "Mrs Hemans did not attempt everything," he claims that "the ambition of most authors would have been content with the range she occupied. Her only limits were *nature, principle,* and *truth.* . . . None could be more alive than she was to the respectability (so to speak) of all that reason discovers and religion reveals of the spiritual meanings of the world around us, in the least as well as the grandest of its parts" (*PWH,* 5, 6–7). Though William does not compare her directly to male authors, he ranks her with writers "of the loftiest school" and quotes "The Diver," which he regards as a "beautiful illustration" of Hemans's "own career" (*PWH,* 7, 4). An apostrophe to a pearl diver, the poem compares the "wrestler with the sea" to the poet who descends into "the gulfs of the soul" to retrieve "bright words." Profundity is the obvious point of connection, but so is pain; both the diver and the minstrel shed "life-drops" securing "treasures" for the world. William admires the dignified lucidity of Hemans's poems; he notes their "perfect transparency" and (mixing the qualities of author and text) their "lofty bearing" (*PWH*, 7). The genteel sadness of her work registers with him as high seriousness, an emotional "calmness" that gives access to truth: "It was a self-possession which never forsook her in the heat of her highest enthusiasm of joy or sorrow" (*PWH*, 6). Felicia Hemans and her poetry seem in the 1850s to have the heroic simplicity one requires of forebears. William ends his "Notice" by quoting the final lines of "A Parting Song"; this melancholy farewell asks, "When will ye think of me, my friends?" and makes a sadly sweet recommendation:

> Thus let my memory be with you, friends!
>   Thus ever think of me!
> Kindly and gently, but as of one
> For whom 'tis well to be fled and gone;
> As of a bird from a chain unbound,
> As of a wanderer whose home is found;—
> So let it be.   (*Hemans,* 425)

The kindly remembrance the poem urges seems, in 1856, to be assured.

Over time, however, William's sense of Hemans's aesthetic merit shifts: the poems come to seem explicit, moralizing, and bland, her worthy truths a matter of sentiment. The introductory comments to his expanded edition of the *Poetical Works* (1878) offer a cooler appraisal, one that eventually becomes received opinion and consigns Hemans to literary oblivion:

> Mrs Hemans has that love of good and horror of evil which characterize a scrupulous female mind; and which we may most rightly praise without concluding that they favor poetical robustness, or even perfection in literary form. She is a leader in that very modern phalanx of poets who persistently co-ordinate the impulse of sentiment with the guiding power of morals or religion. Everything must convey its "lesson," and is indeed set forth for the sake of its lesson: but must at the same time have the emotional gush of a spontaneous sentiment. The poet must not write because he has something of his own to say, but because he has something *right* to feel and say.

The phrase "perfection in literary form" suggests part of the motive for William's altered views; by the 1870s his sister Christina has become the poet of perfect form. "Her skill is exquisite," one reviewer would say,

knowing there would be no disagreement; she is "one of the most perfect poets of the age."[2]

From the vantage point of 1856, when Christina's books are yet to
come, Hemans has genuine appeal. Her collected work expresses a clear
and persistent ambition: to extend the range of subjects for poetry while
defining womanhood and the complexity of women's domestic affections. Voraciously well read, Hemans writes intelligently of such matters
as the Swiss separatists' resistance ("The Vaudois' Wife"), the excavations
at Herculaneum ("The Image in Lava"), and the unfinished work of
global exploration ("The Traveller at the Source of the Nile"). What
Tricia Lootens, one of Hemans's most convincing admirers, has called her
"deeply international" tendency leads her to scour the world and world
history for the heroines of her *Records of Woman* so she may share the
home thoughts of Joan of Arc at the moment of her triumph or celebrate
the bravery of an obscure "forest girl" in preventing a prisoner's torture
(*Hemans*, 380, 389). In *The Prince's Progress and Other Poems*, Rossetti
shows a willingness to pursue similar topics, sometimes fairly closely, as
in the long treatment of domesticity in "The Lowest Room," and at other
times more distantly, as when she imagines the interventionist courage of
"A Royal Princess." But for her, the single most influential feature of
Hemans's work is her conviction about the genius of women artists.[3]

Inspired by Germaine de Staël's depiction of the all-talented Corinne,
Hemans's own "Corinne at the Capitol" revels in the improvisatrice's
triumph on receiving the Roman laurel and celebrates her song with extravagant oxymoron: Corinne's "burning words" flow "With a rushing
stream's delight" (*Hemans*, 461; 37–40). Ellen Moers's inaugural study *Literary Women* has traced the impact of the fictional Corinne throughout
the nineteenth century and the enthusiasm that greeted "the myth of the
famous woman . . . performing to the applause of the world." It is only
necessary to mention the circumstance that made Corinne especially exhilarating for Christina Rossetti: she alone of the women Moers treats had
firsthand knowledge of the oral tradition, since her father, the Italian ex-
patriate Gabriele Rossetti, was an actual improvisator. Her glee at this fact
may be surmised from the earliest extant Rossetti family letter in which
the six-year-old Gabriel writes excitedly to his aunt that "Papa" was at "a
party where there was the Turkish Ambassador, who asked papa to
improvise" (*LDGR,* 1:1). But if Hemans's poem stimulates Christina
Rossetti's already awakened artistic desire, it also provides an explicitly

cautionary lesson. As soon as the "radiant" Corinne is crowned, her happiness is put into question, and Hemans ends the poem by admitting the
sorrow that Susan Wolfson elegantly describes as the "pathos of celebrity":

> — Oh! art thou not
> Happy in that glorious lot?—
> Happier, happier far than thou,
> With the laurel on thy brow,
> She that makes the humblest hearth
> Lovely but to one on earth!   (*Hemans,* 461–62; 43–48)

The adulation of all of Rome does not, evidently, compare with the affection of "one" beloved, and, in Leighton's trenchant assessment, "artistic triumphalism" must be "paid for in loneliness." When Hemans writes
of a historically existent artist, the sculptor Properzia Rossi—whose career she found described in Vasari's *Lives* (the source Robert Browning
turns to for "Andrea del Sarto" and "Fra Lippo Lippi")—there is a similar double message. At the outset, Hemans gives a vivid rendering of Rossi
at the very moment of artistic inspiration. In the privacy of her studio,
the lonely sculptor conceives of one final statue, a "forsaken Ariadne,"
that she hopes will stir the man she loves to recognize her talent and
regret his indifference:

> It comes,—the power
> Within me born, flows back; my fruitless dower
> That could not win me love. Yet once again
> I greet it proudly, with its rushing train
> Of glorious images:—they throng—they press—
> A sudden joy lights up my loneliness.   (*Hemans,* 353; 38, 25–31)

In a later section when the statue is finished, the artist laments the "worth-
less" fame that does not win her an "abiding-place" in her beloved's
heart (83).[4]

Having thus presented Corinne at the peak and Properzia Rossi at the
end of their respective careers, Hemans revisits the theme of art's futility
in "Women and Fame." Cast in the form of an apostrophe, the poem
shows its speaker fending off the "charmed cup" of immortality and confessing that as a woman she needs domestic sympathy and "kindly looks
to cheer [her] on" (*Hemans,* 442). Rossetti may possibly have the sound

of Hemans's line in her head when, at the close of "Goblin Market," Laura celebrates the sisterly affection that serves "to cheer one on" when life proves "tedious" (*CP,* 1:26; 564). Hemans, in any case, ends her poem by mournfully lamenting that fame cannot assuage loneliness:

> Fame, Fame! thou canst not be the stay
>   Unto the drooping reed,
> The cool fresh fountain in the day
>   Of the soul's feverish need:
> Where must the lone one turn or flee?—
>   Not unto thee—oh! not to thee!   (*Hemans,* 442)

The modern reader sees clearly—as Rossetti probably also did—that the incompatibility Hemans alleges between art and love is a narrative simplification. The conflict presented is merely circumstantial, and while it causes pain, it does not provoke deep ambivalence. There is unhappiness and "feverish need," but no self-scrutiny about the commitment to a goal that somehow also brings grief. Fame is not the phantom of Rossetti's "Fata Morgana," bewilderingly pursued in laughter and in tears (*CP,* 1:49); in Hemans's poems it is always already achieved and a bringer of unwanted consequences. Even as an insight into gender relations, the dichotomy is underdeveloped, since Hemans never explores the impediment that art puts in the way of love. Clarification on this score will not come until Barrett Browning's *Aurora Leigh* and the famous self-crowning scene in which Aurora is interrupted by her cousin Romney Leigh, who derides the folly of a woman's pursuit of art. When Aurora, in turn, refuses his proposal of marriage, the plot is set in motion and the whole thrust of the novel-in-verse is to transform the Leigh-Leigh antipathy into a loving aesthetic partnership. Rossetti, however, is not a writer of epic narratives, and her response to Hemans's dichotomy comes in a lyrical monologue by an actual woman artist who acknowledges her unhappiness, but without indicting literary success as the cause.[5]

Fame's disavowals notwithstanding, the resounding effect of Hemans's work, especially her *Records of Woman,* was to encourage women writers to acknowledge women artists and think of themselves in relation to these figures, to write of their precursors and by this means, implicitly, speak of their own aspirations. As the modes associated with Hemans, the woman's monologue and the portrait of the rhapsodic artist, became part of the expectation about how poems work, women became eager to acknowledge their debt to Hemans herself. Not surprisingly, the elegies written at her death in 1836 attest to this continuity. Letitia Landon's appears first; fitted out with an epigraph from Hemans's "The Nightingale's Death-Song" as well as internal allusions to her song "Bring Flowers"— the epigraph and echo being the tacit conventions of the literary elegy— Landon's poem offers specific and generous praise. Hemans's range is said to be extensive, her subjects being drawn "from far and foreign lands," but even "common" domestic scenes grow "fair" in her work (*Landon,* 169–72). Her "song is sorrowful," her thought "lofty," and, in a sad collision of life and art, Hemans endures the same isolation as her own heroines:

> Ah! dearly purchased is the gift,
>   The gift of song like thine;
> A fated doom is hers who stands
>   The priestess of the shrine.
> The crowd—they only see the crown,
>   They only hear the hymn;—
> They mark not that the cheek is pale,
>   And that the eye is dim.   (*Landon,* 171; 49–56)

This elegy was well received, often reprinted, and now has a secure place in the documentary record of the English Corinne's fame. An immediate response to Landon's poem came from Elizabeth Barrett, whose own elegy, "Felicia Hemans," pays similar tribute to the poet's gifts. Barrett praises the elevated solemnity of Hemans's thought—the "mourning" tonality of her "abstractions high and moving"—and grieves at the artist's private loneliness while "the world's cold hand her brow was wreathing" (*EBB,* 46). In an interestingly collegial move, Barrett enforces her regard for Hemans by acknowledging Landon's lament for the "bay-crowned Dead" and identifying both poets in the title: "Stanzas Addressed to Miss Landon, and Suggested by Her 'Stanzas on the Death of Mrs Hemans.'" Since homage tends to amplify homage, Barrett pays Landon, who is her exact contemporary, the extraordinary compliment of hailing her also as "bay-crowned." Enfolded into the elegy, Landon is then instructed not to mourn that Hemans's gift of song was so personally costly. And Barrett, with a set of self-revealing questions, asks her to think further about the artist's dedication to her art:

Would she have lost the poet's fire for anguish of the burning?
The minstrel harp, for the strained string? the tripod, for the
   afflated
Woe? or the vision, for those tears in which it shone dilated?

(EBB, 46; 18–20)

Not only do Barrett's lines affirm the legend of Hemans's suffering, they
affirm Landon's and her own willingness to endure "anguish" for the sake
of their art. The passage is a startlingly direct attempt at tradition building by a poet who is not yet the successful author of *Poems* 1844 and not
yet placed on the young Pre-Raphaelites' 1850 list of "Immortals." It is
a not-so-covert expression of Barrett's own ambition and, what is important for the present purpose, a very public indication that Landon,
too, deserves admiration.[6]

Respecting Letitia Landon: Barrett's Elegy and Rossetti's "L.E.L"

Barrett and Landon are both important to Rossetti. At the middle of her
career, she will turn to the author of *Sonnets from the Portuguese* and acknowledge "the Great Poetess" as an important influence on her own
sonnet sequence *Monna Innominata* (*CP*, 2:86); shortly thereafter, she will
accept "with enthusiasm" an invitation to write "a life of Mrs. Browning," whose "many-sidedness" she admires (*L*, 3:41; 1:348). (The plan
comes to nothing when she learns that Robert Browning objects to any
biography of his wife.) In Rossetti's early years, however, it is Landon who
is the significant influence, Landon—with her varied tonalities and playful form—whose appeal is demonstrable. And it is Landon, commemo-
rated in yet another Barrett elegy, who inspires Rossetti's own "L.E.L."

   Landon's poetry, like Hemans's, was part of the excitement, the aes-
thetic atmosphere, of the Rossetti household. Her books were in—or
rather missing from—the family library. In a letter of 1848, Gabriel tells
William that he has "picked up . . . L.E.L.'s Improvisatrice, for which
I gave ninepence," and asks, "by the bye, have you got her Violet and
Bracelet with you? I cannot find them in our library" (*LDGR*, 1:41). Pre-
sumably Christina has both *The Golden Violet* (1827) and *The Venetian
Bracelet* (1829) and is absorbing an influence very different from Felicia
Hemans's: no one has ever described Landon's poetry as dignified
or praised its "lofty bearing" or attributed to her an unfailing authorial

"self-possession." Instead, as Glennis Stephenson characterizes her work, it is flamboyantly given over to "enthusiasms and excesses" that range from foreign diction and prominent anaphora to "erotically suggestive images." Insofar as her sense of grammar occasionally forsakes her, she is rightly placed among the sibyls, whom Germaine Greer memorably describes as "slip-shod." And yet, as Dolores Rosenblum suggests, "Rossetti owes more to Landon than to Hemans" for reasons having to do with her rest- and death-seeking moods and certain habits of style. Landon's song "Farewell, Farewell! I'll Dream No More" is fairly typical; Frederic Rowton, the midcentury editor of *The Female Poets of Great Britain,* singles it out, in fact, as representative of the "sad desolate tone" that "pervades nearly all [Landon's] compositions":

> I'll turn me to the gifted page
>   Where the bard his soul is flinging;
> Too well it echoes mine own heart
>   Breaking e'en while singing.
> I must have rest! Oh, heart of mine,
>   When wilt thou lose thy sorrow?
> Never, til in the quiet grave:
>   —Would I slept there to-morrow!
>   (17–24; qtd. in Rowton, 429)

What Rossetti might have noticed in such a poem is the nearly motiveless but plainly aesthetic quality of its gloom; stimulated by song (having deliberately consulted the bard's "gifted page"), the poet thinks of escaping "sorrow." The sentiment is purely lyric, indulged for its own sake and without benefit of noble thoughts or a moral lesson. Landon is as interested in the poeticity of her poem, in its lilting rhythm and conspicuous rhyme, as in its theme; and for Rossetti—who is in every way a stronger poet—such song encourages her own love of playful solemnity. She too works in this vein, choosing three- or four-beat lines and feminine rhymes to sing fervently of release into fervorless rest. Her early poem entitled "Sound Sleep" is an acoustic extravaganza:

> Some are laughing, some are weeping;
> She is sleeping, only sleeping.
> Round her rest wild flowers are creeping;
> There the wind is heaping, heaping

> Sweetest sweets of Summer's keeping,
> By the corn fields ripe for reaping.   (*CP,* 1 : 57)

Hardly one of Rossetti's finest, the poem is a self-delighting performance in falling rhythm with enough incidental repetition and feminine rhyme to attest to the sonority promised in the title. Ostensibly concerned with waiting for the final resurrection, the time when "grave-bands shall be riven" (20), the stanzas take their form from Rossetti's inordinate pleasure in their chiming sound. Critics have long known how to appreciate rhyme: theorists of various persuasions agree that the more emphatic the demands of rhyme, syntax, and meaning, the more compelling the language that answers these demands; thus a verse, phrase, or rhyme word that "fulfills at one stroke" two or three "orders of cogency" is theoretically exemplary. But this poem's monorhyme defies such logic and insists on sounds *themselves,* sounds that by sheer excess evade any explanation of their "inescapable aptness." One would never seriously consider Landon a poet's poet, but she does seem to have approximated that role for the young Rossetti, helping to keep her attentive to the pleasures of her chosen art.[7]

When Landon considers the plight of the woman artist, pursuing Hemans's theme of woman and fame, she does so without the latter's "constraining sense of edification" and is less concerned to instruct her Improvisatrice in the sad truth of art's insufficiency than to show her at "the mercy of passion." The suffering of Landon's heroine, the sweet pain that comes with her beloved's absence, was not lost on the author of "The Convent Threshold." Nor was Landon's ability to internalize the artist's struggle; for Landon, unlike Hemans, focuses on the allure of art itself and the self-division that afflicts its devotee. In "A History of the Lyre" from *The Venetian Bracelet,* the highly accomplished Eulalie struggles with the temptation of fame:

> I am vain—praise is opium, and the lip
> Cannot resist the fascinating draught,
> Though knowing its excitement is a fraud—
> Delirious—a mockery of fame.   (*Landon,* 122; 244–47)

One might note, in passing, that the line break on "lip," with its slight puckering of the mouth, may be the source of Rossetti's description in "A Triad" of the showy woman "with lips / Crimson" (*CP,* 1 : 29). Of paramount interest, of course, is Eulalie's failed resistance to the "opium" she does and does not value and its clear foreshadowing of the vacillation in "A Pause of Thought," where Rossetti's speaker regrets the emptiness of her chosen pursuit:

> Sometimes I said: It is an empty name
>   I long for; to a name why should I give
>   The peace of all the days I have to live?—
>   Yet gave it all the same.   (*CP*, 1 : 52)

Landon's image for what tempts Eulalie's aesthetic appetite might also have impressed the young Rossetti:

>   I have fed
> Perhaps too much upon the lotos fruits
> Imagination yields,—fruits which unfit
> The palate for the more substantial food
> Of our own land—reality. . . .   (*Landon*, 124; 332−36)

One hardly needs to be reminded of "Goblin Market" and the fruits that cloy Laura. "A History of the Lyre" is blank verse, a mode whose expansiveness Rossetti probably distrusts, certainly never attempts, and yet there are appealing stylistic features that persuade her of Landon's genuine talent. Three brief examples will suffice. Landon's Eulalie has, first of all, an eye for shaded, half-hidden natural detail:

> Look on those flowers near yon acacia tree—
> The lily of the valley—mark how pure
> The snowy blossoms,—and how soft a breath
> Is almost hidden by the large dark leaves.
> Not only have those delicate flowers a gift
> Of sweetness and of beauty, but the root—
> A healing power dwells there; fragrant and fair,
> But dwelling still in some beloved shade.
>   (*Landon*, 120; 178−85)

Rossetti has a similar tendency to notice what is buried in the leaves, though she typically delivers such observations with greater economy and vividness—as in "Autumn Violets," where the flowers "lie hid in double shade of leaves, / Their own, and others dropped down withering (*CP*, 1 : 194). Next, Landon's Eulalie conveys her sense of isolation with characterizing geographical imagery; her world seems "A northern clime, where ev'ry thing is chill'd" (*Landon,* 121; 223). Rossetti's "Enrica, 1865" uses much the same strategy to distinguish an Italian visitor from the Englishwomen of the "rigid North" who "chilled" beside the Southerner's "liberal glow" (*CP,* 1:194). Finally, Eulalie is energetically scornful, sometimes tripling, alliterating, and ranking the faulty according to the severity of their offenses:

> My days are past
> Among the cold, the careless, and the false.
> What part have I in them, or they in me?
>   (*Landon,* 122; 249–51)

Rossetti will put such bitterness to startling use in the line "I bore with thee, thy hardness, coldness, slights"; the speaker in this instance is Christ, who pleads with the listener to come into the kingdom won by divine suffering (*CP,* 1:66). The force of the accusation and its transformative impact reside in the felt bitterness of the three words, each delivered in fewer syllables until the merest "slights" bear a shockingly accumulated weight.[8]

Not all Landon's speakers are artists and not all are melancholy; some are, in fact, so insouciantly whimsical that even in her heyday Landon's work was regarded in some quarters as irredeemably superficial. A prime example is the coy song in *The Golden Violet* recommending flighty changeability as the way to hold a lover's interest:

> Never does Love find a tomb
> Sudden, soon, as when he meets
> Death amid unchanging sweets.   (*Landon,* 100; 8–10)

This is hardly an admirable sentiment, and yet, as Leighton suggests, Landon's concern is with "the difference between public face and private mask" and a poetic defense against softness and sentimentality. In promoting frivolousness as a guise to protect the vulnerable, Landon's speaker wittily intones a spell-like chant to enforce her instructions:

> Never let an envious eye
> Gaze upon the heart too nigh;
> Never let the veil be thrown
> Quite aside, as all were known
> Of delight and tenderness,
> In the spirit's last recess;

And, one spell all spells above,
Never let her own her love.   (*Landon,* 101; 31–38)

There is genuine skill here. The incantatory rhythm charms the hearer
into becoming a charmer. The short lines speed toward the concluding
spell-of-spells and the third "never" delivers the clinching imperative to
secrecy. Rossetti is not the poet to be irritated by this coquette's falsity; instead, she detects the element of self-mockery in her tone. Rossetti's own
"Winter: My Secret" works variations on Landon's savvy admonishment
against letting any "eye / Gaze upon the heart," and turns coyness into
her own poem's teasing strategy.[9]

When Letitia Landon died in 1838, Elizabeth Barrett again paid tribute with an elegy that includes, in the customary way, an epigraph and
citation from Landon's own "Night at Sea":

"Do you think of me as I think of you,
My friends, my friends?"—She said it from the sea,
The English minstrel in her minstrelsy,
While, under brighter skies than erst she knew,
Her heart grew dark, and groped there as the blind
To reach across the waves friends left behind—
"Do you think of me as I think of you?"   (*EBB,* 178; 1–7)

Landon's "Night at Sea" had been written just a few months earlier as the
newly married poet was en route to Africa. While biographers make
it clear that there was already obvious cause to regret this marriage, the
poem is discreetly nostalgic; Landon pictures the night sky and then
describes turning away to dream of friends in England:

'Tis night, and overhead the sky is gleaming,
Thro' the slight vapour trembles each dim star;
I turn away—my heart is sadly dreaming
    Of scenes they do not light, of scenes afar.
        My friends, my absent friends!
            Do you think of me, as I think of you?
                                        (*Landon,* 205; 5–10)

Because Landon's death on October 15 was sudden and mysterious, mere
months after her July departure, this lonely stanza struck her contemporaries as frankly autobiographical and tragic. Barrett's natural response
was to incorporate its unrhymed, self-isolating final line into her elegy

and entitle it "L.E.L.'s Last Question." As we have seen, Barrett had already admired Landon in print as one of the reigning "bay-crowned" poets, and in her letters too she approves of Landon's "*raw* bare powers," which she regards as "more elastic, more various, of a stronger web" than Felicia Hemans's. The elegy describes Landon's work sympatheti-cally—"Love-learnèd she had sung of love" (15)—and honors her with traditionally elegiac questions about her hasty departure from this life: was Landon, having asked if friends were thinking of her, too impatient to wait for a reply?

> Could she not wait to catch their answering breath?
> Was she content, content with ocean's sound
> Which dashed its mocking infinite around
> One thirsty for a little love?   (*EBB,* 179; 36–39)

Both Landon's and Barrett's poignant questions, especially this last with its mention of "a little love," would make their way into the collective memory of nineteenth-century readers, including Christina Rossetti's, where they become irrevocably intermingled.[10]

Early in 1859, some twenty years after Landon's death, Rossetti invokes the example of Elizabeth Barrett and writes a poem named for "L.E.L." This is a time when Rossetti is at her creative height—"Goblin Market" is soon to be transcribed—and she is thinking about the poets she ad-mires. Because "L.E.L" has a complex history, it is best to begin by indi-cating some things the poem does not do and then to consider such mat-ters as the reticence of its speaker, the probable reasons for its deferred publication in *Victoria Magazine,* and Gabriel's last-minute emendations for its inclusion in *The Prince's Progress.*

First of all, "L.E.L." does not mention Landon's death. Avoiding el-egy altogether, Rossetti borrows Landon's own genre and gives voice to the poet who gave voice to the Improvisatrice, Eulalie, and others. There is both homage and economy in this method, for the very form of "L.E.L." implies approval of Landon's many monologues by women artists.

Second, in identifying the poem, Rossetti does not use the name Letitia Landon. Having once published under the nom de guerre of Ellen Alleyn, Rossetti is fully aware of the distance that separates a writer from her signature and takes the latter for her title (*L,* 1:37). With this choice, she disavows access to the historical Landon, the pretty author who was surrounded by scandal, and takes her literary persona as the speaker, the woman who exists by virtue of Rossetti's reading of her poems. Basic information about Landon's biography was readily available in Laman Blanchard's *Life and Literary Remains of L.E.L.* And rumors might have been learned from any number of sources, particularly William Howitt, a Rossetti family friend who had included Landon in his *Homes and Haunts of the Most Eminent British Poets* and who privately encouraged the hypothesis that Landon's death was a suicide (*Landon,* 15). The precise details of Landon's troubled life are of no concern to Rossetti in the poem; she is very much interested, however, that the poet's social manner was said to have been "all gaiety and cheerfulness," for this provides evidence that Landon was as elusive as every other human being, including Rossetti herself. Instead of writing "L.E.L." as a full dramatic monologue in which "Letitia Landon" mulls over the known facts of her life, brooding perhaps on her early fascination with Africa and the marriage that eventually took her there, Rossetti takes up the preoccupations in Landon's poetry—Landon's emphasis on loneliness and masking—and allows L.E.L. to speak of these things.[11]

Third, assuming that the poet will be recognized by what some have called her "tantalizing initials," Rossetti makes no explicit mention of Landon's fame. Regarding it as a false measure of excellence rather than a general and reliable extension of praise, Rossetti has a tendency to make celebrity the occasion for humor: she quips to her publisher, for example, about the pleasure of attaining "fame (!) and guineas" and offers a friendly reviewer the self-mocking confession that her "soul exults in praise and grovels after pelf" (*L,* 1:146, 2:84). Landon's importance as a literary figure is signaled instead by an attributed epigraph from Elizabeth Barrett (now Barrett Browning), the meteorically eminent author of the recently published *Aurora Leigh.* Repeating and updating Browning's own gesture of addressing Felicia Hemans through Landon, Rossetti presents "L.E.L." with two women's names in visible proximity: "L.E.L. 'Whose heart was breaking for a little love.' E. B. Browning." The epigraph also reappears in the body of the poem, emphasizing that one author's recognition of another is literally the central idea. The line's genesis, however, is a bit of a mystery and an unexpectedly strange example of the roundabout workings of poetic influence. Despite the attribution, which also appears in the manuscript as "L.E.L. by E.B.B.," and contrary to the occasional anthologist's footnote, the epigraph is not an accurate citation of "L.E.L.'s Last

Question." Rather, it is a recollection of Browning's poem enriched by a lingering echo of Landon's "Night at Sea." The seafarer's lament, "my heart is sadly dreaming" (*Landon*, 205; 7), mixes with Browning's description of "One thirsty for a little love" (*EBB*, 179; 39) to become Rossetti's "Whose heart was breaking for a little love" (*CP*, 1:153). A poet's misquotation might be viewed not as ordinary carelessness but rather as an acknowledgment—all the more forceful for being involuntary—that she has admired a resonant passage and unknowingly made it her very own. Others' lines speak so movingly to Rossetti that she cannot tell she has substituted her words for theirs. When reprinting "L.E.L." in 1875, Rossetti retains the epigraph but no longer attributes it to "E. B. Browning," having by this time realized its metamorphosis.[12]

Embedded in the poem, the hybrid line about "a little love" still performs its lovely act of poetic tribute, if not quite the one Rossetti originally supposed, and gives shape to the stanzas about L.E.L.'s loneliness. Here, then, are the first four of its half-dozen stanzas:

> Downstairs I laugh, I sport and jest with all:
> But in my solitary room above
> I turn my face in silence to the wall;
> My heart is breaking for a little love.
> Tho' winter frosts are done,
> And birds pair every one,
> And leaves peep out, for springtide is begun.
>
> I feel no spring, while spring is wellnigh blown,
> I find no nest, while nests are in the grove:
> Woe's me for mine own heart that dwells alone,
> My heart that breaketh for a little love.
> While golden in the sun
> Rivulets rise and run,
> While lilies bud, for springtide is begun.
>
> All love, are loved, save only I; their hearts
> Beat warm with love and joy, beat full thereof:
> They cannot guess, who play the pleasant parts,
> My heart is breaking for a little love.
> While beehives wake and whirr,

> And rabbit thins his fur,
> In living spring that sets the world astir.
>
> I deck myself with silks and jewelry,
>   I plume myself like any mated dove:
> They praise my rustling show, and never see
>   My heart is breaking for a little love.
>   While sprouts green lavender
>   With rosemary and myrrh,
> For in quick spring the sap is all astir.   (*CP,* 1:153−54; 1−28)

Taking up the theme of Landon's own "Night at Sea," Rossetti transforms the emigrant's sense of isolation into an internal condition. With a self-barricading gesture adapted from "Winter: My Secret" and also "Memory," whose reclusive speaker has "shut the door to face the naked truth" (*CP,* 1:148), Rossetti's L.E.L. chooses solitude. From the separate room that is the emblem of the lyric genre's privacy, she confesses her unguessed secret, the loneliness others "never see." In keeping with one of Rossetti's characteristic insights about words and wordlessness, L.E.L. reveals the two kinds of reticence at work in her life. On the one hand, there is the "downstairs" gaiety, the wall of banter that prevents others from intuiting her trouble, and on the other, the literal silence of the wall she faces in her retreat. The most appealing feature of this poem, perhaps, is the restrained way it makes a kind of song out of L.E.L.'s sense of exclusion, rather than a confession or a dramatic monologue. Though lyric tradition allows her to specify L.E.L.'s anguished thoughts and give details like those troubling Landon's own Eulalie, who has "been deceived/ And disappointed" (*Landon,* 121; 243−44), Rossetti follows the lead of more guarded poets and amplifies L.E.L.'s pain indirectly. The lonely woman observes that the "living spring" has set "the world astir" (21), and, as so often in Rossetti's poetry, emotion is intensified by a reminder of some unsensed sensation. In "Dream-Land," bliss registers as the trickle of rain the sleeper cannot feel (*CP,* 1:27), while here L.E.L.'s sadness takes the form of attention paid to an exuberant seasonal renewal she does not share. Rossetti supplies busy sound effects ("beehives . . . whirr"), delicate details ("rabbit thins his fur"), and musically named herbs (lavender, rosemary, myrrh). The "birds pair every one," and so too the springtide passages as rhymes, half-lines, and terminal words ("begun," "astir") bind them in acoustic partnership. Formally, the vernal images arrive in monorhymed triplets launched by a brisk new rhythm ("Rívulets ríse and rún") so that the poem's own language stirs and proliferates and thrives in accord with the "quick spring" it celebrates. L.E.L.'s invigorated notice of this burgeoning life indicates her own unspent reserves of ecstasy and her plight: amid spring's abundance, the "little" she needs is lacking.[13]

To bring the poem to a close, Rossetti supplies a final pair of stanzas allowing L.E.L. to hope that her loneliness will be assuaged in the "new spring" of eternity:

> Perhaps some saints in glory guess the truth,
>   Perhaps some angels read it as they move,
> And cry one to another full of ruth,
>   "Her heart is breaking for a little love."
>   Tho' other things have birth,
>   And leap and sing for mirth,
> When springtime wakes and clothes and feeds the earth.
>
> Yet saith a saint: "Take patience for thy scathe;"
>   Yet saith an angel: "Wait, for thou shalt prove
> True best is last, true life is born of death,
>   O thou, heart-broken for a little love.
>   Then love shall fill thy girth,
>   And love make fat thy dearth,
> When new spring builds new heaven and clean new earth."
>   (*CP,* 1 : 154–55; 29–42)

To fully appreciate these lines, it helps to know their genesis in the poem's publication history. Important though "L.E.L" clearly is to Rossetti, she is in no rush to publish it. Having transcribed it in time to appear in the *Goblin Market* volume, she is content to keep it from public view, and only after Barrett Browning's *Last Poems* appears posthumously in 1862 does she contribute it to the *Victoria Magazine*. That Rossetti waits until the completion of Landon's admirer's career to publish "L.E.L" is perhaps a matter of shyness; she may have needed to feel more established as a writer, to have a first book behind her, before openly acknowledging precursors. Dissatisfaction with the draft may be a factor as well, for on its appearance in *Victoria Magazine* Rossetti amends the last lines to allow a touching new emphasis. In the 1859 manuscript, the commiserating sentiment attributed to the final angel is somewhat moralized and abstract:

> Love only shall be worth,
>   Hate only shall have dearth,
> When new spring builds new heaven and clean new earth.
>   (*CP,* 1:288; MS 40–42)

Though intended as words of comfort, this glimpse of L.E.L.'s heavenly future seems faintly accusatory about the apportionment of love and hate, while the insistent "only" conveys a hint of eternal severity. In the 1863 magazine version, the altered lines emphasize fulfillment and— ever so decorously—hint at the lack that afflicts a loveless woman in life:

> Then love shall fill thy girth,
>   And love make fat thy dearth,
> When new spring builds new heaven and clean new earth.
>   (*CP,* 1:155; 40–42)

In the apocalyptic "new spring," according to this revised promise, love will fill and fatten a woman's spiritual "girth" and turn her earthly infertility—the grief the poem does not otherwise name—into joy. The understated figurativeness of these lines points to the motive for the poem's general reticence and indirection. To have the lonely L.E.L. explicitly lament her childlessness or talk plainly of what truly hurts would increase her risk, or any speaker's for that matter, of pain and humiliation. So, in her reserved way, Rossetti preserves various kinds and degrees of silence on L.E.L.'s behalf; and when joy comes into the poem, it is intensified by the pressure of all that has gone unsaid. The new ending is a typically strong revision, but it is not the last.

In its early incarnations, that is to say, in both the manuscript and the *Victoria Magazine* versions, "L.E.L." has an alternating scheme with only a single rhyme pair in the quatrains preceding the "little love" refrain *(abcb)*. When Christina and Gabriel were going over the poems to be included in *The Prince's Progress,* the rhyme scheme caught his attention and, in a flash of collaborative inspiration, he doubled the pattern *(abab)*. Specifically, he could hear that a change in only one line per quatrain would enhance the poem's euphony and the reader's acoustic pleasure. At his suggestion, the *Victoria Magazine*'s first stanza,

> Downstairs with friends I laugh, I sport and jest:
>> But in my solitary room above
> I turn my face in silence to the wall:
>> My heart is breaking for a little love,

becomes a bit jauntier:

> Downstairs *I laugh, I sport and jest with all:*
>> But in my solitary room above
> I turn my face in silence to the wall;
>> My heart is breaking for a little love.

Similarly, the magazine's desolate second stanza,

> I feel no spring, while spring is bursting forth;
>> I find no nest while nests are in the grove:
> Woe's me for mine own heart that dwells alone,
>> My heart that breaketh for a little love,

is slightly adjusted to sustain the double rhyme pattern while enforcing L.E.L.'s exclusion:

> I feel no spring, while spring is *wellnigh blown,*
>> I find no nest, while nests are in the grove:
> Woe's me for mine own heart that dwells alone,
>> My heart that breaketh for a little love;

and so on through the poem (*CP*, 1:288). When Gabriel submitted his changes to Christina with "a brotherly request" that she use them, she fired back her enthusiastic approval—"Adopted, your enormous improvement"—later adding that they "greatly improv[e] the piece" (*L*, 1:242; *PW*, 482). There is little question that Gabriel's collaboration enhances the poem, especially in the final two heavenly sections. For the word "piteously" in the magazine's penultimate stanza,

> Perhaps some Saints in glory guess the truth,
>> Perhaps some Angels read it as they move,
> And cry one to another piteously,
>> Her heart is breaking for a little love,

he substitutes a quaintly phrased synonym:

> Perhaps some saints in glory guess the truth,
>> Perhaps some angels read it as they move,

And cry one to another *full of ruth,*
"Her heart is breaking for a little love."
(*CP,* 1:288, 154; 29–32)

And for the final stanza's saintly urging to let "patience" heal the "hurt,"

Yet saith a Saint: Take patience for thy hurt;
Yet saith an Angel: Wait, for thou shalt prove
True best is last, true life is born of death,
O thou heart, broken for a little love,

he recalls the nearly archaic "scathe," a term acoustically anticipated by the line's already-resonating *s* and *a* sounds:

Yet saith a saint: "Take patience for thy *scathe;*"
Yet saith an angel: "Wait, for thou shalt prove
True best is last, true life is born of death
O thou, heart-broken for a little love.
(*CP,* 1:288, 154; 36–39)

Gabriel's new rhymes are not, as it happens, imports from his own lexicon; when writing of heavenly beings, he prefers such words as "mystic," and "occult." Instead he finds the terms in Christina's own poems; "ruth" is from her sonnet describing St. Elizabeth of Hungary as "Harsh towards herself, towards others full of ruth" (*CP,* 1:122). The word "scathe," which comes out of Malory, appears in one of her "Old and New Year Ditties" where the new year is asked, "Bring you scathe, or bring you grace" (*CP,* 1:89). Gabriel catches Christina's sense of such terms' solemnity and her feeling that a slight strangeness of diction helps locate a sentiment as other-worldly. In "L.E.L." the words help distinguish the spirits' solicitude from human friends' ordinary inattention. Her brother's changes to her poem are precisely the kind Christina herself might have made had he challenged her to add more rhymes, as formerly he challenged her to games of *bouts-rimés.* She seems to have been delighted. This flexibility about her poem amounts to a recognition on her part, if not an implicit theory, that good collaboration is like good translation: the second-comer to the text is stimulated by something that is inherently fine. To Christina, a first-rate suggestion feels less like tampering than like convincing praise. Gabriel's best responses might best be compared to her own remembrance of the line from "L.E.L. by E.B.B.," a spontaneous adjusting that signifies deep aesthetic respect.

Listening to Herself: On Consulting Gabriel

The successful emendation of "L.E.L." raises the broader issue of the Rossettis' joint artistic efforts, a vexed matter among critics who have sometimes mistrusted Gabriel's involvement with Christina's poetry and worried about violations of her creative autonomy. Gabriel's "absolute confidence in his own aesthetic judgments" was—and still is—a well-known aspect of his personal charisma; it made him the leader of the Pre-Raphaelite Brotherhood and a sought-after friend to many outside that early band of poets and painters. But what has not been sufficiently re-marked is the fervor of his confidence in Christina's talent. From her teenage years onward, he attends to her poems like a true admirer, know-ing them well enough to "resuscitate" passages "from memory," enter-taining friends of an evening by reading "a vast amount of Christina aloud" and, when the time comes, eagerly promoting her books (*L*, 1:239; *LDGR*, 2:667). Even before the success of *Goblin Market*, he is the one who circulates her *Verses*, the collection printed by their grand-father in 1847, as a way of fostering her professional ties with such women artists as Bessie Parkes and Mary Howitt; and in later years he pursues editors, hunts down "notices," alerts reviewers to "a new vol-ume before long," and eagerly tracks the evidence of her growing repu-tation, reporting, for example, that William Gladstone could repeat her "Maiden-Song" by heart (*LDGR*, 2:528, 548, 665). The best record of Christina's response to this brotherly enthusiasm is to be found in the intensely collaborative letters of February–April 1865 in which she wel-comes his aid in assembling the manuscript of *The Prince's Progress, and Other Poems*. Though only Christina's portion of the correspondence is extant, her replies indicate that she and Gabriel discuss nineteen of the volume's forty-seven poems as well as a few they set aside. Together the letters of 1865 and the volume of 1866 give us a picture of Christina as a writer very much in contact with her precursors, accepting, resisting, modifying what they offer, and presenting the results to a living poet for his reaction. That Gabriel assumes his role with unstinted vigor, urging changes, cuts, and exclusions, is a consequence, as I hope to show, of his inveterate but now-forgotten habit of canvassing friends for revisions to his own poems. The Pre-Raphaelite circle's mode of authorial collegial-ity provides a helpful context for reviewing the Rossettis' emendations while attending not only to their aesthetic merit but to their implications for Christina's place among women writers.[14]

Knowing that the siblings will occasionally agree to disagree, the place to begin is with "The Prince's Progress," Christina's weirdly probing adaptation of the abandoned-woman narrative. In this, the volume's title poem, a princess dies of loneliness in the requisite fashion while awaiting the lover who comes too late; Rossetti keeps her heroine narratively out of sight, never allowing her to utter the doleful "aweary, aweary" traditionally ascribed to the fatally lovelorn (*AT,* 43). The "agony" of "unrequited" love does not compel her to yearn for death, in the manner of "Properzia Rossi," or for freedom from "the inward burning of those words—'in vain'" (*Hemans,* 352–55; 20, 25, 100). She does not profess the Improvisatrice's "deep happiness to die" or expect to "live in Love's dear memory" (*Landon,* 79; 1517–20). Rossetti, whose superlative mournfulness underwrites a long-standing joke with Gabriel about poetry as "the legitimate exercise of anguish," makes her princess a mute and sleeping beauty, thereby sparing her much torment (*LDGR,* 1:163). In particular, Rossetti relieves her of the obligation to provide a love-smitten description of her betrothed prince. The physical attractiveness of the beloved male is a prominent feature of the tradition; some of the erotic charge of Landon's poetry comes from her heroine's spoony appreciation of the hero's sexiness. Lorenzo, in one instance, is positioned beside a statue of Antinous and does not suffer from comparison with the "glorious" figure "of Parian stone":

> They were alike: he had the same
>   Thick-clustering curls the Roman wore—
> The fixed and melancholy eye—
>   The smile which passed like lightning o'er
> The curved lip. . . .   (*Landon,* 70; 937–41)

"What a man!" quips Germaine Greer. Glamorous and himself susceptible to the brilliant and beautiful Improvisatrice, he nonetheless forsakes her out of loyalty to another woman, and his defection, a necessity of the genre, is both fated and excused. Rossetti will have none of this, narrating instead the dawdlings of an easily beguiled prince as he squanders precious time, first with a "wave-haired milkmaid," then an alchemist, and lastly a "winsome" lady rescuer, thereby failing to live up to his betrothal (*CP,* 1:95–110; 58, 178, 344).[15]

The actual writing of "The Prince's Progress" begins with a dirge composed in 1861 and subsequently published in *Macmillan's Magazine;*

in 1865 this song becomes the elegiac coda chanted by the princess's
ladies as they condemn the hero's tragic belatedness:

> "Too late for love, too late for joy,
>   Too late, too late!
> You loitered on the road too long,
>   You trifled at the gate:
> The enchanted dove upon her branch
>   Died without a mate;
> The enchanted princess in her tower
>   Slept, died, behind the grate;
> Her heart was starving all this while
>   You made it wait."   (481–90)

According to William, it was Gabriel who suggested that Christina "turn
the dirge into a narrative poem of some length," though it is not clear
who initiated the idea of making it the title work (*PW,* 461). Hoping to
duplicate her success with *Goblin Market,* Christina is on record as wanting to match it in length and presumably also in format; the inevitable
comparison of the long title narratives is mildly unfortunate, since every
reader feels, along with Rossetti herself, that her "prince lacks the special
felicity of [her] goblins" (*L,* 1:230). Joan Rees is nearly alone among critics in making "The Prince's Progress" seem exciting—not simply interesting, which several have done, but emotionally compelling. She does
so by focusing on the alchemist, who enlists the prince in a search for the
elixir of life: "Like any Christian ascetic," says Rees, the alchemist "is a
dedicated soul" whose poignance derives from Rossetti's deliberate ambiguity about whether, given the grotesquerie of his dying (the dipping
of "the dead finger" into "the broth"), he is to be considered a "fool or
knave; / Or honest seeker who had not found" (242–43, 261–62). Rees
may be correct in believing that Rossetti's poem laments the uncertainty
of all dedication, but her interpretive privileging of a subordinate figure
tacitly concedes that Rossetti's characterization of the prince is flawed. A
poem about failure can be a success—but not in this instance. In con-
ceiving of a fervorless suitor, Rossetti presumes in advance that he will
never be thrilled and terrified by the suffering that love requires of him.
Unlike the novice of "The Convent Threshold," he does not bloody
himself grappling with his own thwarted desire. Nor is he an obsessed
pursuer, one whose beloved, in the manner of great love poems, "stays

inaccessible" and who haunts him with that very inaccessibility. Instead, the prince is forgetful, and his poem suffers a comparable narrative lassitude.[16]

It should, therefore, come as no surprise—and certainly not as a sign of any special severity—that Gabriel feels the tale needs a bit of enlivening. Though his reasoning is not summarized in Christina's reply, his thoughts about genre are on record and are pertinent to "The Prince's Progress"; he confesses, for example, "to a need, in narrative-dramatic poetry . . . of something rather 'exciting', and indeed I believe something of the 'romantic' element, to rouse my mind to anything like the moods produced by personal emotion in my own life. That sentence is shockingly ill worded, but Keats' narratives would be of the kind I mean" (*LDGR,* 1:255–56). Since his own "Blessed Damozel" is inspired by the sorrowful lines of Keats's ghostly Lorenzo in "Isabella"—"I am a shadow now, alas, alas! / Upon the skirts of human nature dwelling" (*Keats,* 217)—it is fairly clear what Gabriel means here; the narrative genre at its best rises to the yearning intensity of lyric. He might, therefore, be expected to propose that Christina lyricize her prince's adventures, that she give his tempters the chanting, beckoning allure of the goblins or grant them the bewildering power of the "Fata Morgana." But, and this *is* a surprise, the "something rather 'exciting'" Gabriel proposes is a tournament. He would have Christina plunge her gently hapless prince into what reviewers liked to call "the fury and the headlong madness" of combat. Christina is appalled; she who has never attempted a military episode of any kind is utterly unprepared to add such an element to her story: "How shall I express my sentiments about the terrible tournament. Not a phrase to be relied on, not a correct knowledge on the subject, not the faintest impulse of inspiration, incites me to the tilt; and looming before me in horrible bugbeardom stand 2 tournaments in Tennyson's *Idylls.* Moreover the Alchemist according to original convention took the place of the lists: remember this in my favour, please" (*L,* 1:225–26). A tournament is so antipathetic to her poem's design, and to her own strengths as a poet, that Christina is rightly "disposed to be stiff-necked" about it— a description Gabriel himself uses when declining a suggestion (*LDGR,* 1:227). But at the same time Christina jokingly compares the necessary inspiration to the volcanic "upthrust" mentioned in her poem (49) and genially invokes an aphorism from her and Gabriel's childhood: "However, if the latent epic should 'by huge upthrust' come to the surface someday, or if by laborious delving I can unearth it, or if by unflagging prodment you can cultivate the sensitive plant in question, all the better for me: only please remember that 'things which are impossible rarely happen'—and don't be too severe on me if in my case the 'impossible' does not come to pass" (*L,* 1:232). To get some idea how few phrases were available to her and how troubling a tournament scene would be, one need consider only a single line, a much-revised allusion to the *Iliad* that occurs in "The Lowest Room." Rossetti's first attempt at describing Homeric combatants appears in the draft as "they fought with arrow sword or spear"; the heroes' implements are then generalized as "weapons forged of men" and re-altered to "weapons toughly forged." The line is next recast entirely with a new grammatical subject and a return to specific weaponry, "Crest-rearing kings with goodly swords," and finally adjusted to "Crest-rearing kings with whistling spears" (*CP,* 1:302; MS 45). Clearly, fighting is not Rossetti's forte; and had she offered many lines in this mode, male reviewers of the kind just mentioned would have been as unsparing to her as to other women poets whose combat scenes they scorn as the "confused enumeration of a few unconnected particulars," which "might with equal propriety belong to a tournament, a chase, and to a battle."[17]

Gabriel's blundering idea about a tournament is hardly consistent with his brilliant suggestion that "Goblin Market" replace that poem's manuscript title, "A Peep at the Goblins" (would the volume have been called *A Peep at the Goblins and Other Poems?*), or his deft rhyming in "L.E.L."; and it is sufficiently bizarre to raise questions about the overall value of mentoring advice and "prodment." In recent years critics have complained that Gabriel's involvement was both intrusive and artistically damaging. Allison Chapman has looked at the 1865 correspondence and takes a very dim view of the siblings' collaboration. On her reading, the letters show that "D. G. Rossetti advised, cajoled, and bullied in his attempt to influence the selection of poetry and its arrangement." The concern goes beyond Gabriel's tone, for Chapman finds that he tampers with Christina's "poetic form, style, meter, and subject matter" in an artistically unacceptable attempt "to mould Christina Rossetti's literary persona and poetry to his requirements." Close readings of two poems, "Seeking Rest" (*CP,* 3:180) and "'There remaineth therefore a rest'" (*CP,* 3:226), which were both drastically cut by Gabriel (and never published), leads Chapman to regret Christina's "submission to D. G. Rossetti's advice" and to condemn it as a disfiguring "complicity." Greer looks elsewhere for evidence, and while she gives Gabriel the aesthetic credit Chapman denies him, the resultant critique is very hard on Christina. After examining every textual change in "Goblin Market" ("thirty-nine lines out of a total of 567"), Greer (who assumes all are Gabriel's) concludes that his changes are "genuine revisions of an authorial kind," and she is not at all sure Christina "could have made them without prompting." Her dismay about collaboration comes down to a fear that an artistically inferior Christina was dependent on her dominating brother's genius. What Chapman and Greer have in common is a reluctance to consider the possibility that an author might legitimately seek and welcome "genuine revisions" inspired or suggested by another writer. Despite the sophistication and scrupulosity of their approaches, both critics assume that a proposed emendation is the expression, as Greer says, of a "masterful attitude to the work of another." Neither has a model for envisioning the process except in terms of ownership and hierarchy (*his* words in *her* poem); however, the collegial reading that went on among the poets in the Pre-Raphaelite circle, a phenomenon well documented in Gabriel's letters, provides a near-at-hand example of a historically specific mode of authorial cooperation. Instead of collaboration, it might be called consultation, and it is their normal practice. Manuscripts are always in circulation as these writers routinely seek one another's advice.[18]

The most active solicitor is, of course, Gabriel as he sends drafts to William Allingham, Ford Madox Brown, and his siblings William and Christina, asking not only for their "*severest* criticism" but for positive suggestions about language, narrative structure, and even recommendations on which materials to withhold from publication (*LDGR,* 1:227). Follow-up letters show that Gabriel carefully attends to even the minutest annotations. In one typical instance, he begins by reminding Allingham of his previous objection to a pair of lines in the sonnet "Lost on Both Sides." Admitting that they "are certainly foggy," Gabriel now presents two new versions and asks, "Would they be better thus?" and "What say you?" (*LDGR,* 1:212, 213). Then comes a further question that is especially pertinent for understanding his correspondence with Christina: "Or can you propose any other improvement?" (*LDGR,* 1:213). The evidence is clear that Gabriel occasionally accepts a friendly "improvement," in one case, an entire line suggested by William (*LDGR,* 2:733). Such authorial humility does not mean, however, that every suggestion is taken. Most are fended off, usually with a joke and the mildest hint of rebuttal: "Many thanks for your minute criticism on my ballad, which was just of the kind I wanted. *Not,* of course, that a British poet is going to knock under on all points;—accordingly, I take care to disagree from you in various respects"; Gabriel adds that he will not "bore" his friend with "counter-analysis" (*LDGR,* 1:232). These exchanges, in which no feature of Gabriel's poetry is exempt from criticism, establish the genial-severe milieu in which Christina and Gabriel confer about everything from the minutiae of her rhyme scheme in "L.E.L" to the lameness of the final stanzas in her ballad "The Ghost's Petition" and the pressing business of which poems her new book should include—or exclude.

When Gabriel submits his poems to others, he sometimes wants help with alterations in the tale itself, as is the case with his ballad "Stratton Water." Because he doesn't regard it as finished, he asks first "if any feature" suggests itself which might contribute "to the story." (A tournament perhaps?) Then after sketching out a new and still-unwritten conclusion, he appeals to his correspondent: "Tell me what you think, or whether the present ending seems the more or less hackneyed of the two" (*LDGR,* 1:227–28). This willingness to reject a trite conclusion is particularly relevant to the discussion of Christina's "The Ghost's Petition." In this engagingly eerie piece, a spectral husband describes himself in cryptic terms as "a shadow, come from the meadow / Where many lie, but no tree can stand," and then adds that "We are trees which have shed their leaves" (*CP,* 1:145–49; 41–43). Rossetti has the deceased man speak in this fashion for the same reason that Keats's Lorenzo complains of being "a shadow now" and Shakespeare's aging lover bemoans "yellow leaves" and "bare" trees in sonnet 73. Each has endured an unwelcome transformation, and each speaks enigmatically because he has become an enigma. Robert's riddling "Petition" is meant to tell his wife something like, "The man you mourn for does not exist in the condition you imagine." Then, almost as proof of the difference that has so treacherously deformed him, the husband rebukes his widow with the unfeeling brusqueness of a *Minstrelsy* ghost and tells her to stop weeping:

> "I could rest if you would not cry;
>   But there's no sleeping while you sit weeping—
> Watching, weeping so bitterly."   (49–51)

This fine bit of gothic harshness is then marred by four stanzas of mawkishness. As his wife complies, Robert offers her the solace of rearing their previously unmentioned baby. One stanza will give the flavor of this emotionally and syntactically strained denouement:

> "Nurse our little baby for God;
>   To sing his praises, when grass and daisies
> Cover us both beneath the sod."   (*CP*, 1:283)

Gabriel isn't unduly dismayed; he sees the good poem here and proposes to Christina, whom he knows to be a great slasher of stanzas, that she lop off the hackneyed ending. She agrees without demur to "cut it short" and wisely closes her poem at exactly the point where the wife recoils from her husband's rebuff (*L*, 1:239). Uncomforted and set emotionally adrift, she has the final word:

> "Yet I'll dry my tears for your sake:
>   Why should I tease you, who cannot please you
> Any more with the pains I take?"   (73–75)

Part accusation, and part compliance with a freedom she does not want, the wife's rhetorical question implies a clear, dry-eyed answer: there is nothing to be gained if I "tease you," and so I won't. At the same time, her response points to an unspoken and harder question about why her husband has grown estranged. By so nearly broaching the issue of his cruel faithlessness, she poses a strong question; and Gabriel's advice has helped Christina to locate it effectively.[19]

When Gabriel moves beyond urging the deletion of a few stanzas to proposing the exclusion of whole poems, his collaborative zeal might seem, at first glance, to have accelerated into unconscionable presumption. Certainly, the idea of his discarding any of Christina's finished work—she refers in one letter to "your ousted"—is initially startling; and yet Gabriel's participation in the winnowing of material for the new book is a routine part of the tactful assistance the poets in his circle provide one another (*L*, 1:209). As Gabriel ponders his own first book, he frankly asks his friends what to "omit altogether" and to identify "any you don't think worth including" (*LDGR*, 1:332, 377). There is a bit of nervousness, naturally, and he jokes, "A good number of my perpetrations I have already excluded," and reserves final judgment to himself: "Of course you know our common race too well to think that I should *always* benefit by a warning though one rose from the grave—but I am sure I should get something out of you" (*LDGR*, 1:332). A writer's own opinion, whether it be a half-formed preference or what Christina calls "a spite" toward a piece, can become clearer by having someone else float the possibility of its omission. When Gabriel's correspondents identify items for excision, he concedes some—"*The Mirror* I will sacrifice to you"—but not all and sometimes brings up the question of bulk: "I would throw the *Bride's Chamber* over altogether if I could muster energy to supply an equal amount of new matter" (*LDGR*, 1:382–83). This process, which looks a bit like bargaining, is precisely that used by Christina and Gabriel as they go about finalizing *The Prince's Progress*. When discussion turns to the subject of omissions, four candidates for ouster are quickly dubbed "the squad"; Christina surrenders some, preserves others, cautions that she may yet reinsert her "favourites," and reminds Gabriel that "diminution of bulk is abhorrent" (*L*, 1:228, 209, 234). Far from succumbing to any bullying on Gabriel's part, Christina entertains his suggestions as part of the collegially abetted scrutiny so vitally necessary to the completion of her book.[20]

Some of the Rossettis' most important exchanges concern the three major poems they consider omitting: "A Royal Princess," "Under the Rose," and "The Lowest Room." The first two, which treat female courage and a daughter's illegitimacy, are retained; while the last, a discontented treatment of domestic contentment, is rejected, or, to be precise, deferred until a later edition. This part of the Rossettis' correspondence is crucial, less for the sake of Gabriel's opinions than for the light it sheds on Christina's maturing poetics as she moves away from the narrative themes and topoi traceable to the influence of Felicia Hemans.

Interestingly, it is Christina who first wonders whether "A Royal Princess" might not be "advantageously" ejected since it is "rather a spite" of hers (*L*, 1:234). This stigmatizing of her poem may be no more serious than Gabriel's calling his pieces "perpetrations" or it may, in fact, register some lingering dissatisfaction with the exhibitionist role assigned to her royal heroine. An interior monologue that explores the princess's crisis of altruism, the poem had already undergone extensive cutting before its first publication in 1863.[21]

Passages about loneliness, martyrdom, love of parents, and a romantic subplot had all been excised in order to emphasize the development of the young woman's social conscience; additional slight changes in 1865 further clarify her new sensibility by hinting at a previous indifference to the "trodden-down" peasantry (*CP,* 1:149–52; 36). Upon overhearing some callous impudence about the starving poor, for example, the princess of the 1863 version recognizes the speaker as her own page, "a pretty lad, in dress perhaps too gay" (*CP,* 1:285; 65). On emendation, she describes him as "a lad I reared and bore with day by day" and seems willing to assume blame for his unreproved heartlessness (*CP,* 1:151; 65). In the version Gabriel sees, the princess awakens to the people's need just as an uprising begins; when the castle comes under fiery assault, she bravely resolves to face the mob and give them all she has "to buy them bread" (103).

What Rossetti is working with in this slightly preposterous tale is the intervention formula inherited from Hemans's *Records of Woman.* Though examples abound, "The American Forest-Girl" includes a particularly vivid episode in which a daring "forest" maiden interrupts a captive's execution—"'He shall not die!'"—and prompts a change of heart among the warriors:

> A sudden wonder fell
> On the fierce throng; and heart and hand were still'd,
>   Struck down, as by the whisper of a spell.
> They gaz'd,—their dark souls bow'd before the maid.
> (*Hemans,* 390–91; 68–71)

The flaw in this depiction of an individual's soothing influence on collective ferocity is as visible to Rossetti as it is to Hemans, who in other poems acknowledges the real-world futility of youthful courage. Her "Casabianca" has attracted recent interest, and readers now agree that the poem grieves for the boy on "the burning deck" as "both patriotic martyr and senseless victim." Rossetti, in any case, is not inclined to depict actual martyrdom or to go beyond the moment of ethical challenge. In a significant modification of the received topos, she stops the action and allows her heroine to admit the enormity of her personal risk and to fortify herself with the words of the biblical Esther:

> I, if I perish, perish; they today shall eat and live;
> I, if I perish, perish; that's the goal I half conceive:
> Once to speak before the world, rend bare my heart and show
> The lesson I have learned, which is death, is life, to know.
> I, if I perish, perish; in the name of God I go.   (104–8)

In keeping with her authentically lyrical impulse, Rossetti lets the reader overhear the princess's self-exhortation and feel the urgency of the hypnotizing repetitions by which she steels herself to confront the "shrieking" incendiaries (95). It almost works artistically, but only because the poem ends here within the privacy of its moral climax. To think one moment ahead into the narrative is to realize that incantations from the Book of Esther have no predictive force and that the princess, almost certainly, will meet a hideous death. But to judge a poem by projecting its unwritten episodes is to disallow Rossetti her tale altogether.[22]

When Gabriel does exactly this, i.e., when he questions the recklessness of the princess's gesture, impressive though it may be, Christina responds somewhat dryly that she hasn't supposed that the princess would die: "I do not fight for the *R.P.*'s heroism; though it seems to me that the royal soldiers might yet have succeeded in averting *roasting*. A *yell* is one thing, and a *fait accompli* quite another" (*L,* 1:242). The implicit argument here is that Gabriel's question is far too literal-minded—which it is—and that by invoking such an aesthetically irrelevant norm, he has dispelled her own objection to the poem. She now seems satisfied that her modification of the interventionist plot is, to borrow Greer's phrase, a "genuine revision," and so "A Royal Princess" stays in the new book. It should be noted, however, that this is the last poem in which Rossetti implies or contemplates any such public display of valor.

When canvassing opinions about which poems to exclude, Gabriel explicitly asks his friends whether they see "any objection . . . in the treatment . . . of the subject." The poems he feels particularly concerned about are "Jenny," which he retains, and "Dennis Shand," which he omits at Allingham's suggestion. Of this last, he wants to know, however, whether it displeases because of "anything" besides "its impropriety?" (*LDGR,* 1:383). Topic alone is never sufficient reason to suppress a good poem, but what Gabriel dreads is misjudging his tone or displaying some subtle form of aesthetic incompetence. So he is on the alert when Christina tells him that her new poem, "Under the Rose," is "a longish thing (not only finished, but altogether written just now; and indeed finished since last I wrote to you) which no one has yet seen," and adds somewhat hesitantly, "I don't know whether you will deem it available" (*L,* 1:230). Taking the word "available" to mean "acceptable," Gabriel raises the delicate issue of Christina's treatment of the potentially offensive subject of illegitimacy.

Revision is already under way when Christina replies and it does not seem likely that the poem's inclusion is actually in doubt. Nonetheless, her long comment makes clear that while she has chosen an "unpleasant-sided subject," she does not consider her treatment at all coarse:

> But do you know, even if we throw *U. the R.* overboard, and whilst I endorse your opinion of the unavoidable and indeed much-to-be-desired unreality of women's work on many social matters, I yet incline to include within female range such an attempt as this: where the certainly possible circumstances are merely indicated as it were in skeleton, where the subordinate characters perform (and no more) their accessory parts, where the field is occupied by a single female figure whose internal portrait is set forth in her own words. Moreover the sketch only gives the girl's own deductions, feelings, semi resolutions; granted such premises as hers, and right or wrong it seems to me she might easily arrive at such conclusions: and whilst it may truly be urged that unless white could be black and Heaven Hell my experience (thank God) precludes me from hers, I yet don't see why "the Poet mind" should be less able to construct her from its own inner consciousness than a hundred other unknown quantities. Practical result: if you retain *U. the R.,* I think it would be well placed last in the secular section. (*L,* 1:234)

This explanation is convincing: the poem is an unexceptionable monologue in which the illicit "circumstances" of the girl's begetting and the "accessory" sneers and innuendoes of her tormenters are all filtered through her innocent sensibility. It is particularly noteworthy that Christina's defense is keyed to her own sense of the daughter's restraint, i.e., her slender interest in the details of maternal shame (she knows merely that her mother was "scarce sixteen" when overwhelmed by the "secret bitter throes" of childbirth) and her disinclination to renounce the woman who disavows her (*CP,* 1:164). Significant, too, is Rossetti's belief that this daughterly mildness somehow offsets the "unreality of women's work on many social matters," for here again it is the legacy of Hemans that is the poem's background. The older writer, who sanctifies the domestic affections and repeatedly celebrates "the sweetness of a mother's voice . . . the blessing of her eye," occasionally reinforces her praise of maternal love by condemning its opposite, the negligence of a promiscuous mother, and by narrating this sinner's sure and inevitable punishment (*PWH*, 330). In "The Lady of the Castle," for example, a beautiful woman abandons her child for a life of pleasure only to return years later, degraded, poor, and yearning to be forgiven. In a fleeting moment of failed recognition, her now-adult daughter shrinks "from the weeper's touch" and the prodigal dies of instantaneous heartbreak:

> —'twas but a moment—yet too much
> For that all humbled one; its mortal stroke,
> Came down like lightning, and her full heart broke
> At once in silence. . . . (*Hemans*, 412; 84–87)

Death at the feet of an "undefiled" daughter (73) is perhaps the most blatant example of what Virginia Blain calls Hemans's "penchant for the dramatic moment." Just as Rossetti declines to narrate abruptly effective interventions, so too she resists the sudden authorial vindictiveness of Hemans's tale and relies instead on precisely the formal means she specifies to Gabriel. She writes from the daughter's perspective of a protectively bitter tenderness toward the "lady" understood to be her mother, and sets forth "the girl's own deductions, feelings, semi resolutions" as a purely internal meditation "in her own words." The poem stays.[23]

"The Lowest Room" is a poem about which the Rossettis reach an agreement though not a settlement, and thereby hangs a rather complicated tale—complicated for what "The Lowest Room" shows about a wrong artistic road Christina seems to be taking and for the soul-searching it occasions a decade later when Gabriel, by then suffering the long aftermath of a nervous breakdown, attacks her for including it in her collected works of 1875.[24] Conceived and written in 1856, at the time of William's adulatory edition of Hemans, Christina's poem faces up to the serious task of assessing womanhood and the value of the modern woman's life. Ambitious in scope and broadly discursive about gender and nineteenth-century culture, the poem sets out its materials in Hemans's manner, that is to say, it considers the satisfactions of the domestic sphere and draws an explicit lesson at the poem's end. The speaker, an unmarried woman, recalls a time twenty years earlier when she and her younger sister found themselves disagreeing about the relative merits of ancient and modern culture. The elder sister, who had been reading Homer, challengingly proposed that "those days were golden days, / Whilst these are days of dross" (*CP*, 1:200–207; 35–36). The younger sister countered with the opinion that Homeric men were repellently barbarous and declared her preference for modern days, specifically for the modern home and Christian values:

> "To me our days seem pleasant days,
>   Our home a haven of pure content;
>
> . . . .
>
> Homer, tho' greater than his gods,
>   With rough-hewn virtues was sufficed
> And rough-hewn men: but what are such
>   To us who learn of Christ?"   (149–50, 153–56)

Remembering all this, decades after their quarrel, the elder sister praises her younger sister's "mild" ways, her "few soft words," and then moves forward in time to approve the wifely happiness this gentle woman has achieved in the intervening years (161–62). Her summing up is a virtual paean to marital contentment:

> My sister now, a stately wife
> Still fair, looks back in peace and sees
>   The longer half of life—
>
> . . . .
>
> With little grief, or fear, or fret:
> She, loved and loving long ago,
>   Is loved and loving yet.   (230–32, 234–36)

Bland and vapid as the lines appear to the modern reader, they were the prevailing mode when Rossetti wrote them, and had been ever since *Records of Woman* appeared in 1828. A passage from "The Switzer's Wife" serves to illustrate what had become the conventional strategies for celebrating domestic joy and how closely Rossetti follows its template; the wife is described as

> she, that ever thro' her home had mov'd
>   With her meek thoughtfulness and quiet smile
> Of woman, calmly loving and beloved,
>   And timid in her happiness the while.   (*Hemans*, 349; 67–70)

The ideality of the married woman's circumstances are suggested by the hint of duration; she moves "ever" as if her cottage were a vast eternal space, archetypal by implication. The abstractions "thoughtfulness" and "happiness" suggest that contentment is akin to beatitude. Repetition in the phrase "loving and beloved" affirms a perfect symmetry in the reciprocated affection that blesses a "meek," "timid," and "quiet" woman. Despite the losses and political upheavals Hemans typically includes (in this instance the husband goes off to lead an insurrection), nothing in the poems disrupts the domestic ideal, and as Wolfson points out, nothing challenges "the norm of separate spheres and its gendered system of obligations." This norm, and the conventions that endorse it, are echoed throughout the 1850s and 1860s in countless poems by numerous writers, i.e., by the women who are collectively dismissed in William Rossetti's later preface as "that very modern phalanx of poets" who follow Hemans's lead. One such writer is Adelaide Procter, who, in "A Woman's Answer," ascribes the approved domestic sentiments to a contemporary wife and allows her to say, "I love, too, to be loved; all loving praise / Seems like a crown upon my Life." The elements of female serenity, enduring affection, and symmetrical love are all in place.[25]

When Gabriel looks at Christina's "The Lowest Room," what he sees is its derivativeness, its all-too-obvious similarity to the poetry of the sentimental "phalanx" of Hemans's followers. This seems to be the import of what Christina refers to as the "taunt" that accompanies his proposal to omit the poem from her 1866 volume: "*Lowest Room* pray eject if you really think such a course advantageous, though I can't agree with you: still it won't dismay me that you should do so; I am not stung into obstinacy even by the Isa and Adelaide taunt in which I acknowledge an element of truth" (*L,* 1:234). Isa Craig, as it happens, is the editor of the fund-raising pamphlet in which "A Royal Princess" first appeared, and Adelaide Procter is one of the few poets whose work Christina is on record as being unimpressed with, having once mentioned her to Macmillan as a poet "I am not afraid of" (*L,* 1:189). Between the siblings, Gabriel's remark is code for aesthetic feebleness and Christina, in acknowledging "an element of truth" in the comparison, is admitting that sections of her poem, taken out of context, can seem weakly domestic and moralized in Procter's (and ultimately Hemans's) own manner. She had already set it aside in 1862, omitting it from *Goblin Market and Other Poems,* and to do so again is not particularly disturbing; she knows, however, that it has strengths Gabriel does not see.

To read "The Lowest Room" as merely a hymn to domesticity is to accept the ending and miss the poem. It is to overlook the elder sister's Homerically normed restlessness with the modern woman's lot. Sitting at her embroidery, and recalling how Helen, in the sixth book of the *Iliad,* "delights in the fact that she is a theme of epic poetry . . . and weaves the stories of the battles fought for her into her web," Rossetti's needlewoman becomes troubled:

> "Oh better then be slave or wife
>   Than fritter now blank life away:
> Then night had holiness of night,
>   And day was sacred day."
>
> "The princess laboured at her loom,
>   Mistress and handmaiden alike;
> Beneath their needles grew the field
>   With warriors armed to strike."   (69–76)

The epic portrayal of meaningful womanhood is a painful thing for her, inseparable from its impossibility, and the cause of what she calls "Old Homer's sting" (28). In the course of their "Fight over . . . Homer," the antagonism the elder sister misunderstands as "envy" of the younger is, in fact, resentment of her own gendered fate. She strives, finally, for the self-subdued calm that readers have variously regarded as saintly or bitter wisdom:

> Not to be first: how hard to learn
>   That lifelong lesson of the past;
> Line graven on line and stroke on stroke;
>   But, thank God, learned at last.   (265–68)

Rosenblum has noted the circularity of the "lifelong lesson" insofar as it suggests a "Christian humility" that requires "total self-abnegation," while the latter is intolerable without the former. In any case, the note of exasperated self-congratulation indicates that "total self-abnegation" has not been achieved and that the speaker still feels the "sting" of roiled discontent. Rossetti is intelligently unwilling to represent this modern woman as complacent in the role history awards her.[26]

A decade later, when Christina includes "The Lowest Room" in her 1875 collection, Gabriel sees the poem in a new light. Instead of the blandness of its domestic and Christian sentiments, he now sees the vehemence of its Homeric ideals; and it is not piety but discursiveness that seems a problem. Though he does not specify passages, it is clear enough how some of the elder sister's views on ancient culture could strike him as clumsy provocations to a quarrel and, worse yet, regrettable indications of the author's unsophisticated thinking. The admiration, for example, of man-to-man combat and the contempt for modern warfare hardly amount to a legitimate insight about power, especially since the culmination is an anachronistic rhetorical question about gunpowder:

> "Then men were men of might and right,
>   Sheer might, at least, and weighty swords;
> Then men in open blood and fire
>   Bore witness to their words,
>
>   .   .   .   .
>
> "Then hand to hand, then foot to foot,
>   Stern to the deathgrip grappling then,
> Who ever thought of gunpowder
>   Amongst these men of men?"   (41–44, 49–52)

The preference for "sheer might" and "weighty swords" confuses courage with bloodshed, not to say bloodthirstiness; and Gabriel sees, rightly enough, that appalling misstatements of this kind spring from an assertiveness that eludes Christina's control. What look to be failures in ethical thinking are the unfortunate consequence of a polemically topical mode. As was his strategy when he first objected to the poem, Gabriel again finds the manner derivative. On this new occasion, in a letter dated December 3, 1875, he gives the style a name and a pedigree that have become famous (if not infamous) in modern scholarship; Christina's poem, he says, is "echoish" of Elizabeth Barrett Browning and "tainted" by her "falsetto muscularity":

> A real taint, to some extent, of modern vicious style derived from the same source—what might be called a falsetto muscularity—always seemed to me much too prominent in the long piece called *The Lowest Room*. This I think is now included for the first time, and I am sorry for it. I should also have omitted *No thank you, John* (and perhaps the preceding piece ["The Queen of Hearts"] also). The *John* one has the same genesis more or less, and everything in which this tone appears is utterly foreign to your primary impulses. The *Royal Princess* has a good deal of it unluckily, but then that poem is too good to omit. If I were you, I would rigidly keep

guard on this matter if you write in the future, and ultimately exclude from your writings everything (or almost everything) so
tainted. I am sure you will pardon my speaking so frankly.
(*LDGR,* 3:1380)

This is a shocking passage, and several things must be said about it. First
of all there is the plausibility of the claim about Browning's influence. If
Gabriel is thinking of the vigorous quarreling and opinionatedness in
Aurora Leigh, he has the chronology wrong. "The Lowest Room" was
finished before Browning's poem and a full month prior to Gabriel's receipt of a presentation copy from the author herself. "Lady Geraldine's
Courtship," however, the precursor to *Aurora Leigh,* is an entirely possible model of the "modern vicious style." The poet-speaker Bertram
courts Lady Geraldine with waves of talk about contemporary literature,
the disparity between rich and poor, technological progress, and so on.
His disparaging comparison of modern and ancient men anticipates the
elder sister's in "The Lowest Room":

> When we drive out, from the cloud of steam, majestical white
>   horses,
> Are we greater than the first men who led black ones by the
>   mane?   (EBB, 123; 207–8)

While a single rhetorical question is a scanty sample, it is probably
enough to show that Bertram lacks sufficient contour as a character to
make his views compelling. Gabriel, as early as 1855, complains that the
poem is "quite uncongenial" and serves clumsily as the "medium of the
social and other views" that readers assume to be the author's own
(*LDGR,* 1:267).[27]

Next, there is the intemperateness of the letter. Even if Gabriel is correct about the lineage of the modern opinionated style, his harshness
about the "taint" and his sweeping inclusion of unquestionably fine poems in the stigmatized "falsetto" category belie his objectivity as a critic.
The motive behind his rudeness to Christina becomes apparent in a letter to their friend Theodore Watts; playing coarsely with her title,
Gabriel describes "The Lowest Room" as a "vile trashy poem . . . fit for
one room viz. the bog" and caps his annoyance with an ill-tempered exclamation: "So now the world will know that she can write a bad poem"
(*LDGR,* 3:1390). Gabriel may think he has concealed his anger from

Christina, for he opens with praise that seems generous and specific—"
"To-day I have been looking through [the volume] with the same intense
sympathy which your work always excites in me"—and he praises some
of the "newly added" titles as "most exquisite," "one of your choicest
masterpieces," "lovely, and penetrating in its cadence." The political
sonnets on the Franco-Prussian War are "very noble . . . I dare say, the
best thing said in verse on the subject" (*LDGR*, 3:1380). But this does
not soften the shock of the dispraise that follows. It might be noted that
Gabriel's letters to other poets at this time are a similar mix of flattery and
contempt. William Bell Scott's collection of 1875 is extolled for its "extraordinary beauty" and then subjected to merciless comment on the
"unkempt quality" evident "somewhat throughout," on flaws in the
rhythm, and on some "questionable" additions. When Gabriel sees that
he has "been dwelling at some length on—I will not say objections, but
critical impeachments not passing the point of query," he merely begs
"pardon" for what he calls "a moment's chaff" (*LDGR*, 3:1331–33).
Richard Watson Dixon receives a far milder although comparably mixed
letter (*LDGR*, 3:1334–35, 1377). Without pausing to explain the accumulating personal crises that torment Gabriel in 1875, it might simply
be regretted that this once generous friend whose suggestions were always valued is now sourly impatient with every new book he reads. Apparently unaware that he is passing far beyond the limit of friendly critique, he inflicts on Christina the same kinds of irritated complaint he
sends to others. She cannot know that she has received what has become
his standard-issue letter; to her it seems that his spite against an early
poem has caused him to condemn some of her best work.[28]

Finally, there is Christina's response. Caught off guard and stung by
such harshness from her erstwhile collaborator and once best critic,
Christina writes three replies. Brief and firm, they are touchingly admirable for what they show of her willingness, despite provocation, to
think calmly about her art. The unkindness she has to ignore, but not the
aesthetic misjudgment; and so she sets about distinguishing the true from
the false in Gabriel's assessment of her "primary impulses." Her first letter is directed to George Hake. As Gabriel's personal secretary since his
collapse in 1872, Hake understands the vagaries of Gabriel's moods. He
is also becoming a friend of Christina's (eventually asking her to be god-
mother to his daughter) and it is his presentation copy that Gabriel has
"rummaged" for the new inclusions (*LDGR*, 3:1378). Seizing on this

pretext, Christina alerts Hake that she will reply soon: "Please tell Gabriel, with one love, that I find matter for thought in his thoughtful critique, and much matter for pleasure in his commendation. I hope to write to him one day, and in my turn say my little say" (*L,* 2:72). Tactfully deferring her expected reply, Christina's promise to "say my say" means that she intends to have it out with Gabriel, but it will be a "little say." This last phrase conveys perfectly, perhaps involuntarily, the sense that Gabriel has treated her "with insufficient regard, not taken [her] seriously enough"; he has slighted her work and she feels belittled by him.[29]

In saying her say to Gabriel directly, Christina speaks not as an offended sister, but as a poet who takes another poet's criticism as a stimulus to aesthetic self-scrutiny. Her two letters are quite brief, but they lay out the offending poem's history, clearly bracketing it as "youthful" work composed in the years before the *Goblin Market* volume, but also asserting its worth as a piece published in *Macmillan's Magazine* in 1864. Carefully avoiding mention of Elizabeth Barrett Browning, whom she will not wrangle about, Christina nevertheless indicates her concern with the allegation of being "echoish." Gabriel has identified a tone as "foreign" to her "primary impulses" and she is thinking about this:

> Now for a little bit about my new ed. It gratifies me much to receive your sympathetic praise, & find you care to accept the copy I store for you. The whole subject of youthful poems grows anxious in middle-age, or may at some moment appear so: one is so different, & yet so vividly the same. I am truly sorry if I have judged amiss in including the 'Lowest Room',—which, however, I remind you had already seen light in Mac's Mag. To my thinking it is by no means one of the most morbid or most personal of the group; but I am no good judge in my own cause. (*L,* 2:74)

In the week that passes before her next letter, she moves toward a clearer realization of the poem's weakness: "After impervious density I begin to see light (I think) on your objection to 'the Lowest Room'; & I already regret having inserted it, you having scale dipping weight with me. Bulk was a seductive element . . . I still don't dislike it myself, but can lay no claim to impartiality" (*L,* 2:76). Were this a poem instead of a letter, the double negative in "don't dislike" might seem to reverse the acceptance of Gabriel's "scale dipping" judgment in the way the final line, "I do not deprecate," overturns all that precedes it in "'A Bruised Reed Shall He Not Break'" (*CP,* 1:68); but it is probably a simple admission of nostalgic fondness for an early piece of truly ambitious work. When speaking of poems she is rightly willing to stake her career on, "No, Thank You, John" and "The Queen of Hearts," Christina's aesthetic confidence is emphatically explicit. From the outset, she disallows Gabriel's claim that these two are of a piece with "The Lowest Room," and she re-clusters them with one of her paramount favorites, the outspoken and cryptically indiscreet "Winter: My Secret": "As to 'John', as no such person existed or exists I hope my indiscretion may be accounted the less: & 'Flora' (if that is the 'next' you allude to) surely cannot give deep umbrage. The latter I hardly think as open to comment as 'My Secret,' but this last is such a favorite with me that please don't retort 'Nor do I——.' Further remarks, if any, when we meet" (*L,* 2:74). Christina does not bore Gabriel with a long defense, she simply contradicts him: her favorite work does not give offense. One might wish that she had become stiff-necked, that she had remarked on the caginess and the reticences in these poems, that she had given some hint as to what she considers the "essential qualities . . . on which her claims to serious and respectful treatment rest." Would that she had provided a "counter-analysis" (Gabriel's word to Allingham) and said something about the blending of the playful and the austere in her work, about how vociferousness itself is a favorite interest, and how she represents wordy behaviors in well-crafted poems with clear momentum and tantalizingly clever endings. What a boon to criticism had she told him that, in her view, the pressure of those speakers who say too much registers against her poem's careful saying of less. She does not tell Gabriel anything so defensive, but with characteristic ambiguity indicates, "Further remarks, if any, when we meet." This might mean that she will have more to say, since she is still thinking about her "essential" qualities, or that she will listen if he has more "impeachments" to offer. Whatever the import of her sentence, it is not a refusal to confer. In fact, when the Rossettis again discuss individual poems, Christina alludes to Gabriel's past bad behavior as "fraternal stone-throwing" and thus insures the civility she requires when eliciting his assistance (*L,* 2:125). In addition, as noted earlier, she will eventually have her say about Elizabeth Barrett Browning. The preface to *Monna Innominata* will compel readers ever after to think about the two great women sonneteers in conjunction with one another and about the other Rossetti, also a sonneteer, who wrote *The House of*

Life. More immediately however, Gabriel has caused her, despite his dis-courtesy and obtuseness, to see that "The Lowest Room" might well have remained among the ejected. This is not to say that readers of nineteenth-century poetry will not find "The Lowest Room" interesting—for its depiction of ideals that stand provocatively apart from prevailing senti-ment, for the way domesticity is historicized, for the young Rossetti's mapping of aesthetic onto cultural differences as she pits Homer against Hemans. But it *is* to say that despite its interesting presentation of "social and other views," the poem lacks the restraint, the irony, and wiliness of form that are unmistakably the primary impulses in Rossetti's poetry.[30]

"Your Secret Ways": Rossettian Understatement

What Christina had not yet achieved in "The Lowest Room" and what Gabriel's free-wheeling charge of "falsetto muscularity" seems to ignore altogether is her mastery of understatement. What makes his too-memorable phrase so startling, even aside from the prickly gender slur, is its daft characterization of Christina's mature poetry as shrilly pitched and hard-driven by authorial conviction. It is almost as if he has briefly mis-taken her for one of the wrangling antagonists in the *Goblin Market* vol-ume, though even there, as we have seen, her fascination is with the em-barrassment of their stridency and vehemence. In *The Prince's Progress* noisy rivalry persists as an issue, though softened or internalized, as with the discrepancy between sociability and silence that informs "L.E.L." The assertiveness of the earlier speakers may tone itself down to unwary chattiness or bluntness, but the risk, as in "The Queen of Hearts" and "Jessie Cameron," is always and inevitably that of overexposure. Gabriel, as it happens, is mildly uncomfortable with the latter poem, though as we shall see, it manages to keep its dignity and maintain an enigmatic reserve. Others such as "By the Sea" and "Weary in Well-Doing" achieve the heights of lyric inexplicitness and arrive there by means of distinctively Rossettian tact; the first, a nineteenth-century favorite, is notable for the delicacy of its revisions, the second for its beautifully perturbing close.

Despite Gabriel's comment in 1875 about "The Queen of Hearts," the collaborative letters of 1865 bear no trace of even the slightest objection to it. Far from causing "umbrage," it is the source of playful allusiveness as Christina tells of her "lynx-eyed" search for errors in her final proofs (*L,* 1:229). The heroine, Flora, is tantalizingly clever, a cardplayer whose skill defies close scrutiny, and a worthy counterpart to the half-sequestered speaker of "Winter: My Secret." Both poems celebrate the power of concealment and both provide a rare glimpse of the usually self-effacing Rossetti all but boasting about the enticing tactfulness of her style. The new poem, like its precursor, teases by its riddling openness; playing with the language of card play, it invites the reader to explore its gaming figure in the hope of discovering the secret of how Flora wins:

> How comes it, Flora, that, whenever we
> Play cards together, you invariably,
>> However the pack parts,
>> Still hold the Queen of Hearts?   (*CP*, 1:132)

As a particularly desirable court card, the symbolic Queen provides a perfect "balance between lucidity and obscurity"; such "encoding ensures that" Rossetti's poem "will be both enigmatic and soluble." Interpreted narrowly, it seems to tell that Flora excels in the competition for lovers' hearts; but such a reading is too easy, and there are visible hints about another possibility. Part of the special craftiness of this poem is the way the stanza form dramatizes the players' rivalry. Pentameters tell of strategies for discovering Flora's winning ways, and trimeters reveal consequences:

> I've scanned you with a scrutinizing gaze,
> Resolved to fathom these your secret ways:
>> But, sift them as I will,
>> Your ways are secret still.   (*CP*, 1:132)

The expansion and contraction of lines, what Rossetti refers to as the "inning and outing," enact the surge of analysis and its thwarting by the secret's resistance. Once the alternation of couplet lengths is felt as a pattern, it becomes wittily predictive. Unchanging shape affirms what the opening lines assert: Flora "invariably" wins, and her special talent at cards remains unaccountable. In addition, the graphic placement of lines on the page alludes to placing of words *within* those lines and to the mystery of versecraft. What is encoded as "my fun" in "Winter: My Secret" here becomes a game with unfathomable "ways" of achieving success. Flora's interrogator meanwhile tells of "shuffle, shuffle . . . shuffling" the deck with a repetitiveness that is mimetically right but also manically garrulous. Without much insight, she rolls out abstractions about her own "forethought" as opposed to Flora's "instinct" and with gabby inadvertence reveals her back-stabbing willingness to cheat:

> I cut and shuffle; shuffle, cut, again;
> But all my cutting, shuffling, proves in vain:
>   Vain hope, vain forethought too;
>   That Queen still falls to you.
>
> I dropped her once, prepense; but, ere the deal
> Was dealt, your instinct seemed her loss to feel:
>   "There should be one card more,"
>   You said, and searched the floor.
>
> I cheated once; I made a private notch
> In Heart-Queen's back, and kept a lynx-eyed watch;
>   Yet such another back
>   Deceived me in the pack:
>
> The Queen of Clubs assumed by arts unknown
> An imitative dint that seemed my own;
>   This notch, not of my doing,
>   Misled me to my ruin.   (*CP*, 1:132)

In all this, Flora has only a single line of reported dialogue, her laconic and monosyllabic notice that "There should be one card more." The differences between the cardplayers' verbal styles serves as a caveat to readers who might think of Rossetti as a spontaneously simple poet. The simplicity is a choice, and Flora's taciturnity is Rossetti's delighted self-parody of her own restrained mode with its spare diction, compact syntax, and high degree of line integrity. By this point, the reader knows that Flora herself cannot, and would not even if she could, explain the dynamics of her card-craft; and the poem ends with a flurry of guesses that leave her secret intact:

> It baffles me to puzzle out the clue,
> Which must be skill, or craft, or luck in you:
>   Unless, indeed, it be
>   Natural affinity. (*CP*, 1:133)

Creativity is as ineluctable as sex appeal; and to a mere onlooker, someone else's ability to attract admirers or draw cards out of a random pack or pull words out of thin air is one of life's permanent mysteries. A riddling poem may set up a playful affinity between cards and hearts and the poet's own language, but as a theory of creativity "natural affinity" has no explanatory force whatsoever. It cannot even account for its own dazzlingly unprecedented rhyme; the comic morphology of three-words-to-one ("indeed, it be"/"affinity") belies the semantic claim to naturalness. *Affinity*'s "natural affinity" is with such words as *divinity*—perhaps referencing the poet's god, Apollo—but also *Latinity, consanguinity,* and even *asininity.* In the end, Flora's garrulous partner is no nearer than at the outset to understanding her rival's or Rossetti's talent.[31]

Verbal style is the paramount issue in "Jessie Cameron," another of the finest poems in *The Prince's Progress,* for Rossetti is at pains to defend the heroine's outspokenness and to distinguish it from garrulousness. Whereas in "The Queen of Hearts" the speaker's transparent chatter displays a lack of understanding, the bold Jessie's "somewhat heedless" speech is a sign of her unflinching self-possession (*CP,* 1:116–19; 17). The ballad begins with a voluble wrangle as a beseeching young man presses his love suit on the unwilling Jessie. She tells him, even more emphatically than the speaker of "No, Thank You, John," that "I'm no mate for you" (12); and when he forces her to repeat herself, she protests so feistily that Gabriel suggests the lines' deletion:

> She was a careless, fearless girl,
>   And made her answer plain,
> Outspoken she to earl or churl,
>   Kindhearted in the main,
> But somewhat heedless with her tongue
>   And apt at causing pain;
> A mirthful maiden she and young,
>   Most fair for bliss or bane.
> "Oh long ago I told you so,
>   I tell you so today:
> Go you your way, and let me go
>   Just my own free way." (13–24)

In the same letter in which she gladly agrees to pare down "The Ghost's Petition," Christina defends this stanza as "essential" to her "conception of the plot and characters" (*L,* 1:239). She might have added that the explicitness of the passage, with its somewhat atypical forwardness in telling the story, encourages sympathy with Jessie's frankness. By virtue of the stylistic parallel, the narrating voice actively supports the blunt resistance that is both the provocation and emblem of the fatal impasse soon to come. As the story unfolds, the young couple's verbal stand-off becomes a literal one and the unyielding pair drown in the incoming tide:

> They stood together on the beach,
>   They two alone,
> And louder waxed his urgent speech,
>   His patience almost gone:
> "Oh say but one kind word to me,
>   Jessie, Jessie Cameron."—
> "I'd be too proud to beg," quoth she,
>   And pride was in her tone.
> And pride was in her lifted head,
>   And in her angry eye,
> And in her foot, which might have fled,
>   But would not fly.   (37–48)

Set against the fact of Jessie's calamitous plain-speaking, Rossetti then provides a long denouement on the community's muddled way of speaking about Jessie and her suitor. The remaining stanzas are launched with a set of folk speculations about the tragedy. "Some say" the young man was a gipsy; "some say" his grandmother was a witch; and "some say" they avoided the witch's hut for fear of glimpsing an unnaturally "unked sight" (49, 53, 60). Such rumormongering owes something to Wordsworth's "The Thorn" and its garrulous narrator's interest in the gossip about Martha Ray. For both poets, the more "some say," the less telling their words become. In "Jessie Cameron," the failure of the couple's drowned bodies to wash up on shore puts the community in a quandary. The knowledge of "where the bodies be" is a "secret" kept by sea-winds, sea-birds, and sea-waves (95). One mystery signals another, and the truth of Jessie and her suitor's final moments is, after much talk, abandoned as imponderable:

> Whether she scorned him to the last
>   With words flung to and fro,

> Or clung to him when hope was past,
>   None will ever know:
> Whether he helped or hindered her,
>   Threw up his life or lost it well,
> The troubled sea for all its stir
>   Finds no voice to tell.   (101–8)

The final inexplicitness of "Jessie Cameron" holds out the possibility that Rossetti herself is preserving the secret of Jessie's unguarded utterance, viz., the open secret that courtship and marriage may not be good for maidens. The poet who so often writes of muteness and things that can't be said brings Jessie's tale to an end not by benefit of a mollifying coda but by invoking the ballad convention of inarticulate phantom voices. Henceforth, "watchers" at night hear "wordless, urgent" sounds, which they take to be the couple's ghostly arguing:

> Only watchers by the dying
>   Have thought they heard one pray
> Wordless, urgent; and replying
>   One seem to say him nay.   (109–12)

Though some detect Jessie's "nay," all tonalities and inflections dissolve into an obscure wind-borne anguish:

> And watchers by the dead have heard
>   A windy swell from miles away,
> With sobs and screams, but not a word
>   Distinct for them to say.   (113–16)

By multiplying these superstitious responses, Rossetti shows that fearless speech—and its motives—remain a pressing issue. As implied in the "outspoken" stanza Gabriel finds grating, Jessie's voice becomes a posthumous "bane" to those who did not make out her plainly uttered desire to go her "own free way"; she survives in the indistinctness of a haunting sound.

The blurring of voices in the slowly building close of "Jessie Cameron" is a fairly unusual version of Rossettian inexplicitness. More typical is the compression of "By the Sea," a brief and poignant lyric that attracted anthologists, who published it twice with illustration before its inclusion in the 1875 volume. A mere three stanzas, the poem opens by asking, "Why does the sea moan evermore?" (*CP,* 1:191). Presented so as to preserve its mystery, the melancholy thought borrows the form of such permanently enigmatic questions as those posed in Ecclesiastes: "What advantage does man gain from all the toil that he will toil under the sun?" (Eccles. 1:3). By way of reply, Rossetti amplifies the question with a close paraphrase of the scriptural proverb "All the rivers run into the sea; yet the sea is not full" (Eccles. 1:7):

> Why does the sea moan evermore?
>   Shut out from heaven it makes its moan,
> It frets against the boundary shore;
>   All earth's full rivers cannot fill
>   The sea, that drinking thirsteth still.   (*CP,* 1:191)

Instead of providing solace, Rossetti's stanza emphasizes the distress of the biblical sea. The anticipative "moan" of the first line recurs in the second while a formal pun in the third shows the sea fretting simultaneously against shoreline and line boundary. In the final verse, the poet of cloying hunger and disrupted desire expands the proverb to include the image of saline insatiability: the salt sea "drinking thirsteth still." Then, with a characteristic adjustment of visual focus, a move that suggests the possibility of some miraculous abatement of the sea's restiveness, Rossetti turns the gaze to the shore and the teeming life in tidal pools:

> Sheer miracles of loveliness
>   Lie hid in its unlooked-on bed:
> Anemones, salt, passionless,
>   Blow flower-like; just enough alive
>   To blow and multiply and thrive.
>
> Shells quaint with curve, or spot, or spike,
>   Encrusted live things argus-eyed,
> All fair alike, yet all unlike,
>   Are born without a pang and die
>   Without a pang, and so pass by.   (*CP,* 1:191)

To be reclusively "unlooked-on" and uniquely "unlike" is appealing. To be born and to live "without a pang" is more attractive still. And yet, the insentience of these creatures is troubling: they are only "just enough alive . . . to thrive," or, as Rossetti writes elsewhere, they are "short of life" (*CP,* 1:29). The crucial word here is "passionless." In manuscript, it appears midline in a smoothly uncomma'd polysyllabic phrase, "Salt passionless anemones" (*CP,* 1:298). But in one of her adroit small emendations, Rossetti refits the adjectives behind the noun and stiffens the rhythm with pauses: "Anemones, salt, passionless." The word "passionless" now feels chosen—oddly less passionless—and placed to be noticed and balked at. If to live and die passionlessly and "without a pang" is hardly to live, then perhaps the pangs are essential signs of life. But to put the matter this way is already to overstate the poem's delicate approach to its insight. Rossetti's meditation doesn't go beyond its images; satisfied with the merest intimation, it pauses at the boundary shore of its newfound paradox, viz., that painlessness is a greater deprivation than pain.[32]

This gem of a poem was not always so exquisitely subtle. In manuscript, under the title "A Yawn," these evocative sea-thoughts are set within a first-person lament that feebly prefers the condition of the sea creatures just described. Without irony or any awareness of self-contradiction, the disheartened speaker envies the "happy" life of the "quiescent":

> I would I lived without a pang:
>   Oh happy they who day by day
> Quiescent neither sobbed nor sang;
>   Unburdened with a what or why
>   They live and die and so pass by.   (*CP,* 1:298)

This clear choice in favor of "unburdened" preconsciousness is uninterestingly reductive. In one of the planning letters of 1865, Christina remarks to Gabriel that "*By the Sea,* has superseded *A Yawn;* for which however I retain a sneaking kindness" (*L,* 1:243). Whether this sentence means that Christina is accepting a suggestion of Gabriel's or that she is simply explaining the fate of the draft, the substitution is a wise one. The decision to excise the frame is either an instance of a brilliantly sensitive collaboration on Gabriel's part as he finds the true poem within his sister's manuscript or a signal example of Christina's admirable passion for understatement. In either case, the cropped form of "By the Sea" allows opposing feelings to remain in suspension. Individuated but preconscious, beautiful but ephemeral, the paired qualities of the sea's "live things" evoke contending responses that are more powerful for being unresolved.

The "pangs" that are the concern of "By the Sea" become particularized in "Weary in Well-Doing," a poem that revises St. Paul's exhortation to "be not weary" by quietly claiming that life's tedious vacuity is God's own contrarian doing (Gal. 6:9). In this poem about suffering, Rossetti avoids that abstraction as somehow indiscriminately oversized and shies away from the grander exhaustions of spiritual aridity. Proceeding instead with the strictest poetic economy, her method is to turn human purposelessness into the briefest of antithetical stories about purpose thwarted:

> I would have gone; God bade me stay:
>   I would have worked; God bade me rest.
> He broke my will from day to day,
>   He read my yearnings unexpressed
>   And said them nay.   (*CP,* 1:182)

Broken into half-lines, the meter mimes the thwarting it reports but also serves to disrupt the impression of continuous vexation. There is a kind of covert resilience in the stanza as the enigma of chronic frustration is parsed into distinguishably acute episodes so that oppressiveness can be reckoned "from day to day" instead of continuously and forever. It is interestingly characteristic that Rossetti, who shows repeatedly—as in "L.E.L." and "Winter: My Secret"—that reticence may be a social defense, should here represent the divine antagonist as one who penetrates and confounds the heart's urgent, wordless "yearnings." The speaker, upon finding her desires naysaid, adjusts her aims and the narrative shifts into the present:

> Now I would stay; God bids me go:
>   Now I would rest; God bids me work.
> He breaks my heart tossed to and fro,
>   My soul is wrung with doubts that lurk
>   And vex it so.   (*CP,* 1:182)

Despite the attempted change, change is not the speaker's to determine. The reversed verbs, as David Shaw remarks, fail to achieve "true chiasmus" and show only that the contest of mismatched wills continues unabated. Her intentions once again sabotaged, the speaker arrives at the heartbroken stage where "doubts" set in and where the hopefulness variously known as energy or appetite for life is on the wane.[33]

   The challenge of the culminating stanza is to imagine how this speaker will sustain herself when tempted, metaphorically, to sit down

listless and refuse to move. Formally, Rossetti provides the speaker a
new way of confronting what vexes by shifting from narrative into
apostrophe:

> I go, Lord, where Thou sendest me;
>> Day after day I plod and moil.   (*CP,* 1:182)

The speaker has not completely lost the self-idealizing capacity to pledge
her will to the Lord; and her words faintly echo the centurion's account
of soldierly obedience, "I say to this man, Go, and he goeth" (Matt. 8:9).
At the same time, grief suffuses the verbs whereby she accepts the Lord's
commission to "plod" dully on and to suffer the churning confusion that
the word "moil" conveys. Finally, there comes a disjunctive "but" and a
troubled query:

> But, Christ my God, when will it be
>> That I may let alone my toil
>>> And rest with Thee?   (*CP,* 1:182)

Posed because the speaker's "doubts" are still so grave, this question virtually takes back the pledge of spiritual surrender that has just been uttered. Neither a real nor a rhetorical question, this grammatically indeterminate form precludes comfort and suggests that the timely relief of
an answering revelation or an inner resolve is not possible. The mismatch
between what one wants and what is wanted of one cannot be tidily set-
tled once and for all. When such clarifications are resolutely attempted
elsewhere in Rossetti's poetry, they tend to be of little avail. "Memory"
reports one such brave effort:

> I broke it at a blow, I laid it cold,
>> Crushed in my deep heart where it used to live.   (*CP,* 1:148)

This deliberate smashing of hidden yearnings proves ineffectual, and the
speaker who claims to "have braced my will / Once, chosen for once my
part" is plainly *not* reconciled to her self-crushing decision. What follows
in "Memory" is an elegy for the heart that dies "inch by inch." In a related way, the final achievement of "Weary in Well-Doing" is the acknowledgment that the issues it raises about the heart's yearnings never
go away. The weariness suggested by the title is not to be remedied by

the self-violence attempted in "Memory," and it will not fade into a passionlessness like that figured in "By the Sea." Weariness is tenacious, a vexation that Rossetti later calls "impatient patience" (*CP*, 2:145). It is the "pang" of desire for a satisfying relationship with one's yearnings. As the sign of desire for desire, it is something the religious poet cultivates as assiduously as the love poet and by the same means: restrained lyric momentum, a paradoxical response to being balked, and a commitment to the pursuit of the inaccessible.

THREE

The Nonsense and Wisdom of *Sing-Song:* A Nursery Rhyme Book

ADMIRERS OF ROSSETTI have looked for a single word that will characterize her: she is said to practice a poetry of renunciation or endurance or
disappointment, abstractions that efficiently map the blank area left by
decades of critical inattention and provide formulas for her newly secured
place in the literary canon. The terms are useful and inevitable and yet
there is something rather jarring about them, especially to readers whose
interest in Rossetti includes nostalgia for a loved nursery rhyme or a remembered epiphany like the nine-year-old Isobel Armstrong's exultant
"That's it" when she came upon "Who has seen the wind?" in the search
for what she "called 'real' poetry." The dour labels register as slightly in-
apt to the scholar-parent who chances upon the witty "What is pink?" in
a thick-paged book for toddlers, or the four pieces in the *Popcorn* collection for seven- and eight-year-olds, or the five recently included in *A
Child's Anthology of Poetry*. Similarly, they seem to discount the experience
of the many who have been moved by the wintry Christmas hymn that
memoirist Elizabeth Danson cites with such fondness:

> Snow had fallen, snow on snow,
>> Snow on snow,
> In the bleak mid-winter
>> Long ago.   (*CP,* 1:217)

Rossetti's image, Danson tells us, "was the first in early childhood, to give
me the frisson induced by thoughts of infinity. It had the same mesmer-
izing effect as gazing out the window at falling snow until I wasn't fully
sure I was stationary, and not floating upwards while the snow stood
still." For those outside the academy who become curious about the

major work of an author of cherished hymns, nursery rhymes, and choral pieces such as "Echo," the scholarly titles promise too little. Portending a study of chastened grimness, they seem to forget or to belie what an early critic saw as Rossetti's *Wonder and Whimsy*.[1]

There is, needless to say, very little scholarship on the lighthearted aspects of Rossetti's work, and a carefully appreciative look at *Sing-Song: A Nursery Rhyme Book* (1872), her collection of 121 poems for children, is long overdue. To be sure, it has been affirmed more than once that the sing-songs are a true poet's nursery rhymes, though such assessments usually stand without comment, as if mere ascription were sufficiently explanatory. Like many true propositions, however, this one is worth verifying, for not only are Rossetti's nursery rhymes wiser, less conventional, and more engaging than the uninitiated reader might suppose, they repay critical scrutiny by making visible, or rather audible, the richly sustained playfulness of Rossetti's serious work. A virtual showcase of special effects, the volume provides a reading experience that is both *dulce et utile,* immersing children and critics alike in what theoreticians like to call the "wildness and shimmering contingency" of language.[2]

And so, let us begin by recalling that Rossetti endows the merchants of "Goblin Market" with "lashing" tails and the crocodile of "My Dream" with a caudal weapon "Broad as a rafter, potent as a flail" (*CP,* 1:21, 1:39), and then turn to her nursery rhyme about the appendage to a pig's coccyx:

> If a pig wore a wig,
>   What could we say?
> Treat him as a gentleman,
>   And say "Good day."
>
> If his tail chanced to fail,
>   What could we do?—
> Send him to the tailoress
>   To get one new.   (*CP,* 2:28)

For a child reading or being read to, these lines afford a funny image of the tailoress repairing a tail while for an adult reader there is the unexpected idea that a "tail" might "fail." An "attempt" might fail or even a "heart" but nothing so humble and unfunctional as a pig's tail. There is the pleasure, too, of the poem's sly comment on sartorial codes and its rejoinder to the familiar adage about clothes making the man. The *pig/wig* rhyme is traditional, as the anonymous "Barber, barber, shave a pig, / How many hairs will make a wig?" teasingly shows, but Rossetti's *tail/tailoress* pun is new and first-rate. Its homonyms strain just enough that the mismatch produces a sudden little explosion of recognition. One might add, adapting a much-cited definition of rhyme, that Rossetti's alignment of "tail" and "tailoress" obeys "the general law of textual effects" by its "folding-together of an identity and a difference." It suggests, falsely but cleverly, that there might be an etymological connection between tailors (from *tailler,* "to cut") and tails, which *might* be cut (as with those three blind mice, their tails curtailed by a "carving knife") and sometimes look as if they have been. Or, as another theorist might tell us, her pun does its work by a "conflation" of meanings and "points to the magical power of transmutation that is always present within language." With extraordinary neatness, this little poem aligns its materials so that the semantic context transmutes a word into its homophone while the allegorical context transmutes a pig into a hominid, and together these toy with the social context in which males are transmuted into tailor-made gentlemen. Rossetti's little "animal poem" is an instance of serious play. Like the rest of the poems in *Sing-Song,* "If a pig wore a wig" is valuable to the admirer of Rossetti's art because it provides direct access to the pleasure of form, the source of the poet's "inward laughter," and demonstrates the range and mix of her tonalities.[3]

Now it is true that there is not a single pig in Rossetti's collections for adults, but there are numerous small animals and one rather conspicuous fish. This last appears in "Maiden-Song," the poem Prime Minister Gladstone was said to know by heart. A jubilant celebration of poetic agency, this narrative could hardly be more festive as its three sisters— Meggan, May, and Margaret—proceed to attract suitors by singing. Margaret is the poem's heroine; and with almost giddy frivolousness, Rossetti measures her virtuosity by its effect on local wildlife. As the maiden sits alone, singing and sewing,

> A beast peeped at the door;
> When she downward cast her eyes
> A fish gasped on the floor;
> When she turned away her eyes
> A bird perched on the sill.   (*CP,* 1:111–16; 46–50)

The gasping fish affords a pleasantly silly glance at Orpheus's power of enchantment while also measuring the reach of the young woman's naturally supernatural power. The exaggeration, by virtue of its comedic self-awareness, signals that "Maiden-Song" is an exercise in wish fulfillment, falling happily short of one critic's gloomy addendum that "only in fantasy" does a woman poet have real power. In its zany way, the nonthreatening arrival of this fish-out-of-water anticipates the invasion of the singer's lyric privacy by the enraptured man who comes to woo her. With her magically lovely voice, Margaret

> Sang a golden-bearded king
>   Straightway to her feet,
> Sang him silent where he knelt
>   In eager anguish sweet.   (219–22)

The poem ends with a grand spectacle as the sisters and their newfound loves join a parade of creatures drawn to Margaret's cottage:

> So Margaret sang her sisters home
>   In their marriage mirth;
> Sang free birds out of the sky,
>   Beasts along the earth,
> Sang up fishes of the deep—
>   All breathing things that move
> Sang from far and sang from near
>   To her lovely love.   (210–17)

For this scene of festal merriment, Rossetti multiplies one fish into a throng of "fishes" (the plural usage faintly echoing a more famous parable) and turns nature's benediction into an epithalamic tribute to "lovely love." The fish of "Maiden-Song" are tokens of a mirth that willingly enfolds plain silliness into nuptial joy. Because such solemnized whimsicality is evident throughout the *Sing-Song* collection, the nursery rhymes serve as a valuable reminder that Rossetti's poetry, at its most serious, is an intense and exalted form of play.[4]

"Find the Answer": Riddles, Puns, and Paradoxes

Rossetti's "Who has seen the wind?" was long a favorite with schoolchildren who were taught to "whoooo" the first word in imitation of the wind's song. Even though Oral Expression classes are a thing of the past, children still become fascinated by the poem's invitation to hear and see evidence of the unseeable.

> Who has seen the wind?
>   Neither I nor you:
> But when the leaves hang trembling
>   The wind is passing thro'.
>
> Who has seen the wind?
>   Neither you nor I:
> But when the trees bow down their heads
>   The wind is passing by.   (*CP*, 2:42)

The gusty stir that causes this trembling and bowing induces a pleasurable awe, and youngsters tend to respond with a mimetic nod. The nursery-rhyme genre traditionally includes wind lore such as the anonymous jingle that begins, "When the wind is in the east, / 'Tis neither good for man or beast," and then surveys all points of the compass to conclude that "When the wind is in the west, / Then 'tis at the very best." The editors of *The Annotated Mother Goose,* from which this example is taken, include an entire chapter on the "Almanack" and note that one collector "devotes twenty pages to the subject" of wind and weather. Gerard Manley Hopkins, who does some elegant wind-miming of his own in "The Windhover," knew and valued these "weather saws," crediting them in his "Author's Preface" as one of the sources of sprung rhythm. In Rossetti's splendid little poem, the repeated question "Who has seen the wind?" takes the place of traditional lore and substitutes for meteorology the enticement of an imbedded contradiction. Focused on a split in perception, the question is conceptually similar to an Icelandic riddle about the shadow "visible to all but tangible to none." Rossetti, as it happens, is good at shadows; in a gothic variation for her sonnet "After Death," she allows the speaker, though sightless, to sense the darkness moving over her: "thro' the lattice ivyshadows crept" (*CP*, 1:38). For her *Sing-Song* poem, Rossetti runs the typical sensory dichotomy in reverse so that the shadow "seen by all, felt by none" becomes the wind "felt by all, seen by none." And she begins at the end; a true riddle would withhold its answer, "wind." Rossetti gives it to us right away and makes us wonder not what the solution is, but what besides wind the wind is, and what it has made us feel. What we discover is a surge of affection for the child (or children) being addressed. The "enthusiasm and tenderness" that Wordsworth once claimed as the true poet's natural endowment are here manifest in the egalitarian reversal of the pronouns: "Neither I nor you," "Neither you nor I," no child and no adult, has ever seen the wind.[5]

The delight of the poem is so innocent that some have attributed it to religious intuition. One of the *Sing-Song* volume's best commentators describes "Who has seen the wind?" as giving "a simple, yet intense, expression to the numinous": "The sense of the wind as *inspiritus,* the breath of the divine, comes through in the word 'trembling'; the leaves that tremble express awe. Reverence is in the line: 'But when the trees bow down their heads.'" As he delicately specifies the poem's unspecified surmise, Roderick McGillis also pays heed to the rhythm, noting the subtle effect of the weightier lines. The triple stressing of "the léaves háng trémbling" has the effect of modulating the breeze while in the penultimate line, "But whén the trées bów dówn their héads," the five stresses "convey the strength of the wind that bends the branches." There is another surge of feeling as well; the scenario of the poem implicitly recognizes that the wind sets words as well as leaves atremble and celebrates the grateful moment when sensation pushes into language as it does, for example, at Lake Como when the "breeze" sings "to senses wide awake" and prompts an answering song that *is* the Como sonnet (*CP,* 2:147). The unseen wind, or what Rossetti once calls "the thaw-wind," is an emblem throughout her work for valued invisible energies (*CP,* 1:35). It is the sign of spring's literally germinating force, and in *Monna Innominata,* the figure for love's awakening amid the "traceless" warming that thaws the "bygone snow" (*MI* 2).[6]

The *Sing-Song* volume includes many poems closer to the traditional riddle, which offers a proposition and instructs the riddlee to "find the answer" (*CP,* 2:36). By mixing paradoxes, puns, and strange metaphors, these poems sportively exploit language for its egregious unpredictability. Often the poems propose enigmas and call attention to what appear to be contradictions of the laws of nature:

> The peacock has a score of eyes,
>   With which he cannot see;
> The cod-fish has a silent sound,
>   However that may be.   (*CP,* 2:34)

Building on the tendency of many nursery rhymes to name the facial features, Rossetti's poem encourages the child to visualize "a score of eyes" and consider the amazing fluke of language whereby this same word applies to iridescent spots on a peacock's tail. Mouths are a marvel, too, and the anomalies they utter can be more puzzling than the "silent" sounds of the cod-fish—as the next stanza proves:

> No dandelions tell the time,
>> Although they turn to clocks;
> Cat's-cradle does not hold the cat,
>> Nor foxglove fit the fox.   (*CP,* 2:34)

The first line's denial is oddly unnecessary—of course, dandelions do not "tell the time"—until the second rationalizes the absurdity with a pun on the name of the tufted clusters which (unbeknownst to American children) Rossetti, Halliwell, and the *Oxford English Dictionary* agree in calling "clocks." The fun of the next couplet's tightly worded contradictions is partly graphic, a thing to see as well as hear. The assertions are true insofar as the string nest (cat's cradle) and the flower (foxglove) are metaphorical names that have nothing to do with actual felines or foxes. Nonetheless, these assertions of falsehood are themselves false; for at the level of the letter "cat's cradle" does indeed "hold" a "cat" and "fox" slips easily into "foxglove." In another example, the eye-paradoxes are paired, and encouragement to solve the riddle is provided by means of an additional punning hint.

> There is one that has a head without an eye,
>> And there's one that has an eye without a head:
> You may find the answer if you try;
>> And when all is said,
> Half the answer hangs upon a thread!   (*CP,* 2:36)

Pins and needles are familiar riddle solutions, but the need to decipher the clue is new: cast in the form of a zeugma, it says that the answer to one of the paired riddles (half the answer) depends (hangs) on visualizing what dangles (hangs) by a thread.

As a set, the *Sing-Song* poems are remarkable for the persistence and sophistication with which they pass to-and-fro between the literal and figural meanings of words and images. The poems with flower names conduct an especially thorough canvassing of imaging strategies. First of all,

Rossetti simply enjoys the acoustic profusion of compound flower names including, among others, cornflower, dragon's-mouth, heartsease, honeysuckle, nightshade, shepherd's weatherglass, snowdrop, sweet william, and windflower. The articulation of these multisyllable names seems a pleasure for its own sake; even in her letters, Rossetti's naming of field flowers tends to fall into falling rhythm. In remembering a favorite country walk, she muses, "I wonder how far I should *now* have to walk before I fell in with willow herb, meadow sweet, & mace-headed rushes" (*L,* 2:166). One poem finds an amusingly unexpected correspondence between nomenclature and habitat. The field flowers are identified with smoothly polysyllabic names:

> In the meadow—what in the meadow?
> Bluebells, buttercups, meadowsweet,
> And fairy rings for the children's feet
>   In the meadow.   (*CP,* 2:37)

The natural magic of the meadow produces bells, cups, and circles of mushrooms while the rhythmic magic of metrical "feet" positions the dancing pun. In the second stanza, the garden flowers are named with a grafting hyphen:

> In the garden—what in the garden?
> Jacob's ladder and Solomon's-seal.
> And Love-lies-bleeding beside All-heal
>   In the garden.

Human art, in other words, creates lexical as well as botanical hybrids. There may be a poetic self-reference here, too, in the hint that much depends on the placement of "Love-lies-bleeding *beside* All-heal." The poet, like the gardener, works with contiguities and juxtapositions, arranging words in bordered lines and bedlike stanzas. The child auditor of *Sing-Song* has a fair chance of becoming a sensitive reader of mature poetry, for he or she is already becoming attuned to playful modes of statement and to the possibility that poems are meaningful even when they are not fully explicit. Familiarity with Rossetti's nursery rhymes creates a readiness for grown-up reticence, understatement, and telling alignments of the kind found in "By the Sea" (*CP,* 1:191).

One of Rossetti's wittiest sing-songs provides a litany of dangerous floral species. Various flowers, either because of such botanical features as thorns, toxins, and leaf shape or because of the figurative implications of their names, are represented as socially off-putting, emotionally distressing, or otherwise daunting. The list animates the inanimate and turns the garden into a lively social world.

> A rose has thorns as well as honey,
> I'll not have her for love or money;
> An iris grows so straight and fine,
> That she shall be no friend of mine;
> Snowdrops like the snow would chill me;
> Nightshade would caress and kill me;
> Crocus like a spear would fright me;
> Dragon's-mouth might bark or bite me;
> Convolvulus but blooms to die;
> A wind-flower suggests a sigh;
> Love-lies-bleeding makes me sad;
> And poppy-juice would drive me mad:—
> But give me holly, bold, and jolly,
> Honest, prickly, shining holly;
> Pluck me holly leaf and berry
> For the day when I make merry.   (*CP,* 2:48)

Animation, as parents and child psychologists attest, is one of childhood's primal discoveries. Clinicians report that "as young as three years of age," children "are very clear" about the difference "between animate and inanimate objects" and soon develop a related "awareness that what is seen is not all and not even the essence of a living thing"; the researcher adds that such discoveries are—as students of metaphor, pathetic fallacy, and riddle all agree— "an important achievement in structuring information about the world." For a child, the possibility of the dragon's-mouth barking or biting is a reasonably silly variation of the game of squeezing a bilabiate blossom to make it open and "talk." For Rossetti herself there is the delight of disrupting such tame floral associations as "beauty, innocence, and passivity" by offering in their stead an impish litany of *fleurs du mal.* When the poet writes that *A* is, or is like, *B*, the meaning is understood to be a partial claim: *A* (a woman) has the property *x* (beauty) and so does *B* (a flower) *in a certain sense.* The challenge is to select an unexpected property (*x*) and to think of the flowerlike woman as thorny or rigid or able to survive in a glass of water or hybridized for intense perfume and color.

Customary exclusions are the poet's opportunity, and as few readers of the *Goblin Market* volume ever forget, one of the women in Rossetti's "A Triad" is said to have "Bloomed like a tinted hyacinth at a show" (*CP,* 1 : 29). The unexpected notion of hothouse cultivation and the nearly audible connection between "tinted," "tainted," and the latter's rhyme with "painted" combine to suggest a worse-than-unladylike showiness.[7]

Rossetti's riddles for children are less harsh than "A Triad," but every bit as alert to the conventions of metaphorical exclusion. A favorite syntax, for example, is the paired claim and disclaimer: an *A* has a metaphorical *x* but has no *y*.

> A pin has a head, but has no hair;
>
> .   .   .   .
>
> A fly has a trunk without lock or key;
> A timepiece may lose, but cannot win;
>
> .   .   .   .
>
> A hill has no leg, but has a foot
> A wine-glass a stem, but not a root;
>
> .   .   .   .
>
> Rivers run, though they have no feet;
>
> .   .   .   .
>
> A baby crows, without being a cock.   (*CP,* 2 : 32)

Here too the humor depends on activating an exclusion; the tongue-in-cheek effort to tame the puns' misbehavior results in surreally visualized *A*'s that *do* have *y*'s: a pin with hair, a wineglass with roots, a river with feet. The sheer profusion of such images is giddily entertaining, and should one wonder how many such possibilities ordinary language use excludes, Rossetti's additional litanies suggest that they are unlimited in number:

> A city plum is not a plum;
> A dumb-bell is no bell, though dumb;
> A party rat is not a rat;
> A sailor's cat is not a cat;
> A soldier's frog is not a frog;
> A captain's log is not a log.   (*CP,* 2 : 21)

For the child audience of these sing-songs, language itself becomes temporarily less transparent, and "that's the fun" (*CP,* 2 : 46). At the same time, the riddling emphasis on negation and difference encourages discoveries of lurking sameness: a "fly" (either a lightweight vehicle or an insect) with a "trunk" suggests a carriage trunk or a (butter)fly's proboscis and leads to the elephant whose trunk is a natural fly swish or, more solemnly, to the trunk that is a torso (container of the heart) for which there is no key. Similarly, for the adult reader, the timepiece that "cannot win" suggests that other temporal contest one never wins because, as a poem from *The Prince's Progress* puts it: "Time will win the race he runs with her / And hide her away in a shroud" (*CP*, 1:140). It is only a step from the playful to the serious paradox; and throughout her career, Rossetti pursues the notion of a win that is not a win and the possibility of losing-in-order-to-win. Like Donne and Herbert before her, she meditates on "the fundamental paradoxes in Christianity: one must die in order to gain eternal life, God becomes man in the incarnation, Christ is crucified but wins redemption for man." Among the devotional poems that come after the *Sing-Song* volume, a typically reverent meditation on losing what is "well lost" closes with the clever solemnity of a bilingual pun:

> My God, wilt Thou accept, and will not we
>   Give aught to Thee?
> The kept we lose, the offered we retain
>   Or find again.
>
> Yet if our gift were lost, we well might lose
>   All for Thy use:
> Well lost for Thee, Whose Love is all for us
>   Gratuitous.   (*CP*, 2:210)

The extravagant four-syllable match between "is all for us" and "gratuitous"—possibly the latter word's only occurrence as a rhyme in all of poetry—goes to the etymological root it has in common with "grace," the Latin *gratus,* meaning "grateful" or "pleasing." The stanza's claim is that God loves us freely (gratuitously) and is pleased to confer on us (to grace us with) the gift of his love (his saving grace). The quality of the rhyme, what an appreciative theorist might call the "extravagance, surprise, excess" of it, makes audible the reassuring excess by which God's "gratuitous" love incorporates "us." Rossetti delights in placing words that seem to have only the affinity of their sound in conjunctions that disclose a deep connection in sense.[8]

On Mayhem and Wisdom in the Nursery

Rossetti finds numerous ways to engage with children in her poems. Some are literally playful as in her version of the classic pat-a-cake game with infants:

> Mix a pancake,
> Stir a pancake,
>   Pop it in the pan;
> Fry the pancake,
> Toss the pancake,—
>   Catch it if you can.   (*CP*, 2:38)

Wonderful for its dipody, this poem can be clapped out slowly with emphasis on each stressed syllable:

> Mix a pancake, stir a pancake,
>   Pop it in the pan [clap];

or at exciting full speed with a clap on alternating stresses:

> Mix a pancake, stir a pancake,
>   Pop it in the pan.

For a very small child who is simultaneously discovering her body and her mother tongue, her hands as well as the sounds, inflections, and cadences of language, this poem taps into multiple sources of preverbal delight. In addition, Rossetti's adjustment of the topos (which is usually a tickling game) brings the distinction between animate and inanimate into play: the tossed and momentarily airborne pancake (should the rhyme be sung during actual pancake-making) has the same mysterious aliveness as a puppet. For children who are far too old for pat-a-cake, those with the manual dexterity to manipulate cards, Rossetti provides a house-building game. The requisite light touch and neat placement make for a pleasing tension:

> A house of cards
>   Is neat and small:
> Shake the table,
>   It must fall.   (*CP*, 2:46)

The cautious assembling of precarious units as "neat and small" as the poem's own dimeters is only half the project, however, and further instructions follow:

> Find the court cards
>> One by one;
> Raise it, roof it,—
>> Now it's done:—
> Shake the table!
>> That's the fun.

The reward for precise building is license to create mayhem: "Shake the table!" By converting her own cautionary words into an anarchic imperative (with an excited change of inflection) Rossetti gleefully indulges the creator-turned-destroyer's mischievous ruthlessness.[9]

Elation is rampant throughout these nursery rhymes; and springtime, as might well be expected, produces celebration. Energized by the noise, busy stir, and sheer proliferation of birds at this time of year, "Wrens and robins in the hedge" provides a lively textual cognate for the birds' covering of the greenery. A happily manic accumulation of verbs in the poem's third line culminates in the jubilant plenitude of a single exclamation that covers the last:

> Wrens and robins in the hedge
>> Wrens and robins here and there;
> Building, perching, pecking, fluttering,
>> Everywhere!   (*CP,* 2:23)

The observed activity compounded by the formal crescendo ("Everywhere!") makes vernal excitement palpable. The prevalence of birds is a well-known feature of nursery rhymes, not to mention Romantic odes, as a genre. In her excellent book *Cradle and All,* Lucy Rollin documents the traditional nursery rhymes' "pervasive anthropomorphic" investment in "wrens, sparrows, English robins" and concurs with Lévi-Strauss's explanation for this: "Birds love freedom; they build themselves homes in which they live a family life and nurture their young; they often engage in social relations with other members of their species; and they communicate with them by acoustic means recalling articulated language." She adds, too, that birds can be symbols of children themselves because of "their size and apparent weakness, coupled with their elusiveness and their ability to survive."[10]

Rossetti was probably familiar with "The north wind doth blow," a rhyme that is still a standard in preschools and nurseries and was available to her in James Orchard Halliwell's midcentury collection:

> The north wind doth blow,
>   And we shall have snow,
> And what will poor robin do then?
>   Poor thing!
>
>   He'll sit in a barn,
>   And to keep himself warm,
> Will hide his head under his wing.
>   Poor thing!   (*NRNT,* 38–39)

The poem encourages empathy, and children typically mime its events with fluttering fingers for the falling snow, shivery hugs for warmth, and lifted elbows to suggest the sheltering wing. Rossetti's own poem about the seasons of a bird's life concedes that winter is a hardship, but aims at a more comprehensive response than simple pathos and asks a question that touches on some remarkably important values in a growing child's life:

> A linnet in a gilded cage,—
>   A linnet on a bough,—
> In frosty winter one might doubt
>   Which bird is luckier now.
>
> But let the trees burst out in leaf,
>   And nests be on the bough,
> Which linnet is the luckier bird,
>   Oh who could doubt it now?   (*CP,* 2:23)

In a symbolic and nonthreatening way, this poem urges children to consider the appeal of security as opposed to autonomy and freedom. Since Rossetti's readers, especially girls, were taught to choose safety, the second stanza's energetic presentation of life "on the bough" is subtly countercultural. Especially noteworthy is that the poem avoids asserting or insisting on the free-spirited choice. It is a measure of Rossetti's respect for children that her poem resists declaring what they should decide. Ending with an ambiguous "now"—which may mean that "now" one knows the wild bird is categorically luckier or perhaps only luckier "for now"—Rossetti keeps "doubt" provocatively viable. The thoughtfully weather-wise child might legitimately worry—as have some poets— about the plight of blast-beruffled linnets (or thrushes) when winter comes again, as it inevitably does. In her next volume, *A Pageant and Other Poems,* published in what the keynote poem calls "the Winter of my year," Rossetti openly sides with the robin on the hedge, whose "ruddy breast" makes "one spot warm where snowflakes lie" and whose songs "break and cheer" the "unlovely" season (*CP,* 2 : 59). But in the nursery rhyme, the choice is not forced and the lively indeterminacy of the twice-doubting parable encourages the child's own thinking.

The contradictoriness of Rossetti's musings on the linnet is characteristic of the volume as a whole. The poems rarely turn explicit, and the few that seem to are not allowed the last word on their subjects; another poem or two will revisit and complicate the issue. A typical example is the brisk little dialogue on the topic of what might be called eye-appeal. Presented with a choice between "A diamond or a coal," the young respondent firmly rejects the unlovely lump of carbon:

> A diamond or a coal?
>   A diamond, if you please:
> Who cares about a clumsy coal
>   Beneath the summer trees?   (*CP,* 2 : 42)

But the near flippancy of "Who cares" and the denigrating tone of "clumsy" introduce the faintest of hints that this judgment is somehow wronghearted or unthinkingly careless. Not surprisingly, when the weather changes so does the reply:

> A diamond or a coal?
>   A coal, sir, if you please:
> One comes to care about the coal
>   What time the waters freeze.

A diamond crystal becomes less desirable when ice crystals form, and the child's tone is suitably altered. And yet, though the reversal is neatly accomplished, its blunt inference about the uselessness of beauty is hardly what one expects from a poet. Even a child might resist so merely pragmatic a little lesson; and that surely is part of the point, for Rossetti doesn't drop the subject here. The very next poem returns to the topic of minerals and gems and, without rejecting jeweled loveliness, offers an additional, wondrous truth about the apparently unpleasing flint:

> An emerald is as green as grass:
>   A ruby red as blood;
> A sapphire shines as blue as heaven;
>   A flint lies in the mud.
>
> A diamond is a brilliant stone,
>   To catch the world's desire;
> An opal holds a fiery spark;
>   But a flint holds fire.   (*CP*, 2:43)

The second stanza's wordplay on "catch" and "holds" plainly enjoys the diamond and opal while at the same time anticipating the altered sense by which the fire-bearing flint "holds" its own against such glittering competition. The awed delivery of the final line is a carefully orchestrated effect: the iambic pattern calls for strict alternation ("ruby red" / "sapphire shines"), but in each instance "flint" produces a rhythm of its own. At its first mention, when "A flínt líes in the mud," the premature arrival of the verb flattens the rhythm as well as the syntactic expectation of another vivid simile. Perhaps too there's a hint (apparent in retrospect) that muddiness be*lies* true worth. At its second mention, "But a flínt hólds fíre," the verb fills the medial syllable; in a telling formal pun, the expected nonstress emphatically holds the verb "holds" so that the line itself exhibits a hitherto hidden energy like the flint's. (To judge the effect, compare a metrically regular version, "But flint can start a fire.") Like the exemplary riddle Andrew Welsh describes, the poem fuses "picture and thought," working from simple image (muddy flint) to unexpected metaphor (the "fiery spark" that has implications for burning "desire") and to the active natural paradox of the flint's internal fire.[11]

Taken together, the poems on gems, coal, and flint amount to a kind of brief against ready-made knowingness. Here and elsewhere in the volume, the recurrence of a motif inevitably creates slight mismatches that turn abstract propositions into stimulating hints. Even a summing up, as with the phrase "who could doubt," actively incorporates a space for doubt and cedes to the child the pleasure of figuring things out. Rossetti, the creator of Laura and Lizzie, certainly has reservations about the effectiveness of conventional wisdom and "wise upbraidings" even when these happen to be accurate (*CP*, 1:14; 142). As the "Goblin Market" narrative shows, the goblin-infested "twilight" is emphatically "not good" for Laura, but as the poem also makes clear, Laura cannot and does not accept cautionary advice of the hand-me-down variety (*CP,* 1:15; 144). The same insight about the transmission of nuggets of wisdom pervades *Sing-Song;* one poem challenges truths that come memorably alliterated, culturally timeworn, and apparently validated:

> Swift and sure the swallow,
>   Slow and sure the snail:
> Slow and sure may miss his way,
>   Swift and sure may fail.   (*CP,* 2:45)

Instead of saying that these assurances about sureness are sometimes right, Rossetti posits the negative: both "may" be wrong and their mutually invalidating truths misleading or inapplicable. Rhetorically, the poem cannot be described as didactic; its point, on the contrary, is precisely antididactic and applies equally to all the *Sing-Song* pieces. Children are to consider and test the tidily packaged bits of insight that jostle one another throughout the volume. The profusion of such thematically competing materials is Rossetti's invitation to enter into the game of thinking and knowing.

To further this all-important project, the *Sing-Song* poems repeatedly credit children with powers of imagination and regularly discredit the adults who overestimate what Wordsworth calls the "half-wisdom" that comes "with lapse of years." Having lost the capacity of imaginative flexibility, the mature speakers in some of the *Sing-Song* dialogues reject the vividness of the child's perceptions, fantasies, and wishes. In one poem about a dream, Rossetti allows this voice of "half-experience" (another of Wordsworth's phrases) fully half the poem's lines, enough to expose its own dullness.

> "I dreamt I caught a little owl
>   And the bird was blue—"
>
> "But you may hunt for ever
> And not find such an one."
>
> "I dreamt I set a sunflower,
>   And red as blood it grew—"
>
> "But such a sunflower never
> Bloomed beneath the sun."   (*CP,* 2:45)

Complacent reasonableness insists on the unreality of the dream's assignment of color to natural phenomena; and as is often the case in real life where children can hardly persuade or outtalk their experienced elders, the adult has the negative last word. The point this sing-song displays, however, is that for all its accuracy, the empirical objection is not well taken. The poem's own acoustics undermine the mature voice by showing the irrelevance of its end rhymes: the adult's lines match exactly (*cd, cd*), but not with the child's (*ab, eb*). At the same time, the trailing off of the young dreamer's account (graphically marked by longing dashes) creates a desire on the reader's part to hear more of what remains untold. The child's dreams, after all, have found omissions, openings, and creative opportunities in the colors of reality. (A century later, Louise Bogan makes much the same point when, writing for mature readers, she notes that "earth's bluish animals are few.") In a second example the adult realist quashes a fantasy of flight.

> Twist me a crown of wind-flowers;
>   That I may fly away
> To hear the singers at their song,
>   And players at their play.
>
> Put on your crown of wind-flowers:
>   But whither would you go?
> Beyond the surging of the sea
>   And the storms that blow.
>
> Alas! your crown of wind-flowers
>   Can never make you fly:
> I twist them in a crown today,
>   And tonight they die.   (*CP*, 2:27)

Here again, the child who cannot win the little disagreement has the transcendently winning point of view. Becoming wind-borne may be taken as a figure for poetic inspiration whereupon the adult logic is manifestly unwelcome, insisting too absolutely on inspiration's fleetingness and the deprivation poets themselves traditionally lament as fading gleams or departing nightingales. The imaginative power the adult decries as ephemeral is, in fact, the power the *Sing-Song* poems in so many ways affirm and celebrate. The effort of these two dialogues is to bring naysaying common sense into the realm of the child, where anti-imaginative assertions can be dissipated into the dreamy context that elicited them. Rather like the aphorisms about snails and swallows, adult knowingness "emerges as something to be questioned." [12]

To Speke of the Wo That Is in Childhood

Not only are Rossetti's sing-songs respectful of the child's imagination, the nursery rhymes as a set acknowledge the distresses and trials of a child's existence. One rhyme, for example, takes note of the well-housed child's aversion to the vagrant poor. A tramping woman seems a frightening stranger, but Rossetti shows her to be a protective mother who croons the volume's prettiest lullaby: "Sleep warm and soft in the arms of your mother, / Dreaming of pretty things, dreaming of pleasure" (*CP,* 2:23). Another rocking-song begins by listing the older siblings' possessions and then tells of the infant's present comfort, the nursing and maternal "swaying, cuddling, or rocking," which as Marina Warner tells us are its first, exclusive pleasures:

> Your brother has a falcon,
>   Your sister has a flower;
> But what is left for mannikin,
>   Born within an hour?
>
> I'll nurse you on my knee, my knee,
>   My own little son;
> I'll rock you, rock you, in my arms,
>   My least little one.   (*CP,* 2:21)

Other rhymes respond to a squall of protest or a rap at the door, acoustic signs of the bodily indignities and baffling exclusions that mar a young child's life:

> Baby cry—
> Oh fie!—
> At the physic in the cup:
>   Gulp it twice
>   And gulp it thrice,
> Baby gulp it up.   (*CP,* 2:20)

The rhyme doesn't alter the taste of nasty medicine, but it transforms what is unavoidably unpleasant into an occasion for the child's gulping triumph. So too with the mail delivery:

> Eight o'clock;
> The postman's knock!
> Five letters for Papa;
>   One for Lou,
>   And none for you,
> And three for dear Mamma.   (*CP*, 2:20)

The knock that might otherwise leave the child feeling slighted or temporarily unnoticed becomes the signal for a festive sorting out. The rhyme admits and mitigates exclusion ("none for you") by turning it into the occasion for a counting game with the flutter of newly arrived letters.[13]

Rossetti's nursery rhymes also transform the verbal reprimand, the abusive genre that occasions so much of childhood's misery, into something less belittling. Her strategy is to treat brawling or recalcitrance as if it were a failure of language. Instead of administering rhymed doses of humiliation, *Sing-Song*'s admonishments rely on verbal wittiness to charm the wayward young. Rollin notes that traditional nursery rhymes include many nasty scoldings, jingles that exuberantly resort to derision and scorn. "Shaming," she reminds us, "is one of culture's most powerful weapons," and generations of parents, nurses, siblings, and teasing peers have not been averse to the nursery rhymes' overt "name calling." Offenders are hailed as "Sulky Sue," "Piss a Bed," or "Mistress Mary quite contrary." Halliwell's collection includes this last as well as the familiar taunt,

> Cross patch,
>   Draw the latch,
> Sit by the fire and spin
>   Take a cup
>   And drink it up
> Then call your neighbours in.   (*NRNT*, 32)

The nineteenth-century authors of new nursery rhymes are usually less insulting, but the polite dressing-down tends to makes up in oppressiveness what it lacks in verbal bite. Jane Taylor, whose permanent contribution to children's literature is "Twinkle, Twinkle, Little Star," addresses many well-forgotten rebukes to "little children, who *know* it is wrong" to bicker and "naughty to quarrel and fight" (Taylor's emphasis). Her poem against "Romping" is a fair and typically dreary specimen of this child-minding literary mode:

> Why now, my dear boys, this is always the way,
> You can't be contented with innocent play,
> But this sort of romping, so noisy and high,
> Is never left off, till it ends in a cry.
>
> What! are there no games you can take a delight in,
> But kicking, and knocking, and boxing, and fighting?
> It is a sad thing to be forc'd to conclude,
> That boys can't be merry, without being rude.
>
> Now what is the reason you never can play,
> Without snatching each other's playthings away?
> Would it be any hardship to let them alone,
> When ev'ry one of you has toys of his own?
>
> I often have told you before, my dear boys,
> That I do not object to your making a noise;
> Or running and jumping about, any how,
> But fighting and mischief I cannot allow.
>
> So, if any more of these quarrels are heard,
> I tell you this once, and I'll keep to my word,
> I'll take ev'ry marble, and spintop, and ball,
> And not let you play with each other at all.

Taylor's self-referential "often" is a sign of her speaker's crabby exasperation and an admission, albeit inadvertent, that such rhymes have little effect on "dear" obstreperous boys.[14]

Rossetti manages, with characteristic whimsy, to completely overhaul this unfortunate genre so that disapproval sounds neither mean nor moralizing and is administered without insult. In reproving two boys for flailing away at each other (with thumbs clenched around fists) her poem addresses them with the resonant names of nursery heroes:

> Hop-o'-my-thumb and little Jack Horner,
>   What do you mean by tearing and fighting?

> Sturdy dog Trot close round the corner,
>   I never caught him growling and biting.   (*CP,* 2:22)

A small feisty boy need not be ashamed to be identified with Charles Perraut's Hop-o'-My-Thumb, the tiny hero who outwits an ogre, or the clever Jack who uses his thumb in "the pie incident" and congratulates himself, "What a good boy am I!" The characterization of the boys' scrappiness might seem funny to them (and produce an immediate change of mood) if they too imagine it as "growling." In any case, it is better to offer the boys the unexpected example of the admired Trot and the gender-specific suggestion about restraint—don't take offense, control your temper, be "sturdy"—than to berate them as "naughty." If the poem works, that is to say, if it puts a stop to the "growling and biting," its success is due in part to its own acoustics. The rhymed lilt of its nonsemantic behavior admits and implicitly admires the nonverbal energy that it would, at the same time, have the children turn into words. The poem, in its performance, acknowledges the element of pleasure in what it asks the child to forgo (the heedless bodily intensity of their noisy scuffle) and the difficulty of what it asks. In another instance, Rossetti provides a litany about "don't" and its linguistic kin.

> Seldom "can't,"
>   Seldom "don't"
> Never "shan't,"
>   Never "won't."   (*CP,* 2:29)

The wittiness here is in avoiding the formulation "don't say *don't*" while itemizing the verbal tokens of uncooperativeness. In reciting these negatives, the poem works without harmful labels—without any mention of laziness or contrariness—and without the traditional rhyme's harsh imperative to "Do as you're bid." Instead, Rossetti's poem provides a chiming opportunity to recite the forbidden words and plays the game of contradiction, paradoxically violating its own instruction to "never" say what it, in fact, does say. Together these scolding poems explore the possibility of nonabusive disapproval and of remonstrance so lightheartedly clever as to be almost a joke. Within the Rossetti family, as every biographer mentions, Gabriel and Christina were affectionately regarded as the "storms" (Maria and William were the "calms"), since they were not, evidently, always on their best behavior. Whether or not this bit of

personal history bears on the tone of the *Sing-Song* reproofs, the fact remains that they are not hurtful. They are unfailingly child-friendly and
the instruction they give tends to be double: along with a prohibition,
they convey a sense that what they proscribe is a laughable thing and that
even censure may be a laughing matter.[15]

Rossetti writes, too, of the mortal shocks children are heir to. A child's
acquaintance with death might begin, for example, with the chance discovery of a bird's corpse. Rather than attempting the usual explanation
that all things die, Rossetti describes a simulated funeral with its three
stages of preparation, interment, and commemoration:

> Dead in the cold, a song-singing thrush,
> Dead at the foot of a snowberry bush,—
> Weave him a coffin of rush,
> Dig him a grave where the soft mosses grow,
> Raise him a tombstone of snow.   (*CP,* 2:21)

As with other denials ("None for you") and affronts that make for tears
("Baby cry!"), the poem aims at transformation. The grim remains at the
foot of the snowberry bush are turned into something else, something less
threatening, the object of a game that solemnly imitates a grown-up rit-
ual. Not uncommonly, the discovery happened more brutally. Given the
realities of nineteenth-century obstetrics and the limited ability of Victorian medicine to deal with infectious diseases, a child's knowledge of
death would often come with the loss of a younger sibling. Smulders offers a pertinent reminder of the very "high rate of mortality affecting infants and toddlers" and that "in all probability, at least one of the six children born to the average mid-Victorian family would not survive beyond
its fifth birthday." It might be noted as well that the families in the Pre-
Raphaelite circle were not exempt from this particular sorrow. Rossetti's
letters include messages of condolence to Emma Brown upon the loss of
a ten-month-old child who was survived by siblings, ages one and six, and,
many years later, to her sister-in-law Lucy Rossetti on the loss of a child
less than two years old, also survived by young siblings (*L,* 1:108–9). Nevertheless, some scholars are disconcerted by the appearance of death in a
book of nursery rhymes. They worry that the so-called dead-baby poems
actualize the threats they find hidden in Rossetti's lullabies, which seem
"tinged with an infanticidal wish that the baby's sleep will continue
indefinitely." At this juncture, Warner's encyclopedic study of ballads,

vernacular poetry, and lullabies provides guidance. Warner is expert at detecting the ways in which "songs of reassurance touch on complex anxieties" and "often situate the child . . . in the perspective of life's risks." But she is not willing to conclude, in the words of another critic, that lullabies and dead-baby poems are "controlled exercises in hate." Instead, she deftly connects the logic of the famous cradle song "Rock-a-bye-Baby," as it imagines the infant falling from a tree—"When the bough breaks the cradle will fall, / Down will come baby, cradle, and all"—with the logic of the reverse-wish. Citing the "blessing in the form of a curse" used by actors who tell one another to "break a leg," and "the traditional Italian good luck wish" that sends one "'In bocca al lupo' (Into the jaws of the wolf)," Warner arrives at a reassuring conclusion. In her view, "lullabies dip infants prophylactically into the imaginary future of ordeals and perils" in order to banish such evils from the child's dreams and from its future. Warner's analysis might help us to see that Rossetti's lullabies, far from wishing the baby dead, work to "cast a spell" against sleep's "twinship with death," and her dirges, rather than venting covert ill-will, might actually perform an important and kindly service to the surviving child.[16]

One of these poems opens with the confounding reality of an empty cradle, the strange vacancy that intimates what Sandra Gilbert poignantly characterizes as "the cryptic absence into which what was so recently a warmly living presence seems to have vanished."

> A baby's cradle with no baby in it,
>   A baby's grave where autumn leaves drop sere;
> The sweet soul gathered home to Paradise,
>   The body waiting here.   (*CP*, 2:22)

Organized as a litany without verbs, the poem forgoes the fully developed syntax that might otherwise attempt to explain the inexplicable. Rossetti does not make the error of expounding the doctrine of immortality to a child, certainly not in the prescribed manner of Jane Taylor's "A Child's Grave," in which a mother speaks as a ventriloquist for the dead and offers reassurance about its joy and heavenly detachment:

> "Mourn not because my feeble breath
>   Was stopped as soon as given:
> There's nothing terrible in death
>   To those who come to heaven.

"No sin, no sorrow, no complaints,
   My pleasures here destroy;
I live with God and all his saints,
   And endless is our joy.

"While, with the spirits of the just,
   My Saviour I adore,
I smile upon my sleeping dust,
   That now can weep no more."

Rossetti's quatrain refers to Paradise but keeps that mystifying place (minus Taylor's imponderable exemptions) confined to a single line and honors the surviving child's sense of loss by returning to the bewildering reality of the cemetery. The mere juxtaposition of "cradle," "grave," "soul," and "body" provides an appropriate shape for bewilderment, the oppositions forming an objective correlative, as some might say, for the discontinuity of death. "Home" is no longer home and the poem ends, as it must, with the incomprehensibly literal displacement from cradle to grave and the palpable mystery of a burial "here." Stephen Booth has recently offered a fierce reminder that one cannot be talked into accepting a child's death: "No conceit . . . can succeed. No way of thinking about the death of a child can make it feel other than wrong. . . . Genuine belief in death as a benefit cannot—and never could—combat knowledge that death is an evil." The notion of "death as a benefit" is absolutely irrelevant to a child, who does not yet have a "genuine belief" in death itself.[17]

This last point, this unknowing, is the occasion for another of the *Sing-Song* poems in which it is not death proper, but the signs of parental grief, the wordless tears and sighs, that prompt the child's troubled question:

Why did baby die,
Making Father sigh,
Mother cry? (*CP*, 2:24)

Adults are mysterious beings, and their silences are daunting. "The young child," as Adam Phillips tells us, notices "that there are areas of experience, realms of feeling, that seem resistant to speech," and this noticing informs Rossetti's poem. The child discovers the parents' apparently deliberate disregard of the catastrophe they do not (cannot) put into words and sees that they behave strangely. Rossetti does not try to answer

2

the child's question, but her poem does speak to it by admitting the need
and the lack of a response:

> Flowers, that bloom to die,
> Make no reply
> Of "why?"
> But bow and die.   (*CP,* 2:24)

The carefully indeterminate "of" preserves two meanings; flowers do not
ask "why" they must die nor can they give a reply to the child's "why."
The poem admits its own muteness as well, tapering down to a single foot
(a rather uncommon feature in nineteenth-century poetry) and showing
how little it has to say. There is a generosity in this, however, for by repeating the "why" and twice allowing the unanswered question to stand,
the poem captures and respects the child's incomprehension. The poem
achieves formal closure with the graceful "bow" of the flowers and the
binding monorhyme, which gives the final "die" an acoustic fitness. The
longing for presence and intelligibility is not dispelled so much as tenderly affirmed, and euphony's coherence softly acknowledges a profound
incoherence. Rossetti's ending resists the temptation of a consoling truth
and preserves instead the interior mood of grief's unknowingness.[18]

Lizards with Parasols and Other Nonsense

The *Sing-Song* collection does not include new variants of such traditional
nursery rhyme formulas as "Hickory, dickory, dock," "Rub-a-dub-dub,"
or "Fiddle, faddle, feedle." Of the two broadly distinguishable modes of
nonsense, the nonsemantic kind involving patterned repetition—of
which "Hey diddle diddle" may be the most famous example—and the
substantive kind, which includes "assertions or implied assertions that are
silly . . . assertions contrary to fact . . . sentences that are syntactically
chaotic; and so on," Rossetti excels at the second. In addition to the scenario of pigs absurdly bedecked with wigs, *Sing-Song* presents counter-
factual, seemingly pointless little narratives about creatures worthy to be
associated with the "cow" who "jumped over the moon" and the less-
familiar "man in the moon" who "asked his way to Norwich" and had a
mishap en route:

> He went by the south,
> And burnt his mouth
> With supping cold pease-porridge.   (*NRNT,* 27)

Rossetti's nursery rhymes revel in the proximity of logical syntax and sur-really disconnected images:

> When fishes set umbrellas up
>   If the rain-drops run,
> Lizards will want their parasols
>   To shade them from the sun.   (*CP,* 2:34)

Reason becomes unreasonable when the double-conditional structure as-sociated with matters of consequence is filled with pictures that jump from category to category (animals, weather gear). The analogy of fish and reptiles beguiles, however, and its expansion by means of subordinate oppositions (*up, down; shade, sun*) proves so enticing that connections do emerge. Willy-nilly, one has the impression of discerning or making some kind of sense about the social conditioning of desire: if some have the re-sources they want when they want them (umbrellas), others will want comparable benefits (parasols). Perhaps too there is the sense that silliness begets more silliness. U. C. Knoepflmacher offers a brilliantly extended reading of this sing-song, noting that "Even the smallest child reader of this poem will quickly realize that fishes whose natural element is water would hardly need umbrellas to protect them from the rain. Whether or not that child already is sophisticated enough to know that cold-blooded reptiles actually welcome the rays of the sun, it probably can figure out—by a process of analogy which the poem encourages—that parasols, too, would impede something that lizards actually want." Knoepflmacher's so-phisticated child might even recognize the paradoxical quality of the lizard's desire and at some future date, perhaps when reading Rossetti's "Goblin Market," see that the nursery rhyme had already introduced the possibility of a breach within the desiring self. Even for the young child, however, the poem's serious triviality shows that wanting what others want (lizards want what fishes have) promotes whimsical incoherencies. Fads, rather like the "Freaks of Fashion" described with high hilarity in one of the *Pageant* poems, are eruptions of nonsense (*CP,* 2:113).[19]

Another of the animal sing-songs, "If a mouse could fly," provides equally provocative nonsense by entertaining the possibility of unnatural powers:

> If a mouse could fly,
>   Or if a crow could swim,

> Or if a sprat could walk and talk,
>   I'd like to be like him.

The second stanza takes the form of a spoiling, no-nonsense, norm-enforcing rejoinder:

> If a mouse could fly,
>   He might fly away;
> Or if a crow could swim,
>   It might turn him grey;
> Or if a sprat could walk and talk,
>   What would he find to say?   (*CP*, 2:36)

The voice of reasoned probability suggests that unnatural wishes, if fulfilled, might have ambiguous consequences: dilute crow, in any case, seems faintly unpleasant. But nonsense, as one commentator says, is "robust under vivisection," and the respondent's intentionally disenchanting question about the communicativeness of sprats opens out into pleasing speculation and further silliness *about* silliness. Maybe a sprat would speak of matters as improbably irregular as his creator's hypotheses about pigs with wigs, fishes with umbrellas, or sprats with the power of speech. If the sprat utters utter nonsense, it might remind us, as Northrop Frye says of symbolist poetry generally, that sometimes "the representational answer to the question 'what does this mean?' should not be pressed." The best nonsense poems, a category that includes "If a mouse could fly," resist closure, forgo the clinching thought or the securely achieved mood, and find ways to keep the reader inside the nonsense parameters. Within that charmed circle, reason is safely demoted to mere crankiness while the abnormal and festively perverse do their countermanding, gently insubordinate work.[20]

It is a commonplace in the scholarly literature on children's poetry that lullabies, nursery rhymes, and nonsense verse are part of the child's "initiation into the mysteries of language." Warner writes that "the lullaby is intriguingly important to language acquisition": while "the singers vent their feelings," the infants are learning "phonetic and prosodic patterns," the sequences of sound, rhythm, and pitch that precede "semantic understanding." Infants, she explains,

> absorb cadence and tonality before they can understand meaningful phrases, and it is now thought that contact with such prosodic

variations "may facilitate speech processing and language comprehension." A language's characteristic vowels and consonants recur in the patter of nonsense songs, imparting the intrinsic music of that speech to the infant, and refrains, ritornellos, choruses and catch lines return to typical sound clusters: *ninna-nanna* in Italian and Greek, *heidschi bumbeidschi* in German, *baya bayu* in Russian, *shoheen-shal-eo* in Irish, *dodo dodo* in French, *cha-chang cha-chang* in Korean, and so forth.

McGillis pursues this line of thinking beyond its relevance to the preverbal child and notes that while Rossetti's *Sing-Song* poems "give pleasure in the way all nursery songs give pleasure," they also teach children "to understand, and to have fun with, the play of language"; above all, they provide an introduction to poetry "as a form of communication that differs from statement." This last is crucial: the *Sing-Song* volume equips children to find present and future pleasure in poetry as a genre. Beyond the manifest delight of games, riddles, and nonsense, Rossetti makes poetic form itself an overt source of delight, toying archly with her medium and always knowing while she writes *for* children that she writes *as* a poet. Marvelously fertile of invention when it comes to special effects with rhythm, juncture, pausing, rhyme patterning, syntax, and stanza shape, Rossetti invites children to play with her as she plays with the constitutive elements of her craft.[21]

There are, as might be expected, self-references to song and numerous puns on meter, as in "Sing me a song," where a lightly stressed line affirms that the dancers are "Light and fleet upon their feet" (*CP,* 2:36). The most flagrant scrutiny of poetic means comes in a two-stanza poem about frogs and toads.

> Hopping frog, hop here and be seen,
>   I'll not pelt you with stick or stone:
> Your cap is laced and your coat is green;
>   Good bye, we'll let each other alone.
>
> Plodding toad, plod here and be looked at,
> You the finger of scorn is crooked at:
> But though you're lumpish, you're harmless too;
> You won't hurt me, and I won't hurt you.   (*CP,* 2:32)

As this pairing clearly indicates, Rossetti enjoys showing what can be done with the resistance of language. Like the famous passage in Pope's "An Essay on Criticism" demonstrating precisely how the poet alters speed, how a line "skims along" or how it "labors, and the words move slow," Rossetti's poem adapts its four-beat rhythm in order to seem appropriately lively or inert. Her opening line hops lightly with unvoiced plosives while its counterpart in the second stanza plods heavy and slow. As in her early poem "At Home," where the phrase "plod plod" mimes a trudge through wet sand (*CP*, 1:28), the amphibian command "toad, plod here" relies on difficult juncturing to impede the line's flow. Every poet knows this articulatory gambit, and Richardson, commenting on a line by Browning, gives us a helpfully precise description of its dynamic: "Rooted in the anatomy of the mouth," the difficult transition from voiced to voiceless consonants creates a tension that "translate[s] psychologically into effort" and slowness. Rossetti provides further evidence of the contrasting mobility of the two creatures by distinguishing the ways they sit typographically on the page. The conventional indentation of the frog's alternating rhyme scheme as opposed to the solid margin for the toad's couplets solicits attention as a little joke of visual form. When "looked at" (as the poem cleverly directs), the one set of lines appears to hop back and forth while the other rests lethargically against the edge of its blocklike quatrain. The word "lumpish" is nicely positioned, too, and to test its mimetically retarding effect one might compare a hypothetical alternative, "but though you're *plump* you're harmless too." The now-perfect iambs propel the syntax smoothly along and miss the "lumpish" distortion caused technically by that word's "self-arrested stress." The actual poem's speed is then dramatically restored as the final line's symmetry colludes with syntax to produce a jubilantly reciprocal "and I won't hurt you." In arranging for the child speaker to utter this caution against hurting animals, Rossetti modifies a theme that is traditional in nursery rhymes and, as Kathryn Burlinson shows, moralizes with a difference. Instead of detailing children's cruelties, as in the familiar "Ding, dong, bell / Pussy's in the well," she assumes that paying attention to living things fosters a "protectionist impulse" toward "lowly but sentient" creatures. We need only add that Rossetti does this ethical work with metrical panache; repeatedly finding new rhythms for ambulation, she goes beyond the frog and toad to mime a grasshopper's iambics, "so light of leap," and the trochaic scurry of a "caterpillar in a hurry" (*CP*, 2:44; 2:28). Motion, after all, is the poet's medium.[22]

While "Hopping frog" gaily exploits the possibilities of non-semantic form, it does not, strictly speaking, propose substantive nonsense, nor for that matter do the poems about farmyard animals. These attend to the border between meaningful and meaningless by reproducing the improbable noises that, in the genre supposedly founded by a Mother Goose, are a time-tested source of entertainment. Transcription is not a science, of course, and the competing versions of animal "vocabulary" say less about the accuracy of "arf" or "bow, wow, wow" than about the pleasure of audible nonsense per se. A brief survey of several collections shows that the pig goes "griffy, gruffy" in one but "hoogh, hoogh, hoogh" in another and "oink, oink" in a third. The hen goes "chimmy-chuck, chimmy-chuck" or "chickle-chackle, chickly-chackly" or "cluck, cluck," and even the cat changes voweling to go "mew, mew" or "miow, miow, miow." Rossetti, who never forgets the near alliance of the nonverbal and the preverbal, suggests in one of her punning litanies that "baby crows, without being a cock" (*CP*, 2:32). An infant's urgent wordless crowing (crying) voices a passionateness that is eventually civilized and repressed, confined inevitably to what Phillips describes as the "noisy silence" coexistent with language. For the poet and her audience, animal noises draw energy from that partially inaccessible "life without words" and, under the cheerful guise of imitating nonhuman creatures, activate and celebrate the plenitude of the purely acoustic. One such poem takes the form of a conversation with Nurse about animal sounds:

> What does the donkey bray about?
> What does the pig grunt through his snout?
> What does the goose mean by a hiss?
> Oh, Nurse, if you can tell me this,
> I'll give you such a kiss.   (*CP*, 2:33)

Here it might seem that onomatopoetic terms can do little more than gesture toward anthropomorphic metaphor, but then Rossetti caps the series with a human mouth noise, the promised "kiss" that sounds and seals the child's pleasure. Since an answer is still needed to the question of what the animals mean, Nurse turns a set of nonsemantic birdcalls into anarchic bits of conversation:

> The cockatoo calls "cockatoo"
> The magpie chatters "how d'ye do?"
> The jackdaw bids me "go away,"
> Cuckoo cries "cuckoo" half the day:
> What do the others say?   (*CP,* 2:33)

This little comedy acknowledges, along the way, that the social call has its own polite babble whereby slurred near-words function as ritualized greeting. Ultimately, poems in animal voices are a reminder that all poetry is, in some sense, translation, a crossing from one language—even if it be the inchoate language of silence—into another. The evidence of the *Sing-Song* volume is that the artist is profoundly gratified and, as in the remarkable dawn song "Kookoorookoo," literally happy to make the crossing:

> "Kookoorookoo! kookoorookoo!"
>   Crows the cock before the morn;
> "Kikirikee! kikirikee!"
>   Roses in the east are born.
>
> "Kookoorookoo! kookoorookoo!"
>   Early birds begin their singing;
> "Kikirikee! kikirikee!"
>   The day, the day, the day is springing.   (*CP,* 2:20)

The charm of this piece is the ebullience with which Rossetti reproduces the cock's "wordless voice" (*CP,* 2:176). Moving back and forth between the avian and the English languages, the text's excitement builds until the bird's repetitions become the poet's own in an exultant, reiterative crescendo: "The day, the day, the day is springing." Though a mere nursery rhyme, "Kookoorookoo" comes close to demonstrating certain claims made about the creative process. The poet's art is sometimes regarded as a kind of induced self-forgetting through immersion in words, the achieving of a state that has over the centuries been variously described as mad, inspired, giddy, or ecstatic. The poet in "the act of composition" is said to become detached from the "declared subject" and attached to language itself. Who can doubt that Rossetti has, momentarily at least, lost herself in the delirium of "Kikirikee! kikirikee!"? In the event, if the testimony of anthologists is any indication, this poem delights its intended audience.[23]

The *Sing-Song* poems are especially alert to the materiality of rhyme. As a stanzaic poet, one who altogether eschews blank verse, Rossetti takes the opportunity to play with the assumption that rhyme provides access to deep semantic linkages or, as Welsh puts it, that rhyme "has a way of moving beyond ornamentation, a way of discovering significant connections between the meanings of the rhyming words." Rossetti exploits all the possibilities for making "sound an echo of the sense," but this means that she is equally aware—and makes her reader-auditors aware—of the sheer arbitrariness of the phonic material that language provides. Indeed, the arbitrariness is something she makes visible. In one of the instructional poems, rhyme serves as a mnemonic device for organizing information about the organization of time. The poem opens with small units—

> How many seconds in a minute?
> Sixty, and no more in it   (*CP*, 2:30)

—and runs through the hours, days, weeks, and months. Since "month" is a word that lacks a perfect rhyme, Rossetti invents an outlandish contraction and runs merrily along:

> How many weeks in a month?
> Four, as the swift moon runn'th.
>
> How many months in a year?
> Twelve the almanack makes clear.
>
> How many years in an age?
> One hundred says the sage.
>
> How many ages in time?
> No one knows the rhyme.

The final mystery of time's unknown limit gestures toward the even stranger ideas of imponderability or infinity and is enhanced by the couplet's inherent contradictoriness. The word "rhyme" rhymes with "time" and is a fit reply, a phonically apt chime that brings the poem to a proper close; at the same time, however, it fails as a reply insofar as it does not supply the requested information. The paradox, as McGillis astutely explains, is that "time and rhyme perform [a] coupling which the poem says is impossible." The poem tacitly admits (though a child may not understand this) that rhyme's force, the authority of its provision of the inescapably right word, is one of art's valued illusions.[24]

In another instance, Rossetti plays archly with perfect rhyme, near rhyme, and nonrhyme. The frequently reprinted and sometimes gorgeously illustrated "What is pink?" provides vivid instruction about colors and color names. Six couplets establish a firm expectation that every color has its echo; but then come the happy exceptions, a lovely half-rhyme for "violet" and the funny shock of "orange." Another member of the small but delightfully tormenting set of English nonrhymes, "orange" is inalterably matchless:

> What is pink? a rose is pink
> By the fountain's brink.
> What is red? a poppy's red
> In its barley bed.
> What is blue? the sky is blue
> Where the clouds float thro'.
> What is white? a swan is white
> Sailing in the light.
> What is yellow? pears are yellow,
> Rich and ripe and mellow.
> What is green? the grass is green,
> With small flowers between.
> What is violet? clouds are violet
> In the summer twilight.
> What is orange? why, an orange,
> Just an orange!   (*CP,* 2:31)

The pleasure of this discovered lack, this wonderful hole in the acoustic tissue of language, is complemented by the playful excess of the word "just." At first glance, it seems dismissive: there is "only" or "merely" the fruit name to echo the color name. But "just" quickly becomes affirmative: the word "orange" is a homonymic *mot juste* that just exactly matches itself. The final exclamation point affirms, too, the glee at the jest: the outrageously rule-bending solution to the problem of the word's match. A fair and "just" rule allows for repetition and self-rhyme.

Rossetti is, as shown earlier, a consummate practitioner of repetition. Lacking a fresh word or a matching sound, she manages by reiteration to convey the impression that excitement or exhilaration is pushing against the limits of available language. The surplus has a resonance that Eric Griffiths, drawing on Wordsworth's avowal that "repetition and apparent tautology are frequent beauties," describes as a kind of verbal luxury. In the *Sing-Sing* poems, the technique is used to mark occasions when delight in the natural world escalates into rapture:

> When a mounting skylark sings
>   In the sunlit summer morn,
> I know that heaven is up on high,
>   And on earth are fields of corn.
>
> But when a nightingale sings
>   In the moonlit summer even,
> I know not if earth is merely earth,
>   Only that heaven is heaven.   (*CP*, 2:41)

The disturbance in the metrical pattern at line 7, the indecision whether to say "I knów not if earth" or "I know nót if earth," might be heard as a flaw or as one of the hazards of nursery rhymes' strong stress. The reader does, however, make a decision (especially if reading aloud), and the slight rhythmic tension is itself a sign of the nonknowing the line speaks of. Then comes the firm and satisfying final line and its admission, by default of a new word, that the beauty of song and moonlight is beyond expression.[25]

Finally, Rossetti's *Sing-Song* volume provides an education for the senses, appreciating not only sounds and sights but even the fragrances that solicit our notice almost like touch. In another of the wind poems, Rossetti acquaints the child with the pleasure of vernal synesthesia:

> O wind, where have you been,
>   That you blow so sweet?
> Among the violets
>   Which blossom at your feet.
>
> The honeysuckle waits
>   For summer and for heat.
> But violets in the chilly Spring
>   Make the turf so sweet.   (*CP*, 2:24)

The wind, much like winter's housebound child, is grateful to the premature violets that don't wait for warmth, the sweet heat-seekers that, in their frail hypersensitivity, shiver fragrantly in the vernal sun. In the context of the violets' nearly tactile eagerness for the new season, the second stanza jokes with a little wait at the line break, the syntax conniving with temporality, so that the honeysuckle "waits" for the next line's promise of "summer" and "heat." In imagining the near discomfort of these delicate early flowers—the daffodil in another poem wears "a scant green gown / While the spring blows chilly" (*CP*, 2:23)—Rossetti acknowledges the breezy tingle that subtly pleasures the flesh of a child or healthy adult. Such delicious small shocks of cold and warmth are a versatile "image" throughout Rossetti's volumes, and, as the devotional poems tend to remember, the earliest flakelike blossoms might yet be covered by "sprays of snow" (*CP*, 2:297). And since inclement weather really can be the bane of a child's existence, as famously bemoaned in the incantation "Rain, rain, go away," Rossetti proposes her own be-spelling way to participate in a wet May's showers. At the outset, this sing-song sounds like little more than an adaptation of the adage about April showers:

> There is but one May in the year,
>> And sometimes May is wet and cold;
> There is but one May in the year
>> Before the year grows old.   (*CP*, 2:27)

The difference comes in the second stanza, where Rossetti's honesty about May's dreariness comes into play:

> Yet though it be the chilliest May,
>> With least of sun and most of showers,
> Its wind and dew, its night and day,
>> Bring up the flowers.

The poem works best if May really is "wet and cold," for in the last line the child is invited—by the rhythm—to help coax the flowers out of the ground. The flawless alternation of the penultimate line, "Its wind and dew, its night and day," establishes a metrical expectation that bears audibly on what follows. As a prosodist might explain, the tendency to preserve stress timing invites a "drawing out" of the first stressed word; or, as anyone reciting aloud intuitively knows, one performs the last line by stretching "bring" into a disyllable. A child who is a willing magician will add pulling gestures and mimetically "brí-ĭng úp" the flowers.[26]

As a seasonal poet, Rossetti does for children in "chilliest May" what she also does for adults in a *Later Life* sonnet from the *Pageant* volume: she attends faithfully to the miseries of winter but notices, with a hopefulness enforced by the severest accuracy, that "ivy thrives on scantiest sunny beam" (*LL* 19). Botanical heat-seeking and light-seeking are recurrent motifs in the late *Verses* as well; one prayerful speaker searches her "heart-field" for "A handful of sun-courting heliotrope" (*CP*, 2:184). For another, the liminal hour occasions what might be called a thermal epiphany: "Wheat feels the dawn" despite "night's lingering cope," and the result is a spiritual aubade (*CP*, 2:181). As in the *Sing-Song* "Who has seen the wind?" this later poem rests on the possibility of feeling a power that cannot be seen and links a riddling perception with religious mystery.

It has been said by various writers, William Carlos Williams among them, that "The only means" the artist "has to give value to life is to recognize it with the imagination and name it." Any who agree with this sentiment will recognize that one of the great achievements of Rossetti's career is that she values and names the sorrows and pleasures of children. Though she knows that there are many things that cannot be said, that there are entire realms of experience where words fail, she does not allow the intensities, the distresses, and the gladness of children's lives to go without saying. In acknowledging these realities, her *Sing-Song* collection provides children with a poetry of their own, a poetry so fine it confers the power to love art. By their inducement to "bring up" flowers, to clap hands, to ponder riddles and nonsense, Rossetti's nursery rhymes develop a spellbound love of playful language and cultivate what might well turn out to be a lasting pleasure.[27]

FOUR

Ambitious Triangles

Rossetti and the Sonnet Tradition

THE BEST KNOWN of Christina Rossetti's sonnets among today's readers is arguably "In an Artist's Studio." Composed December 24, 1856, and unpublished in her lifetime, it first appears in *New Poems,* edited by William Michael Rossetti in 1896, with the note that ensures its fame. Inveterately biographical, William diverts attention from the poem's ekphrasis by identifying the "one face" mentioned in Christina's first line: "The reference is apparently to our brother's studio, and to his constantly-repeated heads of the lady whom he afterwards married, Miss Siddal." The poem next appears in print as the epigraph to H. C. Marillier's catalogue *Dante Gabriel Rossetti: An Illustrated Memorial of His Art and Life,* which ties it directly to the images of the woman whom Christina once described as "my beautiful sister in law" (*L,* 3:92):

> One face looks out from all his canvasses,
> > One selfsame figure sits or walks or leans;
> > We found her hidden just behind those screens,
> That mirror gave back all her loveliness.
> A queen in opal or in ruby dress,
> > A nameless girl in freshest summer greens,
> > A saint, an angel;—every canvass means
> The same one meaning, neither more nor less.   (*CP,* 3:264)

Though prompted by the romance between Gabriel and Elizabeth Siddal in 1856, the poem goes beyond this fact to entertain a serious worry about a time-honored aesthetic circumstance. Foregrounded in the extraordinary half-match of "canvasses" and "loveliness," the audible straining of the Petrarchan rhyme scheme prepares the reader for the disclosure of something amiss in the relation of men's art to women's beauty. A "figure" relentlessly refigured as queen, girl, saint, and angel, "one selfsame" woman becomes a "nameless" icon, a lovely nonself identified with another's talent. With the turn at the ninth line, Rossetti goes to the heart of this confusion and fixes on the voracious obsessiveness that obscures even as it celebrates the beloved model:

> He feeds upon her face by day and night,
>   And she with true kind eyes looks back on him
> Fair as the moon and joyful as the light:
>   Not wan with waiting, not with sorrow dim;
> Not as she is, but was when hope shone bright;
>   Not as she is, but as she fills his dream.   (*CP*, 3:264)

The predatoriness of the verb "feeds" has attracted remark, with the liveliest commentaries drawing on Gabriel's later chloral dependency to say that Siddal's beauty "feeds the artist's ravaging addiction," or on the infamous exhumation at Highgate Cemetery to imply Christina's objection to the ghoulishness of Siddal's "deanimation into an image" for the sake of Gabriel Rossetti's "reanimation" as an artist. Readers differ on whether biographically prescient readings do not themselves do some small violence to Elizabeth Siddal and perhaps to Christina Rossetti. Certainly Rossetti's poem loses some of its subtlety if read with too emphatic a sense of indignation regarding subsequent events; Gabriel Rossetti's confessedly belated marriage to Siddal in 1860, the tragic stillbirth of their daughter in 1861, Siddal's fatal laudanum overdose in February 1862, and the reopening of her grave in 1869 were yet to come. Readings more attentive to the poem's form and, again, to its sound tend to discover the larger topic that is its primary concern. Sharon Smulders, for example, notes that in choosing to end her poem with another off-rhyme, Rossetti emphasizes "the discord between the artist's luminous 'dream' and the woman's 'dim' reality." Alison Chapman stresses Rossetti's acute understanding that "although the model exceeds the attempt to equate her with her representation and to suppress her subjectivity, she can nevertheless only be 'seen' relative to the artist"; the "dilemma" her poem confronts is "that the model is presented to us," whether in painting or poem, "as already a linguistic construct." We might add as well that the genre Rossetti herself chooses for pondering these matters originates in the sighs that once "fed" a fourteenth-century lover's "heart." Written in the manifestly relevant form of a Petrarchan sonnet, "In an Artist's Studio" signals Rossetti's fascination with the tradition that presents many a "nameless girl" as the object of her poet-lover's rapture while keeping her "hidden" behind the screen of his words. Whatever this poem of 1856 may anticipate of the unhappy events in the Siddal-Rossetti marriage, it certainly looks ahead to its author's innovative sonnet sequences, *Monna Innominata* and *Later Life,* in *A Pageant and Other Poems* (1881). Indeed, "In an Artist's Studio" virtually predicts the later sequences' care *not* to lose the distinctiveness of selves, feelings, and moments amid an *intensity* she would have regarded not only as obscuring but as indecorous, even solipsistic. Rossetti's revision of sonnet style avoids amplifications that impose not only on the beloved but also on the reader, to whom she allows the same consideration and distance she allows herself.[1]

Rossetti's Case against Dante and Petrarch

Rossetti's interest in the sonnet is intense and lifelong. In 1849, in the remarkable interval between her grandfather's printing of the *Verses* of 1847 and the Pre-Raphaelite Brotherhood's undertaking of *The Germ,* Rossetti writes some of the finest poems of her career, and many of them are sonnets. After an apprenticeship that includes *bouts-rimés* contests and challenges, her sonnets suddenly learn a complexity that is enriched by wariness, muted irony, and perfected restraint; they achieve the style now admired for "its clear-eyedness about love and life and death . . . its wittiness, the sinewy grip on its formal means, and its spry readerly entrapments." "After Death," "Rest," and "Remember," first appearing in *Goblin Market,* quickly become conspicuous in Rossetti's legacy. In 1875 Edmund Gosse mentions "After Death" among the favorites he dubs the "objective sonnets," Samuel Waddington reprints "Rest" with a half dozen others in his *English Sonnets by Living Writers* (1881), and their reputation endures. "Remember," noted earlier for its gentle interweaving of the dying speaker's resentment and desire, has entered the canon as a yearning love poem, but also as a meditative self-elegy, and even—in a sophisticated anthology for children—as the farewell of a child or possibly a parent who has listened fondly to the other's plans for a now-impossible "future":

> Remember me when I am gone away,
>   Gone far away into the silent land;

> When you can no more hold me by the hand,
> Nor I half turn to go yet turning stay.
> Remember me when no more day by day
>   You tell me of our future that you planned:
>   Only remember me. . . .   (*CP,* 1:37)

We might observe that the speaker's self-divided wish to go-yet-stay and the line's carefully arrested momentum—the slow stressing and repetition of "hálf túrn . . . yét túrning"—are prototypical of both the emotions and the movement of Rossetti's later sonnets. *Monna Innominata* and *Later Life* forgo and even mistrust fulsome single-mindedness; instead, a patiently responsive rhythm attends to the hesitations and half-turns of feeling.[2]

Christina is not the only Rossetti, of course, for whom the sonnet is of paramount importance. As early as 1848, Gabriel is writing the poems that eventually become *The House of Life,* expanding it over the years from the 16 pieces that appear in the *Fortnightly Review* to the 50 in *Poems* and the full complement of 102 sonnets in *Ballads and Sonnets.* And Gabriel shares Christina's interest in the history of the genre; at the time *The Germ* is coming into being, he is deeply involved in translating the love poetry of the twelfth through fourteenth centuries along with Dante's *Vita nuova,* eagerly sending Tennyson a copy of this last, and eventually bringing out *The Early Italian Poets* in 1861. The two appear, at first glance, to have apportioned their precursors' works chronologically so that while he attends to the early poets and the youthful Beatrician Dante, she draws epigraphs for *Monna Innominata* from the later *La divina commedia* and the still later *Canzoniere* of Petrarch. The division—as we shall see—is more than a matter of sibling courtesy.[3]

To begin with, Christina does not share her brother's admiration for Dante's Beatrice, at least not as he expresses it in the introductory remarks to "Dante and His Circle." There he celebrates the ardor of the *Vita nuova,* describing it as "a book which only youth could have produced" and for this reason "sacred to the young"; he adds, making an effortless transfer of his own identification with Dante onto others, that for each (male) reader, "the figure of Beatrice, less lifelike than lovelike, will seem the friend of his own heart." In cherishing this "figure" of Dante's imagination, an image whose vagueness offers no resistance to a nineteenth-century admirer's appropriating "heart," Gabriel shows little regard for what might be surmised of the actual Beatrice of Florence, the woman historically known to Dante. It is precisely Gabriel's admiration of the "lovelike" at the happy expense of the "lifelike" that is the point of difference with his sister.[4]

Many years later, Christina gives her own account of Beatrice in an essay for *The Century Magazine* entitled "Dante: The Poet Illustrated Out of the Poem" (1884).[5] Initially, her emphasis is on Dante's public life as "the leader or the victim of his fellow-countrymen," but then she turns to Beatrice, the "one beloved object," and her representation (and misrepresentation) in the *Vita nuova*. Despite that text's "elaborate continuous exposition" of Dante's love (*P*, 189), Rossetti insists that Beatrice lived her life unaware of her admirer: "not a hint remains that Beatrice even guessed" Dante's love of her. To support this view, Rossetti mentions Beatrice's marriage: "And we may well hope that" Dante's love "was neither returned nor so much as surmised by its object; for, at the age of twenty, Beatrice Portinari became the wife of Simon de' Bardi." Moreover, except for one shadowy allusion, Dante does not mention this marriage, though there is "ample record" of "his bitter grief" at her death.[6]

Moving on to the topic of Dante's own marriage to Gemma Donati and mistakenly thinking it to have been "contracted about a year after the death of Beatrice," Rossetti becomes remarkably contentious. Taking issue with the tradition stemming from Boccaccio that the wife was to blame for the "more or less unhappy" condition of this partnership, Rossetti defends Gemma Donati as the mother of Dante's children and the spouse who, though she never rejoined him in his exile, performed the extraordinary service of protecting his manuscripts. Such evidence suggests "affection on her side." Then, in a startling moment of unguarded biographical speculation, Rossetti all but accuses Dante, the Beatrician lover, of coldness toward his wife: "Perhaps no living woman of mere flesh and blood could have sufficed to supersede that Beatrice whom Dante terms 'this youngest angel' long before her death had (as we trust) exalted her to the society of all her blessed fellows, whether elect angels or beatified spirits." And with sudden vehemence, Rossetti adds, "If so, Gemma is truly to be pitied in her comparatively thankless and loveless lot." The woman Gabriel describes as the "lovelike" Beatrice is cast by Christina as the other woman responsible for the "loveless lot" of the "accepted wife."[7]

Even when she takes up the question of Dante's artistry, owning that it excites "wonder, sympathy, awe, admiration" and that "the Divina

Commedia" provides "a discourse of the most elevated Christian faith," Rossetti's summary of the narrative suggests certain reservations about the figure of Beatrice represented there (*P,* 175). To be sure, she guides her lover to an "unutterable revelation" (*P,* 189), but since "on his own showing" in the poem Dante "lapsed from pure, unbroken faith to his first love," Beatrice meets him "with veiled countenance and stinging words." If the reproving Beatrice of Dante's text is not particularly appealing, neither is the figure that emerges in the interpretive tradition surrounding her. With a glance at her father Gabriele's arcane theorizing, the belief that Beatrice represents (in his words) "the qualities of true Pope and true Emperor," Rossetti pointedly objects to the way "some students speak of hidden lore underlying our poet's writing: in Beatrice they think to discern an impersonation rather than a woman" (*P,* 187). No matter how Rossetti approaches Beatrice, whether as the historical rival to Dante's wife or as the chilly admonisher of Dante the pilgrim or the figment of scholarly extrapolations, the woman she once refers to as "the surnameless Beatrice of Dante's immortalization" seems to her more problematic than inspiring (*CGRFL,* 188).[8]

Within a few years of Gabriel's initial work on his *Vita nuova* translation, and soon after her own "In an Artist's Studio," Christina has occasion to write a brief essay on the life of Petrarch for the *Imperial Dictionary of Universal Biography.* She begins in scholarly fashion by stressing the uncertainties that suffuse the biography and the paucity of what is known about "the turning-point of Petrarca's life, the seeing of Laura which inspired so much of his Italian *Canzoniere,* and of which the traces are discernible more or less openly in his correspondence and in other of his compositions, yet which is shrouded with a veil of mystery, and of which the accounts irreconcilably differ" (*P,* 163). She then summarizes the facts as they appear in "one of the most popular narratives":

> On Good Friday, 6th April, in the church of St. Clara, in Avignon, Petrarca first beheld that incomparable golden-haired Laura, who for precisely twenty-one years swayed, living, the current of his life; whose eyes and voice, habitual reserve and exceptional piety, inspired poem after poem; and from whose thrall not even the lady's death availed to release him. Her bare hand and dainty glove, her sweet speech and sweet laugh, her tears, her paleness, her salutation, are noted with untiring minuteness; he

records how he watched with rapture a young girl washing the veil of Laura; and on another occasion how he beheld a group of ladies with Laura in the midst, like the sun girt by twelve stars. To read these elegant Tuscan strains, one might imagine that this veritable slave of love had few cares or interests or occupations, but what sprang from the master passion. (*P,* 164)

Rossetti's tone here, as it alternately records the exaggeration ("incomparable") and exactitude ("precisely") of the traditional version of Petrarch's love, is sufficiently ambiguous to suggest either that she enjoys the self-mockery she has detected within the Petrarchan love story or, possibly, that she feels a slight disdain for the emotional distortions and resultant follies (a ludicrously displaced "rapture" at the scene of a veil's laundering) that are the signs of enslavement by "the master passion." It is the failure of the "lifelike" in the Petrarchan lyrics that triggers her double response. And when describing the solemn coincidences in Petrarch's narrative, the symmetry between the inception of his love for Laura and her death "precisely to the month, day, and hour" twenty-one years later, Rossetti cannot resist what at this juncture is a slightly irreverent (and hardly necessary) insistence on the inevitable waning of a real woman's beauty: "In 1348 a fearful pestilence ravaged Europe, and amongst its victims was Laura—to other eyes less beautiful than when, twenty-one years before, precisely to the month, day, and hour, she had captivated the heart of her Tuscan lover; but ever regarded by him as invested with the pristine charm" (*P,* 165–66). This passage seems, on the surface, to admire the constancy of Petrarch's loving belief in Laura's continuing beauty, and yet the reminder that over the course of twenty-one years even a Laura loses her looks invokes a realistic norm that is manifestly counter-Petrarchan. Rossetti might have been better pleased if the Tuscan lyrics had exalted the ability to love a woman in the way her own sonnet suggests, to love her "as she is," and bequeathed to poetry the image of a woman who—in a modification of Gabriel's phrase—is both lifelike *and* lovelike. Instead, the example set by the *Canzoniere* commits the future "slave of love" to the worship of an unchanging beauty found only in the "incomparable" woman who "fills his dream."

Eventually Rossetti addresses her doubts about the traditional idealization of women, i.e., the erotic convention of the male's enduring but blind devotion and his portrayal of an improbable beloved who never ages or sickens though she surely dies—and returns "in morte" uttering words of counsel. With a sonnet sequence of her own, Rossetti creates a plausible woman, makes her the speaker, and tells a tale of mutual love that ends in painful, authentically Dantean-Petrarchan separation. When she publishes *Monna Innominata* in 1881, her Italian title says plainly what she is up to; this is the lady's *own* sequence, "monna" being a form of "madonna," though in lyric fashion she remains nameless, "innominata." The phrasing of the attached subtitle, "A Sonnet of Sonnets" gives fair warning, as John Hollander notes, that something formally or generically ambitious is being presented. Formed by analogy with "king of kings" and "song of songs," the prepositional construction implies not only that there are fourteen sonnets but also that the poem is somehow quintes-sential, or if such a boast seems too grand for the self-effacing Christina Rossetti, it announces at the very least that her sonnet's worth of sonnets tells "of" or "about" the possibilities of the love-sonnet genre per se. Rossetti elucidates her aims in a preface (the only one she ever writes) that manages in a few highly compressed paragraphs to distinguish her se-quence from those celebrating Beatrice, Laura, and the "unnamed ladies" of Provençal poetry as well as from Elizabeth Barrett Browning's lovingly triumphal *Sonnets from the Portuguese*. Here is the preface in its entirety:

> Beatrice, immortalized by "altissimo poeta . . . cotanto amante"; Laura, celebrated by a great tho' an inferior bard,—have alike paid the exceptional penalty of exceptional honour, and have come down to us resplendent with charms, but (at least, to my ap-prehension) scant of attractiveness.

> These heroines of worldwide fame were preceded by a bevy of unnamed ladies "donne innominate" sung by a school of less con-spicuous poets; and in that land and that period which gave si-multaneous birth to Catholics, to Albigenses, and to Troubadours, one can imagine many a lady as sharing her lover's poetic aptitude, while the barrier between them might be one held sacred by both, yet not such as to render mutual love incompatible with mutual honour.

> Had such a lady spoken for herself, the portrait left us might have appeared more tender, if less dignified, than any drawn even by a

devoted friend. Or had the Great Poetess of our own day and na-
tion only been unhappy instead of happy, her circumstances would
have invited her to bequeath to us, in lieu of the "Portuguese Sonnets," an inimitable "donna innominata" drawn not from fancy
but from feeling, and worthy to occupy a niche beside Beatrice
and Laura. (*CP*, 2:86)

The language could hardly be clearer: to be "drawn by a devoted friend"
is to pay an "exceptional penalty"; it is to be brilliantly misrepresented.
Rossetti's strong surmise is that if Laura or Beatrice or any of the unnamed
Provençal ladies had spoken for herself, the impression she left would
have been "more tender, if less dignified" than tradition provides. And
we may take this as a preview of Rossetti's own speaker: drawn "from
feeling" instead of "fancy," she lovingly and responsively shares her words
and songs until forced to relinquish her beloved. Rossetti's sonnet sequence, in other words, will address and repair the aesthetic legacy of Petrarchism. This effort to revise the tradition from within is, according to
one school of thought, necessarily self-defeating. In the modern contro-
versy over the love-sonnet tradition, some take the position that the genre
is the literary sign of the patriarchy's hegemony and object strenuously to
the "image — or mirage — of the omnipotent male poet." Some few, in
rejecting this oppressive male figure, would have women authors abandon the sonnet genre altogether. In her widely known essay, "When We
Dead Awaken: Writing as Re-vision," Adrienne Rich confesses her disappointment with the "older women poets" and names Rossetti among
them: "I wanted women poets to be the equals of men, and to be equal
was still confused with sounding the same." Emboldened by Rich's understanding of the "politics of form," it might be possible to wish that
Rossetti had had available an altogether new kind of poetry or that she
had somehow managed to write a century ahead of her time. But that
would be to misunderstand the genuine ambition of Rossetti's project.[9]

When Rossetti imagines a poet who shares "her lover's poetic aptitude"
and locates the lover in "that land and that period" which produces the
troubadours, the reference is to the Provençal writers who inspire
not only early Italian poetry (much of it translated by Gabriel Rossetti)
but the *Vita nuova* and the *Canzoniere*. Though Rossetti does not say so,
she certainly knows that the greatest of the troubadours, Arnaut Daniel,
is so highly esteemed by Dante and Petrarch that both pay him the

extraordinary tribute of direct quotation, in the Provençal tongue, within their own poems. To preface a poem by crediting one's speaker with the "poetic aptitude" of such a troubadour is to announce a not altogether trifling aspiration. Then, with the mention of the "Portuguese Sonnets," the ambition is further clarified. Elizabeth Barrett Browning has already transformed the sonnet tradition by creating an ardent woman who does speak "for herself" and who explicitly asks not to be mistaken for the traditionally unresponsive or "cold" beloved lady:

> am I cold,
> Ungrateful, that for these most manifold
> High gifts, I render nothing back at all?
> Not so; not cold.   (*SP* 8)

Rossetti's admiration of Barrett Browning is adamant, though her overly compacted sentence is occasionally misunderstood. Using a contrary-to-fact logic, Rossetti asserts her conviction that had Barrett Browning undertaken to write as she herself does, i.e., in the person of the woman who must renounce love, then the Lady of those hypothetical sonnets would have been an achievement to rival the portrayals of Beatrice and Laura. Or, as Rossetti puts it in a letter, "a 'Donna innominata'" by Elizabeth Barrett Browning "might well have been unsurpassable" (*L,* 2:299).[10]

Embedded in her description of Barrett Browning as the "Great Poetess" is an awareness on Rossetti's part of the "less conspicuous" women sonneteers who contribute to the English Petrarchan line. The Jacobean Lady Mary Wroth she could not have known, modern scholars having only recently recovered her work, but Mary Robinson's example was near at hand. Robinson is best known today for her 1796 sonnet sequence *Sappho and Phaon* and for the polemics of her subtitle, *In a Series of Legitimate Sonnets:* she regards the Sapphic fragments as "the genuine effusions of a supremely enlightened soul" but feels, nonetheless, that a modern rendering should shape them into complete poems. In the words of Margaret Reynolds, "Robinson tidies up her Sappho and makes her story in 'legitimate' or Petrarchan sonnets which confer poetic stature and artistic control." In another attempt at signaling such "stature," Robinson also publishes a sonnet entitled "Laura to Petrarch," in which Laura offers "friendship" as a cure to Petrarch's "sick passion":

> O solitary wand'rer! whither stray
>   From the smooth path the dimpled pleasures love,

> From flow'ry meadow, and embow'ring grove,
> Where hope and fancy smiling, lead the way!
> To thee, I ween, full tedious seems the day;
>   While lorn and slow the devious path you rove,
>   Sighing soft sorrows on the garland wove
> By young desire, of blossoms sweetly gay!
>   Oh! blossoms! frail and fading! like the morn
> Of love's first rapture! beauteous all, and pure,
>   Deep hid beneath your charms lies mis'ry's thorn,
> To bid the feeling breast a pang endure!
>   Then check thy wand'rings, wary and forlorn,
> And find in friendship's balm sick passion's cure.

Although Robinson claims to dislike "the artificial decorations of a feigned passion," her sonnet is hardly free of artifice and is more invested in the sentimental admiration of "passion" than the Laura she imagines would have been (after all, Laura is trying to persuade Petrarch out of it). The bevy of abstractions ("pleasures," "hope," "fancy," "sorrows," "desire," "rapture," "mis'ry," "friendship") and the apostrophe to "blossoms" are the feigning devices of late Romantic sensibility.[11]

Had Robinson's example not prompted Rossetti to realize that she could do better, there was the still nearer, though utterly different, example provided by Felicia Hemans. Throughout the 1820s and 1830s Hemans was drawn to Petrarch's poetry, but as one of her prefaces explains, only the patriotic material interests her: his allusions to the glory of Italy awaken the "feelings" and make it "easy to sympathize with the emotions of a modern Roman . . . or a Florentine" oppressed by Austria's imperial protection (*Hemans,* 171–72). His celebration of Laura, meanwhile, is completely unconvincing: "the everlasting 'laurel' which inspires the enamoured Petrarch with so ingenious a variety of *concetti* . . . might reasonably cause it to be doubted whether the beautiful Laura, of the emblematic Tree, were the real object of the bard's affection" (*Hemans,* 171). Hemans's arch skepticism is not Rossetti's. Despite her own reservations about the representation of Laura and Beatrice, Rossetti is deeply attracted to the love-sonnet tradition, to Barrett Browning's crucial introduction of the woman-poet speaker, and above all to the important element the Great Poetess rejects, viz., the irremovable obstruction to love. Rossetti's sonnets tell of a shared but still impossible love, a mutual affection that is of no avail. In this, she reveals a commitment to the paradox at the core of Petrarchism, the all-important fact, as Heather Dubrow has recently reminded us, that its success is "built on a bedrock of writing about failure." By the ninth sonnet of *Monna Innominata,* the lovers' relationship is plainly over and the speaker becomes movingly elegiac about "all / That might have been and now can never be." The male beloved's "honoured excellence" is affirmed (*MI* 9), the speaker willingly entrusts him to "any one" who "can take [her] place / And make [him] happy" (*MI* 12), and the sequence ends with a renunciation of love songs, but not a repudiation of love itself. The grief of this love is kept always in the foreground, literally at the beginning of each of her fourteen sonnets, by the carefully paired epigraphs from Dante and Petrarch that corroborate the story of the lovers' separation.[12]

As the *Monna Innominata* preface sets about defining the triangle of Rossetti's ambition, a triangle made up of the magisterial fourteenth-century authors, the "Great" nineteenth-century poetess, and Rossetti herself, the figure who is visibly absent is Dante's modern namesake, Dante Gabriel Rossetti. The translator of the *Vita nuova* has no obvious place in the preface or even the *Monna Innominata* epigraphs, since Christina gleans her Dante verses from the *Commedia.* And yet, Gabriel is present; when Christina distinguishes her speaker from others' resplendently silent ladies, the reference necessarily includes the beloved of Gabriel's *House of Life,* the Lady whose "lambent" beauty outshines the moon (*HL* 20), whose lips "play" with his (*HL* 6), and whose surrender makes "proud Love" weep (*HL* 7) while passion engulfs her in a self-obliterating mystery:

> Lady, I fain would tell how evermore
> Thy soul I know not from thy body, nor
> Thee from myself, neither our love from God.   (*HL* 5)

Christina Rossetti is unwilling to move a poem in this obliquely apostrophic way (such lines can hardly be imagined as spoken conversation) and both unable and unwilling to be so extravagantly sensuous about love's high obscurities. Moreover, as she distinguishes her warmly responsive lady from Barrett Browning's and from Gabriel's, she forms a triangle of nineteenth-century poets within the larger triangle, and enlists them as partners in a virtual symposium on poetic style. In this regard, she hardly needs to be explicit about Gabriel's contribution to the sonnet genre, for to nineteenth-century readers the affinity between *The House of Life* and *Sonnets from the Portuguese* is unmistakably apparent. As Joan Rees points out, even Robert Buchanan, "with his usual capacity for seeing a half-truth about Rossetti," suggests that his sonnets have been "'largely moulded and inspired by Mrs Browning' and invites the reader to compare the two sequences." And when so fine a critic as Dorothy Mermin does align them (intending none of Buchanan's disparagement), she finds similarities in the two poets' "marmoreal cadences, personifications, archaisms, and heated slow simplicities."[13]

Implicit in the preface to *Monna Innominata* and evident everywhere in the poems is Rossetti's desire to write a sequence unlike any other and to combine speaker, situation, and style in ways that are consistent with her own best tendencies as a writer. She is moved by a version of the impulse that Dubrow, thinking of Renaissance authors, describes as the sonneteer's "diacritical desire," including in this phrase the hope of distinguishing not only one's beloved from "counterparts in conventional Petrarchism" but "one's own poem" from others' as well. This cogent formulation provides an approach to Rossetti's choice of epigraphs as well, enabling us to see that she is fully aware of what might be called the virtuosity topos, the strategy of honoring the beloved by extravagantly "manifesting and celebrating" one's own mastery as a poet. One passage, for example, comes from poem 72 of the *Canzoniere*. This long and highly elaborate canzone declares love's inexpressibility: never will "human tongue"—"né giamai lingua umana"—be able to tell what Laura's admirer feels (*C* 72; 10). Despite the disclaimer, the next lines offer indulgent praise of Laura's eyes. In a later poem, the lover acknowledges possible objections to the aesthetic choices he makes in lauding his beloved: "Someone perhaps may think, in praise of her / whom I adore on earth, my style is wrong"—"Parrà forse ad alcun che 'n lodar quella / ch' i' adoro in terra, errante sia 'l mio stile" (*C* 247). Thus the master invites Petrarchans and counter-Petrarchans ever after, including the Victorian Barrett Browning and the Rossettis, to indulge whatever ambivalence they feel toward their great predecessor. Though Rossetti does not ever discuss the formal practice of any poet or identify herself as the hypothetical "someone" who shrinks from reproducing the ornate syntax that propels Petrarchan fulsomeness, it is nonetheless her project in *Monna Innominata* to transform the love-sonnet genre by recasting it in her own luminously reticent style.[14]

It is a well-known truth that artistic stimulation has preeminently to do with artistic form, and yet the temptation presented to readers of Rossetti's preface is to mistake her dismay with beloved ladies, both traditional and contemporary, for the whole story of her response to the poetic triangles suggested there. Rossetti's preface spells out, to be sure, some of the "abstractable" ideas expressed in these poems, but her strongest response—one she cannot state except by writing her own sonnets—concerns the "inherent practice" of love poetry. Style is, in the broadest sense, the issue. And because style is behavior—what a poem *does*—the surest articulation of Rossetti's "diacritical differences" occurs in the lines of her poems. They alone fully reveal how it is that she departs from Dante, Petrarch, Barrett Browning, and Gabriel in the representation of love, or in what McGann elegantly calls "the artistic process of thinking" about love. A preface in prose cannot get to the heart of one poet's response to another, nor could a technical manifesto about style, even had Christina Rossetti chosen to write one and however eagerly critics might have received it. Here it might be useful to recall another Victorian poet's words about admired authors. In a letter to a friend, the twenty-year-old Gerard Manley Hopkins complains that Tennyson's language is too Tennysonian and that Wordsworth's idiom is "a higher sort of Parnassian." Citing the latter's "Composed near Calais," Hopkins freely admits that "beautiful poems may be written wholly" in this mode. Still, this is not a kind of beauty he would ever attempt; for, as he explains, such a style is "too essentially" its author's own: "Its peculiarity is that though you can hardly conceive yourself having written in it, if in the poet's place, yet it is too characteristic of the poet, too so-and-so-all-over-ish, to be quite inspiration." Underneath Hopkins's critical interest in Wordsworth's self-imitating style is a more basic recoil from Wordsworth's poetic "personality." This dual response, however fleeting or subliminal, contributes to the way in which the reader-poet's own poems come to be written. For both Hopkins and Christina Rossetti, resistance to a precursor is stronger than attraction, but the two responses "coexist in a sort of pleasurable agitation." This last element, the exhilarated aspect of the poet's ambivalence, is important too. Rossetti most certainly has reservations about the style of her sonneteering compatriots, especially the "too so-and-so-all-over-ish" quality of the *Sonnets from the Portuguese*. Her mixed response extends to, if it does not actually originate in, her attitude toward the style of Gabriel's *House of Life* and

compels the enormously exciting project of establishing her difference—
an excitement that is compounded by her deep familiarity with the
founders of the tradition. The pages that follow will focus on the artistic process of imagining love, specifically on how the fourteenth- and
nineteenth-century poets in Rossetti's chosen triangle imagine love's inception, its measure, and its distortion of time, in order to show how
thoroughly she engages with their poetic styles.[15]

Memory and Amnesia in *Monna Innominata*

When Dante characterizes the *Vita nuova* as "the book of my memory"
(Gabriel's translation), he identifies what becomes the central trope for
Petrarch and poets ever after who invent, embellish, and cherish a remembered first glimpse of the beloved. In *Canzoniere* 85, for example,
the lover boasts of being indebted to the day and hour—"il tempo et
l'ora"—that brought him the sight of his beloved. Seizing on the acoustic
inevitability of the "Laura"/"l'ora" chime, Petrarch elsewhere recalls the
dates and symmetries of love's history with a specificity that is arresting,
the clustered intrusiveness of the details an endorsement of love's power
to disrupt time and the lover's autonomy:

> In thirteen twenty-seven, and precisely
> at the first hour of the sixth of April
> I entered the labyrinth, and I see no way out.

> Mille trecento ventisette, a punto
> su l'ora prima, il dì sesto d'aprile,
> nel laberinto intrai, né veggio ond' esca.   (*C* 211)

The anniversary of this situated first episode is a recurrent source of glad
gratefulness:

> I bless the place, the time and hour of the day
> that my eyes aimed their sights at such a height
> and say: "My soul, you must be very grateful
> that you were found worthy of such great honor."

> I' benedico il loco e 'l tempo et l'ora
> che sì alto miraron gli occhi mei,
> et dico: "Anima, assai ringraziar dei
> che fosti a tanto onor degnata allora."   (*C* 13)

So frequent are the benedictions of the blessed hour that Musa, in his magisterial commentary, regards "this moment held in the memory" as "the touchstone of the *Canzoniere*" (*C* 530). Rossetti has a somewhat skeptical attitude toward such temporal fixing; and without quite calling it a fictional device, she dryly remarks the inaccuracy of the details. Though Laura's death is said to have occurred on Good Friday, which purportedly fell on the twenty-first anniversary "precisely to the month, day, and hour" of Petrarch's first sight of her, scholars, she notes, detect a flaw "in Petrarca's own record" (*P,* 165). A bit of Rossettian research shows that April 6, 1327, coincided with Monday in Holy Week "but certainly not Good Friday, in spite of Petrarca's distinct statement that so it was" (*P,* 167–68).[16]

Calendric discrepancies notwithstanding, the impulse to celebrate and textually multiply the remembrance of love's beginning is, as Rossetti well knows, a compelling feature of the Petrarchan legacy. In the *Sonnets from the Portuguese,* Barrett Browning records many firsts; there is the admirer's initial letter suggesting they meet:

> This said, . . he wished to have me in his sight
> Once, as a friend: this fixed a day in spring
> To come and touch my hand . . . a simple thing,
> Yet I wept for it!   (*SP* 28)

There are the suitor's enumerated kisses: the first on her fingertips, the second on her forehead, the passionate third pressed on the lips in ecstatically "perfect, purple state" (*SP* 38). Most vivid of all is Barrett Browning's allegorized representation of her speaker's discovery that she loves. The awakening so often depicted as the opening of a battle or a first assault becomes in this instance a hair-pulling attack by "a mystic shape":

> Straightway I was 'ware,
> So weeping, how a mystic Shape did move
> Behind me, and drew me backward by the hair;
> And a voice said in mastery, while I strove, . .
> "Guess now who holds thee?"—"Death," I said. But, there,
> The silver answer rang . . "Not Death, but Love."   (*SP* 1)

Love's first touch is felt as a suddenly domineering, redemptive yank. Tricia Lootens is surely correct in emphasizing the intimacy of Love's gesture and the "strangeness, heaviness, and eccentric richness" of the

entire sonnet sequence as the speaker is transformed from a "patient ascetic" into love's own "prophetess." In *The House of Life,* Dante Gabriel
Rossetti writes, famously—or, as Buchanan thought, infamously—of
love's wedded fulfillment and the couple's blissful "Nuptial Sleep":

> At length their long kiss severed, with sweet smart:
>   And as the last slow sudden drops are shed
>   From sparkling eaves when all the storm has fled,
> So singly flagged the pulses of each heart.
> Their bosoms sundered, with the opening start
>   Of married flowers to either side outspread
>   From the knit stem; yet still their mouths, burnt red,
> Fawned on each other where they lay apart.   (*HL* 6a)

Extravagantly counter-Petrarchan in its emphasis on "consummated, not
frustrated, desire," Rossetti's nuptial eroticism is the natural sequel to
Barrett Browning's scenes of courtship. The style, which his own introductory sonnet describes as aspiring to "arduous fulness," is every bit as
rich as hers. Critics speak of "the pressure" or "closeness" of Rossetti's
manner; and Richardson, in tracing such impressions to their formal
source, shows that "the intensity" of "prolongation" in "Nuptial Sleep"
is an effect of the heavily stressed rhythm ("At length their lóng kíss
sévered, with swéet smárt," "And as the lást slów súdden drops are shed"),
the "indulgent voweling," and a syntax that seems "to be dictated moment by moment, each phrase surging out of the last rather than drawn
forward by a visible goal." In *Monna Innominata,* Christina Rossetti finds
a completely different way, conceptually and formally, to imagine the important firsts in her lover's tale.[17]

   Instead of providing a passage about the fabled first sight of the beloved,
Rossetti arranges for a sort of amnesia to afflict her speaker and creates
from the absence of memory a new experience of erotic yearning. Her
speaker longs to recall the forgotten glance that must have preceded the
forgotten first touch:

> "Era già l'ora che volge il desio."—Dante.
> "Ricorro al tempo ch'io vi vidi prima."—Petrarca.
>
> I wish I could remember, that first day,
> First hour, first moment of your meeting me,
>   If bright or dim the season, it might be

Summer or Winter for aught I can say;
So unrecorded did it slip away,
    So blind was I to see and to foresee,
    So dull to mark the budding of my tree
That would not blossom yet for many a May.
If only I could recollect it, such
    A day of days! I let it come and go
    As traceless as a thaw of bygone snow;
It seemed to mean so little, meant so much;
If only now I could recall that touch,
    First touch of hand in hand—Did one but know!   (*MI* 2)

The epigraphs show that Rossetti's sequence is conceived of as a book of memory manqué. The first establishes the unsettled mood—"It was already the hour which turns back the desire" (*Purg.* 8.3)—and delicately anticipates the pleasure memory customarily brings. The second indicates the substance of the desired remembrance: "I recur to the time when I first saw thee." In *Canzoniere* 20, this line accompanies the lover's lament at failing to praise his lady's beauty; and Rossetti, in having her speaker unable to produce a memory, adopts the Petrarchan lover's sense of inadequacy while displacing it onto a new, counter-Petrarchan symptom. In building her sequence around a lapse of memory, Rossetti quietly avoids the Dantean-Petrarchan illusion that love's inception occurs in a flash of revelatory self-awareness. That the speaker laments this amnesia should not prevent us from seeing how drastically it revises the tradition's most stable myth. *Monna Innominata* acknowledges a time when the beloved is known but not yet recognized *as* the beloved and finds that love's ineluctability is not a consequence of any suddenness but of the growing irreversibility of the transformation it accomplishes. It may be, too, that this forgetting is an honest refusal to invent what passed "unrecorded" or to provide what Gabriel calls a "moment's monument" (*HL,* introductory sonnet). Maybe it is an honesty about how much love leaves *un*changed—which other love poets strain not to believe. As Rossetti's loving speaker proves unable to summon up the first meeting with her friend, her impatience at this defect of memory trails off into subdued puzzlement: "If only now I could recall that touch, / First touch of hand in hand—Did one but know!" Aware of unawareness, Rossetti allows her speaker to wish that at the fortunate moment she had not been, in Hardy's words, "looking away." [18]

Without recourse to the heaviness or closeness of her contemporaries' styles, Rossetti devises a way to recover the remarkableness of the lovers' literally unremarked meeting. She does not need or try to reproduce love's intensity or assume that a feeling is to be judged by the standard of Barrett Browning's "perfect purple" ecstasy. She rejects the "arduous fulness" of Gabriel's manner along with his assumption that the arduousness, the work, of the poem is to bring the reader into the lover's labyrinth of feeling. Using the saddest of opening phrases, "If only," she locates her lover's crisis—gently but definitively—at the word "such": "If only I could recollect it, such / A day of days!" Isolated by the latest-possible caesura, "such" pushes into a steep enjambment that converts the connective (*such as* other lovers do) into an intensifier (*such a* crucial day). The resonant phrasing echoes the subtitle, "A Sonnet of Sonnets," and this time the "singular noun" linked "with its own plural" unquestionably "indicates a superlative: X of X's = Best of all X's." After the exclamation point, with momentum spent, the tone shifts slightly into mild self-reproach: "I let it come and go / As traceless as a thaw of bygone snow." Fainter than the elegist's "snows of yester-year," the unrecorded memory is lamented as an unseeable losing of what is already lost. The care needed to articulate the accumulating *z* and *s* sounds and the frictionless softness of "thaw" give this line something of the slow quietness of the snow fade it describes. Buried in the notion of "thaw" is the sense, too, of that other process unnoticed at the time, the warming of indifference into desire. Love's inception in Rossetti's sonnet sequence is hardly an event at all, but rather a "traceless" change invisible except for its aftereffects.[19]

The backward-yearning drift of the speaker's meditation in *Monna Innominata* 2, and the suggestion of perceptual deficiency on the lover's part, may owe something to Barrett Browning's sonnet 20, in which the avowed lover imagines her life immediately prior to meeting her beloved. Amazed to think that he was "in the world a year ago," she faults herself that she did not "ever cull / Some prescience" of him. But if there is a likeness in the two poets' dismay, their tones are utterly distinct. In celebrating her joy at the presence of the beloved in her life, Barrett Browning's speaker marvels at the lack of precourtship acquaintance and writes of a past that is energized, even as she recalls it, by present knowledge of the beloved's vigor. Specifically, she writes of the "time I sat alone" and

> . . . link by link,
> Went counting all my chains as if that so
> They never could fall off at any blow
> Struck by thy possible hand. . . .   (*SP* 20)

Rhythmically, the reported "blow" surges toward "struck" and imagines liberation with a forceful double dactyl ("blow / Strúck by thy póssible hand"). Images proliferate suggestively to hint that the beloved has been rescued from a condition as tormented as that of Andromeda or a virgin martyr dying in the snow. By way of conclusion, the amazed and grateful speaker invokes the beloved-as-divinity trope to decry her former unknowingness: "Atheists are as dull, / Who cannot guess God's presence out of sight." The exuberance of this boasting self-reproach, the boldness of identifying her unguessed lover with God, the cheerful stab at "dull" atheists—the erotic inflation of it all—may be what Rossetti has in mind when, in her preface, she praises Barrett Browning but demurs at her happiness.

There is an anomaly here to consider. The exaggeration of Barrett Browning's style is an indication that as a writer she maintains, in some crucial respect, a more private perspective than the reserved and evasive Rossetti. Barrett Browning allows no agent of decorum to hover nearby and interfere with the freedom of her Portuguese to speak as she pleases. When imagining how men see "the inner cost" of her love or how her beloved moves amid "social pageantries" admired by "a hundred" eyes, she is projecting spectators who are versions of herself and who not only sense her secret ardor but share her eagerness to love her beloved (*SP* 12 and 3). Hers is an extroverted privacy that remains uninvaded even by the outsiders she fantasizes. By comparison, Rossettian intimacy seems conducted in the presence of an unimpressible skeptic who prevents excesses of style or, in Hopkins's phrase, any display of "too so-and-so-ish" bravura. Rossetti's lover-persona never flaunts—even in her lyric inwardness—the importance of her love and soberly avoids the heroics of godlike men striking off chains. At the same time, this inhibiting pressure creates a resistant counterpressure such that the speaker's manifestly underarticulated style resonates with the excess of what goes unsaid. The difference in the poets' styles crystallizes in the diction of line 7, where, in writing of love's uncomprehended prehistory, Rossetti picks out Barrett Browning's reproachful term "dull" and re-sets it: "So blind was

I to see and to foresee, / So *dull* to mark the budding of my tree." As is
the case so often in her poems, Rossetti's focus is on a commonplace in-
advertency, not a failure of "prescience," and she avoids the aggrandiz-
ing comparison to atheists. With mild diction and extraordinarily deft
compression, she says only, "It seemed to mean so little, meant so much."
With a shift in the verb tense replacing who knows how much explanation of what cannot be explained, this inexplicit line achieves the sweet
force of Wordsworth's hushed exclamation "oh / The difference to me."
The understated style of *Monna Innominata* tells us, with a regret that is
all the lovelier for its patient candor, that love's arrival was not epiphanic,
that the precious moment lost in the fog of the commonplace was not,
after all, a moment, and that true love doesn't need (or need to invent)
such a valorizing episode. The scrupulous restraint and honesty of
Rossetti's style allows us to believe in the profundity of her speaker's love.
The wondering inflation of Barrett Browning's strives to prove the
strength of hers.

   This is not the place to review the tangled love story of *The House of
Life,* with all its ecstasy, grief, guilt, varieties of new love, torment, and
wan hope; but it is worth noting that when Gabriel Rossetti treats love's
inception, he outdoes his precursors, including Barrett Browning, by
imagining how a lover might actually "cull / Some prescience" of the
loved woman before ever knowing her. In "The Birth-Bond," the lovers'
first meeting is suffused with a sensation of déjà vu that is fancifully attributed to their souls' simultaneous origin:

> when first I saw you, seemed it, love,
>   That among souls allied to mine was yet
> One nearer kindred than life hinted of.
>   O born with me somewhere that men forget,
>   And though in years of sight and sound unmet,
> Known for my soul's birth-partner well enough!   (*HL* 15)

To love, in other words, is to retrieve an indefeasible "birth bond" from
the realm of amnesia and, in the same movement, to merge lover and
beloved. Though Gabriel Rossetti does not seem to notice, a reader of
Christina Rossetti's preface cannot help but see that the object of this
mystic appropriation pays an "exceptional penalty." Her lover's acknowledgment extends back into the period of her own self-unknowing and
claims alliance with her unformed identity. The male's joy, as Richardson

says, is "rife with solipsism," and like the dream that aestheticizes the "one face" in Christina's "In an Artist's Studio," it loses sight of the beloved "as she is."[20]

"Happy Equals": Love's New Measure

One consequence of a lover's all-absorbing passion is the luxury of self-abasement it affords. Throughout *The House of Life,* the speaker professes an excessive unworthiness and describes himself in "Equal Troth" as "lacking absolutely" the qualities a lover should possess (*HL* 32). Disclaimers of this sort not only establish the woman's graciousness but rely on her exalted status to solve the problem of love's assessment:

> Not by one measure mayst thou mete our love;
>   For how should I be loved as I love thee?—
>   I, graceless, joyless, lacking absolutely
> All gifts that with thy queenship best behove.   (*HL* 32)

By the sonnet's end, the lover insists on an inequality of which he is the benefactor:

> If not to sum but worth we look—
> Thy heart's transcendence, not my heart's excess—
> Then more a thousandfold thou lov'st than I.

The fervor of this claim builds audibly as the acoustic "sum" of his "heart's excess" expands into the fuller polysyllabics of her "heart's transcendence . . . a thousandfold." This gratitude at being loved with prodigious disproportion is an expression of the same confidence that attributes "all beauties" to her and elsewhere exults that "Beauty like hers is genius"(*HL* 18). The one claim on her behalf that is *not* made, the one traditionally precluded, concerns artistic gifts: there is nothing mutually aesthetic in the "measure" of love in *The House of Life.*

The standard is different in *Monna Innominata,* where from the outset Rossetti keeps her prefatory pledge and creates a speaker who shares "her lover's poetic aptitude." The first sonnet launches this theme by asking, "Ah me, but where are now the songs I sang / When life was sweet because you called them sweet?" and then offering, by way of reply, the loving "songs" that follow. Though the inflection of the question, with its echo of the *ubi sunt* motif, hints at sorrows and sadder songs to come, the very fact of aesthetic admiration ("you called them sweet") is important.

Poets' respect for one another is, as Rossetti well knows, a conventionally male topos. Dante and Virgil, for example, repeatedly encounter admiring fellow artists as they make their way through Purgatory. In canto
2, the musician Casella, who knew Dante in life, sings a line from one of
his friend's canzones; and Rossetti chooses this lovely verse to introduce
her own sonnet 12: "Amor, che ne la mente mi ragiona."—"Love, who
speaks within my mind." Similarly, the Latin poet Statius hails Virgil rap-
turously as he joins the pilgrims' ascent; his greeting, too, provides an
epigraph: "Or puoi la quantitate / Comprender de l'amor che a te mi
scalda."—"Now canst thou comprehend the quantity of the love which
glows in me towards thee" (*MI* 6). In borrowing these particular passages,
Rossetti has the twofold satisfaction of openly aligning her words with
Dante's while also, by taking them out of context, quietly contesting the
tradition that apportions praise by gender and hymns the splendor of inspiring women and talented men. In her sonnet sequence, the poets' love
is supported by their mutual regard *as artists*. For this reason song itself
becomes the source of metaphor when the speaker attempts to take the
measure of their love:

> I loved you first: but afterwards your love
>   Outsoaring mine, sang such a loftier song
> As drowned the friendly cooings of my dove.   (*MI* 4; 1–3)

This unblushing assertion, "I loved you first," reverses the situation in
Sonnets from the Portuguese, where, as the Brownings' personal history
seems to require, the male suitor is credited with setting "an example"
and the loving woman offers a mere follower's disclaimer: "And thus, I
cannot speak / Of love even, as a good thing of *my own*" (*SP* 12; emphasis added). Rossetti's poem pursues a different logic and strives to
avoid discrediting either of the lovers. Broaching the question of indebtedness, her speaker initially considers love in terms of duration, strength,
insightfulness:

> Which owes the other most? my love was long,
>   And yours one moment seemed to wax more strong;
> I loved and guessed at you, you construed me
> And loved me for what might or might not be.   (*MI* 4; 4–7)

She soon finds that comparisons don't serve, however, and with phrasing similar to Gabriel's "one measure," she rejects the whole business of

assayable worth: "Nay, weights and measures do us both a wrong" (*HL* 32; *MI* 4). Her sestet then transforms Barrett Browning's rhetorical disavowal of love "as a good thing of my own" into a wholesale rejection of the trope of ownership:

> For verily love knows not "mine" or "thine;"
>> With separate "I" and "thou" free love has done,
>>> For one is both and both are one in love:
>> Rich love knows nought of "thine that is not mine;"
>>> Both have the strength and both the length thereof,
>> Both of us, of the love which makes us one.   (*MI* 4; 9–14)

Rossetti's poet-lovers are "happy equals in the flowering land / Of love"—with one significant qualification (*MI* 7). Though both are accomplished in the practice of that "measure" which is their versecraft, a shared aptitude does not ensure strictly comparable achievement, and the lover awards her beloved the palm as artist.[21]

   That Rossetti and Barrett Browning both ascribe superiority along gendered lines, deferring to the male lover as the "singer of high poems" and "loftier song," has caused critical dismay over the years (*SP* 4; *MI* 4). Some have been sorry to see the profession of lovers' equality "shade into anxiety and even rivalry," while others have deplored the women's complicity in an aesthetic "subordination" that, as Mermin astutely says, comes "painfully close to the social reality of women's lives." And yet there are two factors to take into consideration here, one having to do with convention and the other with tonality. As noted earlier, the admiration topos is masculine in character, and women's sequences accomplish a disruption simply by inserting women poets into its structure. Secure in the knowledge of their own entirely countertraditional assertions of poetic authority, Barrett Browning and Rossetti allow their speakers to overpraise the men they love. Second, self-deprecation has many tonalities; and Barrett Browning's various ways of humbling her poet-speaker have a certain, if intermittent, appeal for Rossetti. She rejects most but still finds gestures she can modify and borrow. Consider, for example, Barrett Browning's emphasis on her lonely singer's creative depletion:

> . . . Cheeks as pale
> As these you see, and trembling knees that fail
> To bear the burden of a heavy heart—

> This weary minstrel-life that once was girt
> To climb Aornus, and can scarce avail
> To pipe now 'gainst the valley nightingale
> A melancholy music—why advert
> To these things?   (*SP* 11)

The swooning momentum and ornateness of this representation of her "minstrel-life"—the allegorical climbing of Aornus and the metaphorical piping contest with the nightingale—belie its claim of poetic fatigue. The "trembling" weariness is a mere pretext for a vigorous marshaling of the traditional devices of poetic self-reference. Such stylish self-deprecation finds no corollary in *Monna Innominata*. But as Barrett Browning moves into the sestet, she introduces a new thought with the crucial phrase "it is plain." Immediately the images disappear, the syntax disentangles itself— "O Beloved, it is plain / I am not of thy worth nor for thy place!"—and the passage that follows becomes a touchstone for Rossetti's appreciation of the "Great Poetess":

> And yet, because I love thee, I obtain
> From that same love this vindicating grace,
> To live on still in love, and yet in vain—
> To bless thee, yet renounce thee to thy face.   (*SP* 11)

To convey the austerity of her choice, Barrett Browning's Portuguese re- lies on a cautious "and yet" before slowly approaching the terrible "grace" that enables her to love "in vain." Rossetti sees a nearly perfect spareness here with only the legalism of "vindicating" to give texture. And she sees the craft, borrowing both the syntax and the cadencing when her own speaker announces a similar willingness to renounce love:

> And yet not hopeless quite nor faithless quite,
> Because not loveless . . .
>
> So take I heart of grace as best I can,
> Ready to spend and be spent for your sake.
> (*MI* 9; 9–10, 13–14)

The two women's styles momentarily converge. Launched by the same demurring phrase ("and yet") as their speakers discover a similarly neces- sary "grace," both passages suggest an excruciating deliberateness by means of doubled pronouns ("because I love thee, I obtain"; "So take I

heart . . . as best I can"). Rhythmically, both modulate the speaker's anguish by breaking the lines into halting phrases ("And yet, because I love
thee, I obtain"; "Thinking of you, and all that was, and all"). Rhetorically,
both confirm the contradiction of love's refusal with a final antithesis
("bless thee, yet renounce thee"; "to spend and be spent"). Though such
impeded straightforwardness is not Barrett Browning's characteristic
mode, it is the voice that Rossetti values. Needless to say, it is quite different from the marmoreally rich and sonorous voice readers and critics
have heard Gabriel imitating. Poets make their own precursors; they
make a virtue of their ambivalence toward the "great" ones and by a
spontaneous winnowing find, and are enabled by, what they admire.[22]

As with Barrett Browning, so with Dante and Petrarch, which a close
look at the epigraphs to *Monna Innominata* 4, with its comparison of the
poet-lovers, will show. The passage from the *Commedia,* "Poca favilla
gran fiamma seconda"—"A small spark fosters a great flame," anticipates
the ignited response of the Rossettian beloved; though he is the second
to love, there comes a time when his ardor flares up "strong" (*MI* 4). In
similar fashion, the passage from Petrarch previews Rossetti's concluding
move, "Ogni altra cosa, ogni pensier va fore, / E sol ivi con voi rimansi
amore."—"Every other thing, every thought, goes off, / and love alone
remains there with you." Rossetti's speaker, after considering ways to
measure love, will dismiss all such thoughts ("ogni pensier") as irrelevant
to the "love which makes us one" (*MI* 4). When read together with an
awareness of their original contexts, Rossetti's Italian epigraphs also tell a
story about poetic transmission. The first comes from the great invocation to Apollo that begins the *Paradiso.* In praying for a "small spark,"
Dante imagines in the next verses that if the god inspires him, others will
become inspired as well (*Para.* 1.34–35). And indeed, the "spark" is literally transmitted from poet to poet as Dante's image of the "favilla" becomes Petrarch's as well. The latter's poem 72, as it credits Laura's eyes
with driving away all but the thought of love, develops a lengthy conceit
in which her shining glances emit angelic sparks ("faville angeliche"):

> Angelic sparks of loveliness, the blessers
> of all my life, wherein flares up the pleasure
> sweetly consuming and destroying me:
> as every other light
> will flee and fade when whenever yours shines forth,

just so from my own heart,
when so much sweetness pours down into it,
all else, all of my other thoughts depart
and left there all alone with you is Love.

Vaghe faville angeliche, beatrici
de la mia vita, ove 'l piacer s'accende
che dolcemente mi consuma et strugge:
come sparisce et fugge
ogni altro lume dove 'l vostro splende,
così de lo mio core,
quando tanta dolcezza in lui discende,
ogni altra cosa, ogni penser va fore
et solo ivi con voi rimanse Amore.   (*C* 72; 37–45)

With the figural connection in front of her, Rossetti makes telling choices. She isolates Dante's adage; his "spark" that produces a "great flame" has the simple cogency of her own nursery rhyme about the "flint" that "holds fire" (*CP,* 2:43). As for the "spark" in Petrarch, she rejects the elaborate image as too self-involved for *Monna Innominata* 4; her poem, after all, eschews the rhetoric that does the lovers "a wrong" (*MI* 4). But when even he, the master of *concetti,* disclaims distracting thoughts—"ogni penser"— Rossetti takes the plain-speaking lines as her epigraph. She too is inspired by the spark of her precursors and is moved to write of love in the ways they do in her favorite, carefully gleaned verses. The greatest and most complex of love poets include within their range a style that is beautifully pellucid, unadorned, and, for Rossetti, aesthetically moving.

Love and Fame

How one tells of love is a persistent concern of all sonnet sequences; words addressed to the beloved are often about or frankly directed to the poem's audience, and the style that imagines the union of lover and the listening beloved will also be laying hands on the reader. When Petrarch, for example, urges Laura to take pity on him, he assimilates her fame to his own and woos her with the anticipated wonderment of "a thousand others" ("ancor mille") who would, if they could, experience his fervor:

The way I burn, for which you care so little
and all your praise diffused in all my verse
could yet inflame perhaps a thousand others,

for in my thoughts I see, O my sweet fire,
once cold my tongue, once closed your lovely eyes
still full of sparks will be when we have gone.

Quest' arder mio di che vi cal sì poco
e i vostri onori in mie rime diffusi
ne porian infiammar fors' ancor mille,

ch' i' veggio nel penser, dolce mio foco,
fredda una lingua et duo belli occhi chiusi
rimaner dopo noi pien di faville.   (*C* 203)

Such emulous lover-readers are a frequent presence in both the *Sonnets from the Portuguese* and *The House of Life,* where they are explicitly invoked as the artist's admirers. The Portuguese alludes to the contemporaries who pause "to hear my music," then exclaims disarmingly that she writes for posterity:

> Oh, to shoot
> My soul's full meaning into future years,
> That *they* should lend it utterance, and salute
> Love that endures, from Life that disappears!   (*SP* 41)

At the moment she writes these lines, Barrett Browning has already come closer to "achieving full literary canonicity than any of Victorian England's other female poets," though, as Lootens says tactfully, "hers was always an unstable cultural presence." And while not at all frivolous, Barrett Browning's deliberate fusing of the "Love that endures" with the reputation that lasts has been decried by some as naive self-glorification and a factor in the embarrassment some readers feel on her behalf. Gabriel Rossetti, as poet-painter, makes double use of the immortality topos. In the joyful early sonnets, love's "encomiast" imagines that "eyes / Unborn" will some day "read these words" (*HL* 17). Later, when the God of Love grimly predicts the lovers' separation, he offers his devoté the solace of one "last gift," the "laurel" of celebrity as love's chosen singer (*HL* 59). The sonnets on painting are every bit as concerned with the artist's fame. In "The Portrait," where his ambition is to reveal, by the sign of outward beauty, the whole truth of the beloved lady's interiority, he prays,

> O Love! let this my lady's picture glow
> Under my hand to praise her name, and show
> Even of her inner self the perfect whole.   (*HL* 10)

Once again, the god is imagined as bestowing a gift; the finished picture will draw others (as do the poems) to admire Love's own artist:

> Let all men note
> That in all years (O Love, thy gift is this!)
>   They that would look on her must come to me.   (*HL* 10)

With "remarkable self-confidence," the painter assumes "as if by right" the role of gatekeeper, making himself the goal of pilgrimage. To some readers the flagrancy of the portraitist's "masculine assumptions" is exasperating, even though by the end of the sequence it is it clear that eventual recognition will be but poor recompense for his final desolation.[23]

   Against this background of aesthetic anticipation, Christina Rossetti's one sonnet on posterity says both less and more than Barrett Browning's or Gabriel Rossetti's. Just as she lets there be a time before love, she knows there will be a time after and allows the loving speaker to strain forward toward eternity, building her own myth of the self's continuity. Rossetti's lady cherishes no hope that her "soul's full meaning" will reach others (*SP* 41) or that her love-sorrow will "signify" some deep truth to "all hearts" (*HL* 5). On the contrary, she expects that her experience will be warped and trivialized when talked of in "aftertimes" (*MI* 11). Instead of compassion, awe, or envy, there will be gossiplike incomprehension of the kind suggested in the Dante epigraph. The passage "Vien dietro a me e lascia dir le genti"—"Come after me, and leave folk to talk"—is from the episode in which Dante is momentarily distracted by souls who gape at his mortal shadow and is urged by Virgil to disregard their chatter (*Purg.* 5.13). So it is that Rossetti's speaker is distressed by the banality of others' speculations:

> Many in aftertimes will say of you
>   "He loved her"—while of me what will they say?
>   Not that I loved you more than just in play,
> For fashion's sake as idle women do.   (*MI* 11)

Rossetti herself engages in serious play, punning on the "idle" women of fashion who play a debased Petrarchan game of being idolized. Rossetti, who shows elsewhere that the more "some say" about lovers, the less insightful their opinions, here allows her "innominata" to express indignation:

> Even let them prate; who know not what we knew
>> Of love and parting in exceeding pain,
>> Of parting hopeless here to meet again,
> Hopeless on earth, and heaven is out of view.   (*MI* 11)

"Prate" disparages the disparagers, linking them with the fools, rogues, and vulgar types scorned by satirists (who favor this particular verb) and intimating that the opinions of the chattering "many" would, as the expression goes, vex a saint. In specifying their ignorance, however, Rossetti's speaker gives way not to anger but to a gradually debilitating sadness. The linked repetition of "parting," "parting hopeless," and "hopeless on earth," as it adds, drops, and adds again, seems stalled and increasingly feeble. Trapped by grief, she is also trapped by the inadequacy of words. Eric Griffiths, in his fine discussion of Rossetti's habits of style, observes that repetition can be an expression of "exultant fullness" or its opposite, a "clinging lack." He credits Wordsworth with providing the basis for this distinction in the "Note" to "The Thorn," which explains that a speaker who attempts "to communicate impassioned feeling" but is brought up against "the deficiencies of language . . . will cling to the same words, or words of the same character." The present quatrain is a perfect realization of the theory: overwhelmed by permanent separation, the speaker gropes to find adequate language and falls into repetitions that are a sign of "real distress," the authentic trope of a "suffering voice."[24]

Remedy seems unlikely and yet, in an unexpected and vigorous move, the maligned speaker takes up an issue from the preface that goes to the very heart of Petrarchism. There Rossetti deplores the coldness attributed to a lady who is described "by a devoted friend," and here the lady herself undertakes to tell her beloved precisely how she wants him to bear witness to their love. As the second epigraph suggests, he is to honor her by revealing the entire truth, "Contando i casi della vita nostra"— "relating the casualties of our life," all the facts of their case and the circumstances parting them. And as her poem's sestet indicates, this is to happen after death. In the *Canzoniere,* the line chosen as epigraph refers to the deceased Laura's return as Petrarch's visionary counselor

(*C* 285); but Rossetti, unimpressed by the silenced woman's speaking role "in morte," reconceives it as the male partner's apocalyptic obligation:

> But by my heart of love laid bare to you,
>   My love that you can make not void nor vain,
> Love that foregoes you but to claim anew
>   Beyond this passage of the gate of death,
>   I charge you at the Judgment make it plain
>   My love of you was life and not a breath.   (*MI* 11)

At the Last Judgment, before the posterity of "all nations" (Rev. 15:4), the beloved must speak of the loving woman, but not in the fashion of a Petrarchan lover. He is not to tell of his ardor but of hers, and following a directive that is enacted by the sonnet itself, he is to "make it plain" that she loves him deeply. Energized with the exhortatory "by my heart," enforced by the emphasis on vulnerability ("lóve láid báre"), delivered as a single sentence (the only such sestet in all of *Monna Innominata*), and relaunched by the imperative "I charge you," the words prescribing his testimony seem intended to arrive with an extraordinary crescendo. In spite of the anticipatory buildup, the final line, "My love of you was life and not a breath," has a quietness and a restraint that is typically and at the same time surprisingly Rossettian. Because the speaker seems about to say, but does *not* say, that her love was a matter of "life *and death*," there is a sense of grandiloquence avoided. When the last phrase arrives as "not a breath," the negatived particular is so unexpected it gives the reader pause. A complex thought is packed into the article as Rossetti distinguishes "a" breath, something as ephemeral as a whisper of "idle" flirtation or a whiff of gossiping scandal, from "the" breath that is a synecdoche for life itself. The meaning is importantly tautological: my love for you was life, and not just a breath, but my life's breath. And there is more; since breath is also the poet-speaker's medium, the breath of her verbal art form, her love gains life in her love songs. The beloved's task, then, is ultimately to repair the tradition's founding neglect of women's love and women's song, and to do so in precisely the way that has already been set out for him by Rossetti's own sonnets. He is to endorse the poet-lover and the songs that are *Monna Innominata*. In a sense, Rossetti is professing, in her own discreet way, what she believes to be the enduring worth of her sonnet sequence.[25]

For all its definitiveness, sonnet 11 is also atypical insofar as *Monna Innominata* is principally concerned with the present and with the distortion love causes in the perceived flow of events, especially when the lovers are parted. The deepest intuition suffusing these love poems may, in fact, have less to do with the totalizing effect of a lover's passion than with the loving self's unbridgeable solitude. Before and after, but also during, the love that inspires *Monna Innominata,* the loving woman's separateness is never forgotten, never overridden. The sequence opens with a temporary parting, the moment just after the lovers' adieu, the "addio" of the Dante epigraph, and turns, of course, to the question of the beloved's return (*MI* 1): the burden of waiting is universal in love poetry. In Gabriel Rossetti's sequence, "Severed Selves" laments that the lovers' secret meetings are "slow to come" but "quickly past" (*HL* 40). The period between is oppressively narcotic, a "darkened" interval that leaves only an "attenuated dream" of the beloved. In *Sonnets from the Portuguese,* Barrett Browning takes the misery of the time apart as the basis for a bit of ascetic computation: at a point in the courtship when the speaker is still arguing to defer love's consummation until eternity, she suggests that "others" will think such fulfillment comes "'too late,'" but promises that in the transport of their joy, the lovers themselves will "think it soon" (*SP* 40). Well before time's end, however, the Portuguese makes her beloved a gift of her sonnets, expecting that these "flowers" will flourish under his "weeding" (Victorians heard in this a reference to the Brownings' "wedding"), and completely abandons her love-postponing sophistries (*SP* 44). In Christina Rossetti's sonnets, the speaker also considers the joys that come sooner-or-later, and with an illogic of her own turns the duration of the beloved's absence into something beautiful and austerely comforting. The self alone is, must be, capable of self-solace. She begins with a wish, but then resists the torment its fulfillment will bring:

> Come back to me, who wait and watch for you:—
>   Or come not yet, for it is over then,
>   And long it is before you come again,
> So far between my pleasures are and few.   (*MI* 1)

Longing does not give voice to anything so enticing as the summons of "Echo" (*CP,* 1:46), or croon with the sound of lover's repletion as in the song "Come again, come again, come back to me" (*CP,* 2:38). A self-interrupting syntax chops short the lover's plea that cannot shorten longing, "—Or come not yet." In the perversity of its desire for postponement, the ensuing clause delays "pleasures" until the final line where it

sits midway "between" the disheartening "far" and "few." The adroit enactments of such wording, the play of grammar itself, soon become an
aid to the loving imagination, and the displeasure of the beloved's absence yields to the paradoxical luxury of expectation:

> While, when you come not, what I do I do
>   Thinking "Now when he comes," my sweetest "when:"
>   For one man is my world of all the men
> This wide world holds: O love, my world is you.

Manipulating the "when" as adverb and substantive, Rossetti's lover reorganizes time with an inspired grammatical palimpsest. By its tripling,
her sentence literally says, "the time when I am alone is when I speak to
myself of when you come." By a lovely conflation, all three "whens" are
sweet, and longing itself becomes "a natural phenomenon whose beauty"
one observes and might even "wish to preserve." The success of this verbal ploy is apparent in the next lines' recovered fervor amid the rever-
berating whirl of open vowels and the triply repeated "world."[26]

There comes a time, eventually, when the lovers are irrevocably parted
and the speaker struggles to accept this loss as permanent. The Dante epigraph to the final sonnet is literally exemplary, quoting the lovely peace-
fulness of Piccarda Donati, "E la Sua Volontade è nostra pace." This famous sentiment from the *Paradiso*, "And His Will is our peace," evinces
even as it explains the perfect contentment—despite lower or higher
places—of the souls in heaven (3.85). Piccarda's serenity represents the
composure not yet (and perhaps not ever) achieved by Rossetti's speaker.
The Petrarch epigraph is from an anniversary sestina that remarks time's
effect on the lover: "Sol con questi pensier, con altre chiome"—"Only
with these thoughts, with different locks" (*C* 30). Though the interval in
Monna Innominata is uncertain, time and loss leave their mark on Rossetti's
speaker; she surrenders the "fresh roses" once worn in her hair, and her
thoughts take the form of a self-answered question. No longer addressed
to her lover, the passage opens with a kind of near pun, replacing the
"you" of the earlier sonnets with "youth," which is also "gone":

> Youth gone and beauty gone, what doth remain?
>   The longing of a heart pent up forlorn,
>   A silent heart whose silence loves and longs;
>   The silence of a heart which sang its songs

While youth and beauty made a summer morn,
Silence of love that cannot sing again.   (*MI* 14)

Taking recourse in that most familiar of tropes, the silence that falls when the lute is "still" or when "no birds sing," Rossetti's poet-lover knows that an effective way to bring these songs to an end "is simply to announce that [she] is doing so." Though love has proven destructive emotionally and aesthetically, she forgoes the "vain regret" and the final renunciation that close *The House of Life* and the *Canzoniere* respectively and speaks, instead, of her resolute wordlessness. Acoustically, these lines bring the sequence to an end with an impossibly distant rhyme, as "remain" reaches through half-rhymes (with all the *n*'s) to find "again," the distant echo itself a figure of unsatisfied yearning. A discerningly intelligent woman with a distinctive voice and considerable "poetic aptitude" has reached an impasse as a lover. The forlornness at the end of *Monna Innominata* might serve as an emblem of life's other diminishments; but while the loss of the beloved brings the end of love songs, there is no question that Rossetti herself continues to sing. When love's time runs out, there is all that other time—the time of the *Later Life* sonnet sequence.[27]

Later Life, a Sonnet Sequence for the Aftertimes

Organized as an anthology of sonnets, Rossetti's *Later Life* is a formal descendant of the *Canzoniere,* which, despite its concern with dates and anniversaries, privileges narrative a good deal less than readers tend to remember, and is so loosely structured that, as Roland Greene observes, many of the lyrics "can be freely substituted for one another" without damaging the collection as a whole. The nearer model is the second half of Gabriel Rossetti's *The House of Life,* which gathers sonnets on mixed subjects under the title "Change and Fate." "Lost Days" is included there, with its unforgettable image of failures and missed opportunities as so many "murdered" selves (*HL* 86), as well as pieces that touch variously "on art, on poetry, on the way of the world, and on such themes as death and memory." Love is not the overriding concern of this section, nor is it in Christina's second sequence. *Later Life* is presented without an identified or dramatically situated speaker except that she is obviously a poet and possessed of the Rossettian ability to turn youth-and-beauty's loss into unexpected gain. She finds loveliness in unpromising places and preserves moments of rapture, however infrequent, through a process of lyrical recollection. Generally, this sequence receives less attention than *Monna Innominata* and is sometimes hurriedly dispatched as if it were a specimen of discursive prose, its beliefs abstracted and summed up as uncompromisingly orthodox—the adverb giving an indication of the critic's impatience. Lionel Stevenson, ordinarily Rossetti's admirer, describes it as "a sort of dejected sequel to 'Monna Innominata'" in which "Shame and penitence mingle with stoic acceptance of tedium and frustration," while Bellas disparages its craft, objecting to the "slight and approximate rhymes" that strike him as "annoying infelicities." Such descriptions leave the *Later Life* sequence virtually unrecognizable and seem oblivious to the nuances of its bleak beauty. Some of Rossetti's most austerely moving work is done in these sonnets as she creates a reticent and often discomfited speaker who succeeds, nonetheless, in scavenging some of life's fleeting joys.[28]

When Rossetti deprives the speaker in *Monna Innominata* of certain signal remembrances, it is to clear the way for a less traditional account of love and the deep changes it works in the lover, not to discredit memory as a category of the imagination. Since love's mythologies are not a concern in *Later Life,* memory becomes an important element in the momentum of the sonnets, prompting the "progression of thought and feeling" that Rees discerns, along with "striking turns and contrasts" and shifts in tone. Rossetti now pursues memory's various satisfactions, sometimes as an otherwise never-to-be-recovered pleasure and at other times as a blurry trace whose very faintness proves stimulating. Sonnet 17 begins with a slight tug of daydreamy recollection, conveyed with an incommunicativeness that teases the reader into wanting the memory as well:

> Something this foggy day, a something which
>   Is neither of this fog nor of today,
>   Has set me dreaming of the winds that play
> Past certain cliffs, along one certain beach,
>   And turn the topmost edge of waves to spray:
>   Ah pleasant pebbly strand so far away,
> So out of reach while quite within my reach,
>   As out of reach as India or Cathay!   (*LL* 17)

The twice-used "something" is patiently vague about what sets the speaker reaching into the past, and the word "certain" withholds the story of that certain windy beach. There are no details in the scene (no gulls, tidal pools, companions, or horizon line) and only the quality of the strand is noted, the definiteness of its "pleasant pebbly" texture enhanced by the slight effort of the lips to form the alliterating phrase. Yet there is an impression of the speaker's visual acuity: the fog of memory lifts slightly and, with sudden precision, she sees the clearly defined "edge" preceding the waves' dissolution into "spray." The present sense of loss, the speaker's own wave of nostalgia for what is "out of reach," is sharply focused by her remembrance of this "topmost" evanescing peak.[29]

The nonpictorial picturing in *Later Life* is both like and unlike Gabriel Rossetti's in *The House of Life*. Adept at such visually appealing settings as the meadow of "Silent Noon" (a Pre-Raphaelite painting ready-made), he is more often fascinated by scenes that don't come to full realization or that dissolve and blur (*HL* 19). For the eerily tormented "Through Death to Love," he creates a windy skyscape suggestive of panic:

> Like labor-laden moonclouds faint to flee
> From winds that sweep the winter bitten wold.   (*HL* 41)

The long simile (its referent still unspecified) multiplies tumultuous images:

> Like multiform circumfluence manifold
> Of night's flood-tide,—like terrors that agree
> Of hoarse-tongued fire and inarticulate sea.

In this vast chaos of viewless images, the extravagantly inwoven alliteration of "multiform circumfluence manifold" (*mlfm, mfl, mfl*) tells of something that cannot be seen clearly in words that cannot be heard distinctly. The Rossettis' shared interest in things unseen is pursued to utterly different ends, of course, and with varied degrees of obscurity, differences that are almost too apparent for comment. In *Later Life* 17, Christina's dim recollection is prelude to the speaker's sad avowal that the windy beach remains "so far away." The nostalgic mood dissipates, and whatever pleasure memory might have provided is promptly lost in a scattering of complaints:

> I am sick of where I am and where I am not,
> I am sick of foresight and of memory,
>> I am sick of all I have and all I see
>>> I am sick of self, and there is nothing new;

> Oh weary impatient patience of my lot!—
>> Thus with myself: how fares it, Friends, with you?   (*LL* 17)

This is probably not an outburst of thoroughgoing despair but rather, given the overly emphatic anaphora and all-inclusive binaries, a surge of exasperation; Rossetti indulges her speaker and lets the rhetoric accelerate into self-parodic crankiness. The mild satire of the dismissal "Thus with myself," and the colloquial jauntiness of the question "How fares it . . . with you," bring the complaint to a sensibly other-directed close. Such abatement does not, however, erase the speaker's sense of grievance. The sighing oxymoron of "impatient patience" delivers a muted but expressive protest against quotidian dullness and preserves its restlessness without subsiding into mere lassitude.

Wearied but resilient, energized by the awareness of enervation, the speaker's attention to her own mixed feelings produces variations in momentum (in contrast to the pushing urgency of so many of Gabriel's sonnets) and some of the most interesting language in the sequence. In sonnet 6, shapeless discontent has the acoustically firm sound of "lack":

> We lack, yet cannot fix upon the lack:
>> Not this, nor that; yet somewhat, certainly.   (*LL* 6)

The behavior of this twice-present word for the missing *je ne sais quoi* is illustrative of the difficulty it cannot quite identify. It shifts from verb to noun but then, with renewed transitivity, gathers shiftily indeterminate objects to suggest the recurrence of what Griffiths dryly calls life's "unsatisfaction." Precise only about its vagueness, the specified "somewhat" eludes analysis and must be named again in other poems and, in one splendid example, quadruply renamed:

> This Life is full of numbness and of balk,
>> Of haltingness and baffled short-coming.   (*LL* 26)

The playfulness of Rossetti's diction should not be overlooked, for it represents a triumph over conditions that cannot otherwise be changed. Kathleen Blake notes that "a word could hardly stop shorter than 'balk,' in meaning and in the abruptness of the explosive 'k,'" while the phrase "'baffled short-coming' perfectly baffles the ostensible metre." By its trick of hyphenation, the stress on "coming" comes too soon—in literally too "short" a space of time. That the strange new word "haltingness" so precisely describes the flow of its own line lends authority to its larger claim about life itself. We know that at least one Victorian woman felt the truth of these two sonnets, for in the late 1880s, Elizabeth Sharp reprinted them with a handful of Rossetti's "essentially characteristic poems" in an anthology titled *Women's Voices*. In a preface that gives her rationale for collecting two hundred years of little-known poetry by women, Sharp provides a terse account of the obstacles in these poets' lives: "Women have had many serious hindrances to contend against—defective education, lack of broad experience of life, absence of freedom in which to make full use of natural abilities, and the force of public and private opinion, both of which have always been prone to prejudge her work unfavourably, or at best apologetically." Hopeful that these hindrances "are gradually passing away," Sharp gathers poems that regret and defy them. Rossetti, by these lights, affords women a chance to read of the "balk" and "lack" that correspond to the difficulties and "lack of broad experience" in their own lives. In the context of *Women's Voices,* she becomes an almost topical author—but not quite, or at least not explicitly. The strength of Rossetti's late poetry is that it is persistently lyric. Rather than treat the social constraints Sharp refers to as "these deterrent influences," Rossetti confronts life's haltingness with the subtle resistances of the lines and language that dwell on what might be called the climate of existence. In poems that Sharp does not have room for, Rossetti presents seasons and landscapes that are emblematic of depletion and forgetfulness as reported by a speaker whose moods include ennui, austere festiveness, and genuine exhilaration.[30]

Throughout her career Rossetti is good at sensory deprivation, whether as the "charmèd sleep" in "Dream Land" (*CP*, 1:27), the anticipated insensateness of the "Song" ("When I Am Dead, My Dearest") (*CP*, 1:58), or the "salt, passionless" condition of the anemones in "By the Sea" (*CP*, 1:191). Now, in *Later Life,* she projects this condition onto the seasons in a vision of hibernation and unstirred, unroused sense. In sonnet 18, a sort of anti-ode to autumn, Rossetti invokes the image of natural dormancy, not to enjoy the Keatsian repletion of lazing "on a half-reaped furrow sound asleep" (*Keats,* 249) but to consider the nonpleasures endured in the season of rot and dull forgetfulness:

> So late in Autumn half the world's asleep,
>   And half the wakeful world looks pinched and pale;

> For dampness now, not freshness, rides the gale;
> And cold and colourless comes ashore the deep
> With tides that bluster or with tides that creep.   (*LL* 18)

The ambiguity of "half the world's" sleepiness, which might be a faintly scientific reference to hemispheres or a colloquially formulaic generalization, allows the reader to see a landscape, the humans crossing it, and the inanimate forces that somehow ride or come into the scene. Some might see a not-quite-viewable fusion of all three in a world that ails with discomfort. The account quickly turns to the palpable displeasures of raw, dirty weather and its consequences:

> Now veiled uncouthness wears an uncouth veil
>   Of fog, not sultry haze; and blight and bale
> Have done their worst, and leaves rot on the heap.
> So late in Autumn one forgets the Spring,
>   Forgets the summer with its opulence.

By the merest accident of language, the open vowel of "rot" matches that of "opulence," a rare word for Rossetti that does a rare bit of work in these lines. Polysyllabic and complexly voweled, it summons up the impression of a richness convincingly retrieved from amnesia, though re-erased by the remembrance of the late-summer's nearer betrayals:

> The callow birds that long have found a wing,
>   The swallows that more lately gat them hence.

The speaker fends off desolateness by eliding any mention of the impending winter and instead asking, albeit rather bleakly,

> Will anything like Spring, will anything
>   Like Summer, rouse one day the slumbering sense?

The accomplishment of this couplet is the perfect balance whereby it demonstrates and resists the effects of "slumbering sense." Unable to think of spring's coming as the "sweetest when" in the manner of *Monna Innominata* or to hint at a "certain" feature of summers past as in *Later Life* 17, but wanting still to amplify the expression of desire, the speaker asks twice if there is "anything like" what formerly stirred and pleased. The dissatisfaction that in real life leaves emotion blunted acquires the contoured momentum of a double question.

There are comparable effects in the winter sonnet: the same honesty about coldness and sterility, the same emotional resourcefulness. In the stark post-autumn, cheerlessness itself palls; attention turns to what "still" endures and the sparse pleasure that bleakness affords:

> Here now is Winter. Winter, after all,
>> Is not so drear as was my boding dream
>> While Autumn gleamed its latest watery gleam
> On sapless leafage too inert to fall.
> Still leaves and berries clothe my garden wall
>> Where ivy thrives on scantiest sunny beam;
>> Still here a bud and there a blossom seem
> Hopeful, and robin still is musical.
> Leaves, flowers and fruit and one delightful song
>> Remain; these days are short, but now the nights
>> Intense and long, hang out their utmost lights;
> Such starry nights are long, yet not too long;
> Frost nips the weak, while strengthening still the strong
>> Against that day when Spring sets all to rights.   (*LL* 19)

As if in response to the melancholy last question of *Monna Innominata*— "Youth gone and beauty gone, what doth remain?"—the speaker here finds what she needs. Like the winter ivy, she too can thrive on the "scantiest" stimuli. Like the winter robin, the emboldened speaker "still is musical" and with a look skyward sings the intensity of long "starry nights."

Rossetti's sonnets explore what might be called the emotional logic of the aftermath, the means whereby the singer in later life comes upon her songs. Among the most moving, that is to say, the most intelligently and tonally reticent, are the Alpine sonnets that recall hearing the nightingales at Lake Como and crossing the St. Gothard pass. The first of these is briskly assertive about the unreliability of life's pleasures and makes its point with witty impertinence:

> A host of things I take on trust: I take
>> The nightingales on trust, for few and far
>> Between those actual summer moments are
> When I have heard what melody they make.
> So chanced it once at Como on the Lake   (*LL* 21)

Confidence in nightingales, as with so much else taken "on trust," is supported by a shortage of primary evidence. To demonstrate how "far / Between" these moments are, Rossetti splays the phrase across a line break in the midst of a four-verse sentence without end stops (the only such quatrain in the *Later Life* series) and defers "melody" as long as possible. When the "actual" example of the Swiss nightingales materializes, the diffidently impersonal "chanced it" nearly reduces the epiphany to a random accident. It is as if the speaker can only recover the quality of this trusted episode by a reminder that it might not have "chanced" at all. Even as the details seem about to come, a concessive "but" intrudes, along with a defensive explanation: "But all things, then, waxed musical." In other words, the experience at Como is as nonrepeatable as it was unlikely, insofar as "all" the necessary circumstances must be conducive. The moment, however, is nearly recovered:

> But all things, then, waxed musical; each star
> Sang on its course, each breeze sang on its car,
> All harmonies sang to senses wide awake.
> All things in tune, myself not out of tune.

With a triple "sang," the passage becomes its own song of the self awakened to cosmic harmonies. The inertial and drowsy nonresponsiveness that is the underlying metaphor of the *Later Life* sonnets seems overcome by now-remembered rapture. And yet, the slight tepidness in the self-characterization "not out of tune" *is* a bit out of tune and suggests that the original experience was not perfect, which might mean that it can be just as good (though imperfect again) now. Or it might mean, more simply, that nostalgia's access to exhilaration is neither easy nor complete. Not surprisingly, the next line lapses into the dullness that is humanity's default condition; exactly where the reader hopes for a full-throated (not to say Keatsian) celebration of the nightingales' song, the speaker gives a comically prosaic assurance that "Those nightingales were nightingales indeed." Oddly flat and contentless, "indeed" seems proof that the speaker cannot be roused.[31]

But Rossetti knows how to find virtue in scantiness of all kinds, from a deficiency of winter sun to an irresponsive temperament. With a disarming and slightly funny humility, her speaker admits that, once stirred, she hardly requires a nightingale to experience delight. Pivoting on a long-delayed eleventh-line volta, "Yet truly," the poem finally rises to and certifies the speaker's capacity for rapture:

> Yet truly an owl had satisfied my need,
> And wrought a rapture underneath that moon,
> Or simple sparrow chirping from a reed;
> For June that night glowed like a doubled June.

Despite the self-denigrating modesty that almost gainsays the glory of Como's nightingales, the speaker is at last exuberantly in tune. The glow of that June night is doubled again in the layering of the now and then and redoubled by the sheer loveliness of the final line. While the elegant formal pun sets a second "June" to prolong the first in its retrospective glow, language itself, with the slow vowels of "night glowed" and still slower juncture of "doubled June," savors the fullness of the experience. The impertinence of the opening line's "trust" is now transformed, and among the things that can henceforth be relied on—though infrequently and unpredictably—is the artist's own songfulness. There is no facile celebration here of an assured method, no brash confidence that the precious "overflow" of feeling can be unfailingly "recollected in tranquility"; on the contrary, Rossetti's poem makes a characteristically restrained claim for the sporadic but real power of the artistic imagination.

If the Como sonnet can be said to be about the obstacles to art—the shortage of stimuli, the lethargy of the self, and the hesitation of memory—so too the St. Gothard sonnet, in which the scale of the Alps is sublimely oppressive:

> The mountains in their overwhelming might
> Moved me to sadness when I saw them first,
> And afterwards they moved me to delight;
> Struck harmonies from silent chords which burst
> Out into song, a song by memory nursed;
> For ever unrenewed by touch or sight
> Sleeps the keen magic of each day or night,
> In pleasure and in wonder then immersed.   (*LL* 22)

Initial silence gives way to a responsiveness that is, once again, figured as song; here too, just as the speaker seems about to burst into full celebration, a present difficulty is introduced. To recall that she felt keenly is not to recover what she felt, and the poem becomes a sort of elegy for the magic "unrenewed" by a dormant imagination. The evanescence of even the most "overwhelming" sensation seems about to be confirmed when the sestet opens by locating "all Switzerland behind." The lines tell, however, of passing through St. Gothard, and Rossetti, with typical unobtrusiveness, shifts the focus to allow memory to recover what it needs:

> All Switzerland behind us on the ascent,
>   All Italy before us we plunged down
>   St. Gothard, garden of forget-me-not:
>   Yet why should such a flower choose such a spot?
>   Could we forget that way which once we went
>   Tho' not one flower had bloomed to weave its crown?

The grandeur of the crossing is secured by a change of scale, the discovery of a small wildflower growing in profusion. As if to match this surprise, Rossetti makes unexpected music out of a sequence of gutturals and hails the spot as "St. Gothard, garden of forget-me-not." The pleasure of this Eden is then fostered by questions that delight in the fortuitousness whereby "such a flower" ("such a day of days!") fixes the memory that renews and doubles the experience. The appropriately named forget-me-not is both cause and effect of the remembrance that crowns all with this very sonnet, this humble work of cadenced syllables and rhymes. So it is that these oppressive mountains become the occasion, finally, of another meditation on the poetic silence that threatened the lover at the close of *Monna Innominata*. The sequence called *Later Life* clearly finds much to sing about even as it considers the hard question of why sing at all. One reply, chanced upon at the St. Gothard pass, is that song needs no justification. A sonnet in a sequence, a small and proliferating poetic form, is lovely in its superfluousness. Rossetti's sonnet 22 is a manifesto, of sorts, defending the improbability, the irrelevance, the excessiveness of the poetry that comes "later," after love's songs have been sung.

Finally, it is possible to read the "overwhelming might" of the mountains that initially subdue the alpine traveler as a representative figure for the collectively stunning achievement of the poets Rossetti admires. Confronted with the massive fluency of her precursors and contemporaries, she takes herself to a private St. Gothard pass, the interior border between the articulate and the inarticulate regions of the self. Her wonderment at the *Commedia,* the *Canzoniere,* and the nineteenth-century sequences by the "Great Poetess" and her own brother Gabriel is coupled with an awareness of how much of the passionate life is conducted silently. She finds traces of *that* wordlessness even in these works and is thereby encouraged in her own hushed and reticent style. Her narrative restraint about the "few and far between," her focused way with detail, her taking hindrances into the poem's momentum, her preference for understatement: these are her way of offering words that retain their aura of glowing wordlessness even as they proliferate.

Rossetti's Finale

The Face of the Deep (1892) and *Verses* (1893)

IN HER ADMIRING essay occasioned by the centenary of Christina Rossetti's birth, Virginia Woolf greets the poet with cordial intimacy, "O Christina Rossetti . . . I know many of your poems by heart," and casts a cold eye on the buying public's stinginess, noting that "Her annual income from her poetry was for many years about ten pounds." Without delaying over Woolf's resentment on Rossetti's behalf or her well-known hunch about the happy effect on women writers of "five hundred a year" and "rooms of our own," we might confirm that sales figures were not a source of pleasure to Rossetti until late in life. Although her poetry was always well received, she never enjoyed anything like the demand for successive editions that met Gabriel's *Poems* of 1870 nor was she ever to report such jubilant news as that of his letter to their Aunt Charlotte Polidori: "I dare say you have heard . . . of the commercial success of the book. [That the] first thousand sold in little more than a week is not amiss for poetry. The second edition is now out, and I have already received £300 for my share of the profits. Of course it will not go on like this for ever, but perhaps a quiet steady sale may be hoped to go on. I am now about to republish my book of the *Early Italian Poets,* as perhaps a new edition may profit by the luck of the other book" (*LDGR,* 2:880). Aunt Charlotte must have been delighted, since she had often been asked, early in Gabriel's career, for loans she cheerfully gave. Christina's triumph would come at age sixty-three, only a year before her death, when she had the satisfaction of seeing the first edition of *Verses* sold out in a week. The Society for Promoting Christian Knowledge had brought out the book in September 1893 and "by Christmas" her friend Mrs. Garnett loyally complained that "there was no meeting the demand for 'Verses': at one considerable shop she tried at she heard that twenty or thirty applications had had to be negatived for the moment" (*L*, 4:364). By January a deeply gratified Christina would tell William of seeing a *"4th thousand"* copy "which looks grand" (*L*, 4:367).[1]

In her letters, Rossetti usually refers to *Verses* as "my reprint" since, as indicated by her subtitle, *Reprinted from "Called to be Saints," "Time Flies," "The Face of the Deep,"* the poems had first appeared in her volumes of religious prose (*L*, 4:316, 340); there they attracted the attention of those Anglican worshipers whom Lynda Palazzo, in her recent study of Rossetti's theology, graciously admires for seeking devotional guidance on the "journey into spiritual understanding." As a collection, however, *Verses* reached the broader audience who had already made "Up-hill," with its wry cautioning of "wayfarers" about the inn they "cannot miss," a nearly universal favorite (*CP*, 1:66). These readers knew that Rossetti's first two books each included a section of "Devotional Pieces," announced as such in the table of contents and marked by an interior title page, and they valued what they found there. Arthur Symons, for example, admired "Advent" from *Goblin Market* for "startling us perhaps by its profound and unthought-of naturalness"; others singled out "Good Friday" from *The Prince's Progress* and "Who Shall Deliver Me?" from the collected edition of 1875. The division of these first books "into two distinct sections" had been a suggestion of Gabriel's, who early in his own career had been writing what he called "Songs of the Art Catholic." When William and Gabriel were bringing out *The Germ,* their short-lived literary magazine of 1850, they had eagerly included among the "pure" lyrics—such as Christina's "Song" ("Oh roses for the flush of youth") and "Dream-Land"—her explicitly religious "A Testimony," replete with borrowings from Psalm 39 and Ecclesiastes, as well as "Sweet Death." The latter, a traditional meditation on petal-fall, opens in a churchyard and takes up the refrain of George Herbert's "Virtue," gravely modifying his lament that all things "must die":

> The sweetest blossoms die.
>   And so it was that, going day by day
>   Unto the Church to praise and pray,
> And crossing the green churchyard thoughtfully,
>   I saw how on the graves the flowers
>   Shed their fresh leaves in showers,

And how their perfume rose up to the sky
    Before it passed away.

The youngest blossoms die.
    They die and fall and nourish the rich earth
    From which they lately had their birth;
Sweet life, but sweeter death that passeth by
    And is as though it had not been:—
    All colours turn to green.   (*CP*, 1:74)

"Thoughtfully" accepting the evidence of spring's easeful passing into the all-green of summer, the churchgoer imagines death as a change that allows its devastation to be pleasantly effaced, passing "as though it had not been." Rossetti's inference is, of course, too wishful and subsumes too readily the actual terror of individual death, but she redeems her poem by coming to a subtle close. Her seasonal metaphor turns typological and remembers Ruth amid Boaz' autumn fields:

Why should we shrink from our full harvest? why
    Prefer to glean with Ruth?   (*CP*, 1:75)

The final question, spread across the line break, puts delicate emphasis on the word "prefer." Ruth herself, as we know, did *not* prefer to glean but managed to raise her status (another meaning of "prefer" is to promote in rank) to that of Boaz's handmaiden (Ruth 2:9). Rossetti's question, by displacing and faintly punning on its verb, gently wonders at the mysteriousness of human inclination. This final deftness is probably what earned "Sweet Death" its place in the *Germ*.[2]

Many years later, when once again writing of a churchyard, Rossetti again elides what terrifies—the "full harvest" of death—only this time it is because she knows all too well how cruel a death can be and how anxiously a mourner shrinks from posing questions about the soul's status in the afterlife. "Birchington Churchyard" is separated from "Sweet Death" by Rossetti's three decades of experience as a poet and by the culminating agony of Dante Gabriel Rossetti's death on Easter Sunday, April 9, 1882. Christina and their mother, Frances, were with Gabriel throughout the final weeks and the very last minutes of his life. As she would soon write to George Hake, the "amiable" companion to Gabriel after his suicide attempt a decade earlier, her brother was buried in the churchyard of the seaside town where they had hoped he would recuperate

(*L*, 1:432). It is a subdued letter that purports to give "a few particulars of poor dear Gabriel's last days" but is, in fact, solicitous of Gabriel's reputation and aims at preventing blame; she does not want Hake to believe that Gabriel's reliance on chloral had killed him: "The immediate cause of death arose from blood-poisoning induced not by an extraneous cause but by an internal derangement. The last moments appeared to pass (and [I] am assured did really so pass) quite free from pain, nor was there the slightest struggle" (*L*, 3:36, 37). Having performed this tender work, she has one further task: she must make the location of his grave a thing too natural to question. To her it was an added and unintelligible grief that Gabriel refused to be buried at Highgate Cemetery with their father and his wife Elizabeth Siddal. Christina could not have known that Hake was the very person Gabriel had apprised of his aversion to the cemetery in a letter instructing that he "not on any account be buried at Highgate" (*LDGR*, 3:1437), and she probably knew nothing of the now-legendary exhumation that Gabriel's friends had undertaken to retrieve his poems from Siddal's coffin. So she covers over the strange fact of his solitary grave with a description of the prospect from the Birchington churchyard and assures Hake that friends and family had gathered at the last: "The country about Birchington is not very pretty, but the Churchyard where he is buried—not a cemetery; but a small quiet Churchyard—lies high, and commands a fair exposure of land and sea with sunsets over the sea. Two days before Gabriel died William joined us, and we and nurse and three dear friends and Dr. Harris of Birchington were gathered round the bed at the moment of death. Mr Marshall had seen him in the morning, having passed the night on the spot" (*L*, 3:37). Brief and restrained, Christina's remarks are a model of mourner's denial (Gabriel probably did not "really" die "quite free from pain") and decorous irrelevance (Hake does not care where John Marshall spent the night). She substitutes what is acceptably thinkable for what cannot be said about this especially unhappy dying.[3]

Within a few days of this letter, Christina's elegy for Gabriel, "Birchington Churchyard," would appear in the *Athenaeum*. It too takes up the landscape and manages to be both poignantly lovely and austerely uncomforted. This churchyard poem intimates the consolation that is wanted but which, given all she knows of Gabriel's troubled agnosticism, she is far too honest to profess. She had long been distressed that her much-loved brother tended, as McGann puts it, to regard "the whole of

Christian history" as "a poetic construction" rather than the grounds for spiritual trust. And so she begins her poem with the muted sound of the "low-voiced" sea and the sterility of the chalky shore, perfect correlatives for the flattened, dull ache of grief:

> A lowly hill which overlooks a flat,
>   Half sea, half country side;
>   A flat-shored sea of low-voiced creeping tide
> Over a chalky weedy mat.   (*CP,* 2:167)

The dignified laboriousness in the stanza's movement—an effect of the long vowels, the hyphen-bonded accents ("A flát-shóred séa of lów-vóiced créeping tíde"), and the constraining of verbs as participles)—mimes the slowness of the tide and the lowness of emotion. Together the sea and the poetic line cross inevitably "over" their boundaries, while the word "creeping" recalls Tennyson's thought about the feeling of ghostliness that sends a mourner to "creep / At earliest morning" around a loved friend's door (*AT,* 352). The "weedy mat" is a reminder, too, that the Victorians wrapped themselves in mourning "weeds." Attention then moves to the churchyard itself:

> A hill of hillocks, flowery and kept green
>   Round Crosses raised for hope,
>   With many-tinted sunsets where the slope
> Faces the lingering western sheen.

The scene is both religious and domestic. The word "hillocks" is almost affectionately diminutive while the sign of human tendance is preserved in the phrase "kept green." The sacred aura of the place is subtly enhanced by the "many-tinted sunsets" and the "sheen" on the ocean. Set amid moving lights, the crosses "raised" in hope and the hillside that "faces" into the light are touchingly more animated than the earth-bound dead who neither see nor feel the sun. Sadly, then, the focus shifts from the near to the distant prospect, from the grave site to eternity. But grief is severe and Rossetti is so vastly experienced in the ways of poetic restraint that she manages to say no more about hope than she actually feels—and what she feels is inconsolable loss:

> A lowly hope, a height that is but low,
>   While Time sets solemnly,

> While the tide rises of Eternity,
> Silent and neither swift nor slow.

The low voice of the opening stanza's incoming sea is refigured as a "silent" tide, and the attendant abstractions Time and Eternity resist any attempt at allegorically intoned comfort. An assertion of belief or claim about "sweeter death" would bring no solace; the exultation that forms the lovely close to a poem in the previous year's *Pageant* volume, Paul's jubilant words to the Corinthians, would be jarring and false: "He bids me sing: O death, where is thy sting? / And sing: O grave, where is thy victory?" (*CP*, 2 : 123). The mourner at Birchington cannot imagine gaining emotional access to any such sentiment. A mourner's sense of loss, as Stephen Booth vehemently explains, is "altogether immune to invasion by comforting conclusions based on consideration of such 'facts' as the inevitability of mortality, the painfulness of life, the immortality of the soul, and the reunion of body and soul at the Last Judgment." Booth cites precisely the "facts" implied by Rossetti's raised churchyard crosses, and her poem shows that, despite the religious convictions represented by such symbols, there is no acceptance of the terrible fact of Gabriel's death. His passing brings a mood and a pain that will be assuaged only slowly and imperceptibly; and so instead of hope, "Birchington Churchyard" aspires toward calm. The poem's beauty is a temporary relief from numbness; it brings sorrow into words and momentarily fills the vacuity of inarticulate pain. It surmounts muteness to speak of eternity's tide as a silently relentless motion that takes no cognizance of human death and grief.[4]

"Tune Me, O Lord": Invocation, Lamentation, and Consolation

The bleakness of the final image of "Birchington Churchyard" releases Rossetti from the burden of articulating a sentiment she does not feel and maybe also from enacting the one she does. It shows, at the same time, the contours of a difficulty that is paradigmatic for her as a writer. There is a sense in which the struggle enacted in the poem's final lines corresponds fairly precisely to the challenge every poet faces in the late stages of a career, viz., the depletions of one sort or another that weaken the desire to write. An author's gradual fall into silence was once described as writing less and less until one stops altogether, and this seems to be the pattern Rossetti herself feared. She once told Macmillan, in a famous misstatement, that "the fire has died out, it seems"; this was in 1874 when a collected edition and much new work was yet to come (*L*, 2:7). In the 1880s, however, such discouraged comments became more adamant, as when she told Swinburne in 1884 that "dumbness is not my *choice*" (*L*, 3:231) and Frances Kingsley in 1885 that *Time Flies* "exhausted my last scrap" (*L*, 3:284). Viewing Rossetti's work in retrospect, we know better than to take these as serious forecasts, and yet the evidence of the publication history suggests she was losing the "patience and desire" to write (*CP*, 2:181). After its appearance in the *Athenaeum*, "Birchington Churchyard" would be included among the handful of new pieces in the reissued *Pageant* volume (1888) when it was not at all clear that there would ever be another collection of new poems. But for all this, the poems do come—sometimes with worries attached.

In the dozen years it takes her to assemble the devotional poems that eventually become the *Verses* of 1893, Rossetti's attention often turns, not surprisingly, to the wordlessness she dreads, the specter she calls "utterless desire," "voicelessness," "breath that fails" (*CP*, 2:250, 185, 204). The imagined muteness that was once an unfailing stimulus—variously recast as the hushed eavesdropping in "At Home," the lonely withdrawal in "L.E.L.," and the resolve at Lake Como to include song among the "host of things" taken "on trust" (2:147)—now looms as a debilitating threat. The silence that once defined a perimeter, its negotiation a source of enlivening aesthetic tension, now constitutes an all too literal barrier portending the loss of imaginative power. When the late poems assess the waning of spiritual stamina, they often ask, as Rossetti's friend Mary Howitt put it, "to be delivered from *Self*," and in the same words to be blessed with an infusion of aesthetic energy. Since at some level a poet's invocations are all the same, a means to the elevation that is the poem's inception, it is literally the case that the substance of Rossetti's devotional pleading is to recover the ability to write devotional poems. The Lord of Apostrophe is both the Christian's and the poet's deity, and metaphors for spiritual union are musical. "Tuning of my breast," as Herbert puts it, will "make the music better" and Rossetti prays accordingly:

> Tune me, O Lord, unto one harmony
>   With Thee, one full responsive vibrant chord;
> Unto thy praise all love and melody,
>   Tune me, O Lord.   (*CP*, 2:255)

With an access of melody and spiritual trust, poetic song becomes a "hopeful quiet psalm" and the singer tells of searching her "heart-field" for a gift of thanksgiving (*CP*, 2:184). There she finds the "sun-courting heliotrope," a flower that brings the memory of Apollo's sponsorship of poets delicately into alignment with the reverent Christian pun on *sun* and *Son*. Once tuned, the "responsive chord" yields as many tonalities as the vocal cords permit; and the formed breath of the late poems ranges in pitch from a "lonely beseeching cry" to a rapturous "shout" (*CP*, 2:208, 211). Sometimes the prospect of death's imminent silence prompts a kind of spiritual hedonism, and Rossetti imagines an imperative to sing while she can:

> Thou who must fall silent in a while,
>   Chant thy sweetest, gladdest, best, at once;
> Sun thyself today, keep peace and smile;
>   By love upward send
>   Orisons,
>   Accounting love thy lot and love thine end.   (*CP*, 2:269)

The urgency of the exhortation to chant "at once" is felt in the velocity of the phrasing "thy sweetest, gladdest, best," as each of the final *st*'s arrives more quickly than the last. The third line makes "sun" sound like a verb meaning "rise towards the sun" and activates the "horizon" and more exactly the "risen" in "orison." As if to revel in this achieved sense of sun/Son-blessed exhilaration, "orisons" is awarded the unshaded splendor of a line to itself. The acoustic flamboyance of this stanza is a reminder, albeit an unusual one, that a good Rossetti poem is never too far from an awareness that it might not have come into existence. One of the strangest versions of this same hint takes the form of a tormented complaint about shortness of breath:

> Good Lord, today
> I scarce find breath to say:
>   Scourge, but receive me.
> For stripes are hard to bear, but worse
> Thy intolerable curse;
>   So do not leave me.   (*CP*, 2:222)

By alluding to scourging, this prayer holds up the model of the Savior's exemplary docility (Mark 10:34). But in professing a near inability "to say" what is required and by distancing the plea for pain as an indirect citation, the speaker nearly refuses to accept affliction. This ambivalence about the fearsome signs of divine attention are the poem's strength; there is no pretense that suffering is anything less than an ordeal. But there is also the suggestion that suffering might be something more, something attractive. The cascading syllables of the "intolerable curse" are braked and slowed to an abject final whisper of the kind made to a lover, "So do not leave me." Not only does Rossetti suggest that a connection with the divine has the vividness of physical pain, she pushes that idea toward the erotic and welcomes inflicted "stripes" with a submission that borders on masochism. "Good Lord, today" is a double poem—completely conventional and utterly perverse—and its speaker does, in fact, "find breath" to confront the central issue of Christian spirituality, the peril of relying on an unseen god.[5]

For Rossetti, the beliefs that some cherish and others scorn as the conventionally "secure pieties" are not always *felt* to be secure. The chief tenets of her religion remain uncontested, of course, and she refuses to entertain doubt about spiritual realities—as she says in a letter, "I have not *played* at Xtianity, & therefore I cannot play at unbelief" (*L*, 2:167)—but hopefulness often pales against the glare of what she calls the "instinctive dread of death" (*FD*, 63). Confidence in the ultimate value of the life she is committed to is a crucially unstable emotion. Because Rossetti is neither a docile nor an opiated believer, her devotional poems confront all that confounds her ways of making sense of life, helping her, as an earlier poem says, to "fix upon the lack" and to contend with what she now calls "the fume and the fret" of life's seeming pointlessness (*CP*, 2:140, 292). One of her most distinctive modes, therefore, is lamentation, as she lodges complaint after complaint against the temporal process whereby all good things "decrease" (*CP*, 2:181). One poem mourns the cosmos itself:

> A moon impoverished amid stars curtailed,
>   A sun of its exuberant lustre shorn,
>   A transient morning that is scarcely morn,
> A lingering night in double dimness veiled—
> Our hands are slackened and our strength has failed:
>   We born to darkness, wherefore were we born?   (*CP*, 2:252)

The scene at first resembles the paled landscape of "Dream-Land" in the *Goblin Market* volume, and even "Birchington Churchyard" with its verblessness and many participles, but the tone and culminating challenge are new. The extremity of the question approaches defiance; though the "hands" are said to have "slackened," one at least takes up the pen in protest. In other poems, when Rossetti turns, as so often in her career, to the image of the sea, it is with a forceful new severity. Gone are the "flower-like" anemones, the "argus-eyed" sea creatures, and the "pebbly strand" (*CP,* 1:19; 2:145); the darkening waves have become the "very embodiment of unrest" (*P,* 230), no longer teeming with life forms but "lifting" cadaverlike hands:

> The sea laments with unappeasable
> > Hankering wail of loss,
> > > Lifting its hands on high and passing by
> > > > Out of the lovely light:
> No foambow any more may crest that swell
> > Of clamorous waves which toss;
> > > Lifting its hands on high it passes by
> > > > From light into the night.
> Peace, peace, thou sea! God's wisdom worketh well,
> > Assigns it crown or cross:
> > > Lift we all hands on high, and passing by
> > > > Attest: God doeth right.   (*CP,* 2:268)

These waves that wave their "hands" as if drowning are startlingly surreal and at the same time precisely biblical. Rossetti takes the image, along with her title, from Habakkuk, where the prophet questions the Lord's "wrath against the sea" and grieves that "the overflowing of the water passed by: the deep uttered his voice, and lifted up his hands on high" (Hab. 3:8, 10). To amplify the "wail of loss" that needs appeasing, Rossetti creates a high degree of acoustic tension and, because this poem is moving in the prophetically affirmative direction, works audibly toward formal resolution. The first quatrain seems unrhymed, and not until the second do the echoes of the end words emerge; but even here the term "unappeasable" finds only an idiosyncratic match in "swell." In committing what Fried wittily designates one of "rhyme's sins," Rossetti's "mannered, quaint, contrived" pairing virtually puns with the word's "unappeasable" need for a rhyme partner and manages, at the same time, to intensify the reader's own hankering for a perfect chime. Finally, when the third quatrain complements the second with a full set of exact matches, the satisfaction of hearing the words themselves work "well" encourages acceptance of the thought that "God's wisdom worketh well." With the final line's solemn command, "Attest: God doeth right," the language itself sounds biblically and acoustically "right," an echo of Herbert's technique when he ends "Denial" with the phrase "and mend my rhyme." If the poem succeeds, it is because of the skill that brings the prophet's text into Rossetti's own and then, by subduing strange rhymes, mimes the bringing of restless emotions to order.[6]

The closing assertiveness of "Was Thy Wrath against the Sea?" is somewhat atypical in Rossetti's poetry. Keenly aware of what she elsewhere calls "renewed incompleteness," the recurrent anxiety that belies the confidence of this poem's exhortation, Rossetti tends to complain more softly and to be more ambiguous in her assurances (*FD,* 524). One sighing, weary poem asks about the slow coming of time's end using a nearly petulant phrasing, "Will it never," as if restless about minor annoyances:

> Oh knell of a passing time,
> Will it never cease to chime?
> Oh stir of the tedious sea,
> Will it never cease to be?
> Yea, when night and when day,
> Moon and sun, pass away.   (*CP,* 2:274)

Though the questions elicit an answering "Yea," it comes with the tautological information that time will end when the cosmic signs of time end. Vague in content, the answer is also mysterious in origin: the poem is either a lyric whose speaker has grown tired of her own discontent or a dialogue with an unidentified (possibly divine) tutor. The ambiguity raises the question of genre—is there one voice or two? It is important for the poem's effect that the reader remains of two minds about what is happening and slightly agitated. This unsettling formal mystery precludes naive assumptions about access to the greater eschatological mystery— even when the next stanza begins with a seemingly confident "surely":

> Surely the sun burns low,
> The moon makes ready to go,
> Broad ocean ripples to waste,
> Time is running in haste,

Night is numbered, and day
Numbered to pass away.

In retrospect, the "surely" seems to have been concessive, guardedly coaxing, and lacking the force to sustain its meaning through to the end of the sentence. The only sure numbering that goes on—since there is no knowable total of days past or future—is the poem's own play with metrical number. And it gives shape, not to temporality per se, but to human impatience. This covertly self-allegorizing poem examines its own ways of facing uncertainty and all but promises that Rossetti will "never cease to chime." Rhymed and "numbered" language (she repeats this punning hint) is her devotional tool, and throughout the *Verses* she plays repeatedly with the long and short of duration to achieve the paradoxical serenity of aesthetically molded unrest. A pentameter sonnet, for example, opens with the thought that "Time lengthening, in the lengthening seemeth long" (*CP,* 2:275). Acoustically, the line drags out its own length with falling rhythm, softly thickening *th* sounds, and the unelided syllables of "lengthening" while repetition takes the thought back to the beginning of the line and arrests its momentum. Such artistic handling disciplines even as it voices its complaint.

But lamentation is not the only, or even the dominant, mood of the late poems. Some are cheering and almost colloquially heartening; instead of mourning humanity's "deathstruck" condition or bearing witness to divine wisdom, they suggest ways one might "take comfort" in this life (*CP,* 2:182, 297). Neither blithe nor carefree, they offer consolation by admitting the prevalence of discouragement and showing a kindly regard for the "heart disheartened thro' and thro'" (*CP,* 2:190). There is respect for the rigors of despondency and sheer miserableness that strain the "patience" she once called "a tedious, indomitable grace" (*FD,* 68). The poems charm by their understatement and by their refusal to blunder into abrasive imperatives about joy. Rossetti may or may not remember Dr. Johnson's insistence that "The only end of writing is to enable the readers better to enjoy life or better to endure it," but certainly she knows Paul's advice to Timothy. Imprisoned and bound in chains, the apostle exhorts his follower to partake in "the afflictions of the gospel" and to "endure hardness" (2 Tim. 1:8; 2:3). Rossetti borrows this last phrase to introduce a spring poem, or rather a poem that glimpses spring from the perspective of winter. Noting the wind's "keenness," she offers more than a Pauline exhortation to endure the season's bone-chilling cold; she envisions coming sprays of snowlike blossoms:

> A cold wind stirs the blackthorn
>> To burgeon and to blow,
> Besprinkling half-green hedges
>> With flakes and sprays of snow.
>
> Thro' coldness and thro' keenness,
>> Dear hearts, take comfort so:
> Somewhere or other doubtless
>> These make the blackthorn blow.   (*CP,* 2:297)

The secret of this poem is that it takes delight in what it proposes enduring. There is physical pleasure in the alliterated first sentence as the lips shape the *b*'s of "burgeon," "blow," "besprinkling" and then open for the continuants of "flakes," "sprays," "snow." The sound is not mimetic in any strict sense, but the shift in mouth's articulation, from obstructed to free-flowing air mimes the emergence the words describe. An attentive weather-watcher, the speaker plainly enjoys detecting the earliest hint of flakes that are not made of snow. Convincing in its modest precision ("half-green hedges" are still half-brown) the speaker's joy becomes all the more cogent with the second stanza's gentle diffidence. The word "doubtless" makes the poem. Instead of insisting absolutely on a burgeoning not yet in evidence, the speaker offers a plausible claim that "somewhere or other" the season breaks into bloom, which might, of course mean "unpredictably later in life" or even "after life," while the cajoling "doubtless" half-admits to doubts about the coming change. The point is not pressed, and even the dourest of the "dear hearts" would agree that the suggested connection between cold and bloom is not improbable and that it might be, in the words of another poem, "possible, or probable, or true" (*CP,* 2:102). To gauge the effect of the poem's mild unassertiveness, one need only turn to the vigorous expostulation in a passage from *Seek and Find* (1879): "Winter even while we shrink from it abounds in hope; or ever its short days are at the coldest they lengthen and wax more sunny. Winter is the threshold of spring, and Spring resuscitates and reawakens the world. Winter which nips can also brace" (*P,* 227). The seasonal analogy is meant as an aid to reflection, for it is literally true that days lengthen for five or six weeks before the temperature bottoms out; at London's latitude, February 1 is often colder than December 21 when days start lengthening. Nonetheless, in overlooking the disproportion between allegedly abounding hope and midwinter's imperceptible increases in daylight, the passage seems nearly facile. The supposition that winter is bracing offers nothing but its own briskness to invigorate a chilled reader. The poem, however, by its honest admission of the bitterness of bitter weather and its accuracy about the black-thorn yet-to-bloom succeeds in communicating its sense of vernal expectation.[7]

This sensible good-heartedness, this wish to console reliably and without falsification, moves Rossetti to celebrate even fleeting occasions for hope, admitting that they are temporary and perhaps only a brief remission of the sorrows that "overhang" us (*CP,* 2:324). Among the strengths of these late devotional poems is their emphasis on the mood in flux, or more accurately, the sensation of rebound from some pain or frustration that will come again:

> One woe is past. Come what come will
>   Thus much is ended and made fast:
> Two woes may overhang us still;
>   One woe is past.
>
>   As flowers when winter puffs its last
> Wake in the vale, trail up the hill,
>   Nor wait for skies to overcast;
>
> So meek souls rally from the chill
>   Of pain and fear and poisonous blast,
> To lift their heads: come good, come ill,
>   One woe is past.   (*CP,* 2:324)

The poem makes a delicate effort to contain suffering, to distinguish and tally up discrete episodes, not always to take the long view because, both perversely and wisely, we don't want to face unremitting woe. In the interval, the afflicted might become as beautifully reckless as first blooms in a chilly spring. Newly volitional with three brisk verbs, these flowers "wake," "trail" after the light, and refuse to "wait" for what another poem calls the "fattening rain" (*CP,* 1:31). The focused quality of Rossetti's attention to germination, infinitesimal growth, and the not-so-random spread of seed and root makes this brief observation compelling. Just as these flowers "rally" from winter's "blast," the verb suggestive of resilient loyalists and soldiers, so will the meekly woebegone. The very shape of the poem, a roundel with a prescribed rentrement, encourages a rally by its own example, confining "woe" to the framing stanzas while the springtime image flourishes in the interval. There is even an exemplary staunchness in the phrase "One woe is past." It not only resists false hope by refusing to evolve semantically into the "one" that is once-and-for-all or somehow climactic, it also fends off dread; for as many readers will recognize, the phrase denies knowledge of the prediction it echoes, the warning of "two more woes hereafter" (Rev. 9:12). With its extraordinarily subdued use of the carpe diem motif, this roundel remains "unsnared" by improbable optimism, "unscared" of future pain, and affirms, by its own austerity, the value of even small recoveries (*CP,* 2:182).

Occasionally Rossetti's spring poems find winter's lingering chill less oppressive: the "poisonous blast" goes unmentioned, and the emphasis is on the cheering botanical fact that flowers detect the slightest gradations of temperature and can be said to "know" the new season is arriving. Ordinary violets and daisies, because they are "unaccounted rare," become the speaker's personal emblems:

> As violets so be I recluse and sweet,
>   Cheerful as daisies unaccounted rare,
> Still sunward-gazing from a lowly seat,
>   Still sweetening wintry air.
>
> While half-awakened Spring lags incomplete,
>   While lofty forest-trees tower bleak and bare,
> Daisies and violets own remotest heat
>   And bloom and make them fair.   (*CP,* 2:257)

The final image is unexpectedly but delicately sensuous: were these flowers fully personified, the reader would be close to or even inside their bodies, feeling a temperature change along the skin. Because this tactile intimacy is a response to "remotest heat," touching occurs without touch and perfectly symbolizes a spirituality the poem need not actually mention. Rossetti has other images for the hopefulness that persists despite (and in part *because of*) all that is numbing, frightful, or dire. Alone in "a chill blank world," a desolate sky watcher discerns a faint lessening of the gloom. The change detected is "No more than a paler shade of darkness as yet," but it is enough; the coming of light has unmistakably begun and straining attention is rewarded (*CP,* 2:210). A favorite figure is the half-moon, which shows

> a face of plaintive sweetness
> Ready and poised to wax or wane;
> A fire of pale desire in incompleteness.   (*CP,* 2:273)

Hope and vulnerability are here mingled in a glowing state of readiness, and dissatisfaction is a suspenseful sweetness too aesthetically appealing to be desolating. What might feel, in actuality, like mere instability or gloomy anticipation of recurrent loss is tactfully reimagined as a kind of "poised" luminosity.

The watchfulness that underlies so many of Rossetti's images, the empathetic heeding of what evolves, whether it be the emergent day or season or lunar phase, might be taken as a figure for Rossetti's own relation to her art. A contemporary poet-critic reminds us that "absolute attention" must be paid at every moment of "the poem's process" because in the finest instances tones modulate, the end is not foreseen from the beginning, and the poem provokes or yields unlooked-for results. Patience, in other words, with the poem's own mobility is the means to surprising grace. Rossetti often begins with a devotional commonplace and then carefully, almost courteously, allows it to become unfamiliar. In one instance, an easy contradiction tells us that joy is not really joy:

> Joy is but sorrow,
> While we know
> It ends tomorrow:—
> Even so!
> Joy with lifted veil
> Shows a face as pale
> As the fair changing moon so fair and frail.   (*CP,* 2:302)

The austere paradox is familiar, but the buoyant affirmative is unexpected and fixes the proposition so vehemently that one is curious about what else can possibly be added. What comes next seems to portend a stereotypical unveiling; but instead of the "loathsome and foul" hag who is the traditional symbol of deception (*CP,* 1:77), a delicately fair face is revealed. In this scenario, ephemeral joy is not a woman to be excoriated like the "false" temptress in "Amor Mundi," but one who is to be seen as truly lovely and almost excused for her fragility (*CP,* 1:216). The next stanza, as one sees even before reading it, has an identical, manifestly predictive, shape. Given the symmetrical assertion in the first line, "Pain is but pleasure," and the glimpsed exclamation mark, expectation is set for a stanza like the first and a reiterated pattern of contradiction, endorsement, image. But because this is a Rossetti poem, one half-expects something unexpected:

> Pain is but pleasure,
>   If we know
> It heaps up treasure:—
>   Even so!
> Turn, transfigured Pain,
> Sweetheart, turn again,
> For fair thou art as moonrise after rain.

With the unforeseen figure of address, "Pain" is startlingly greeted as if she were a paramour. Like Rossetti's other lovers who "turn with yearning eyes" (*CP,* 1:63), this "Sweetheart" is asked to "turn" her face to the speaker so her beauty may be celebrated. The success or failure of the poem rests on the conviction with which pain's loveliness is conveyed, and the last phrase manages this with a pristine and almost anticlimactic image. The evocative phrase "after rain" comes, as Rossetti tells us in *Seek and Find,* from the book of Samuel, where it describes new grass "springing out of the earth by clear shining after rain" (2 Sam. 23:4; *P,* 236). In adapting this botanical observation to the radiance of moonrise, Rossetti turns it synesthetic and gives light itself a soft, misty texture. The association with rinsed freshness turns pain into a tenderly intimate cleansing. All this is subtly corroborated by an evolving sound pattern; the poem unobtrusively reweaves the vowels and consonants of "pain" through "fair" "turn" "again" "moonrise" until they become "rain," whose very sound is an affirmation that "pain" may turn into something else.[8]

Perhaps the least expected turn in a devotional poem is to humor; and yet, because an unremitting struggle with ephemerality and depletion can leave the poet *as poet* feeling "unrefreshed from foregone weariness," Rossetti is not unwilling to parody her own mode of lamentation (*CP,*

2:139). In a solemn bit of spoofery, one of the sonnets from the *Time Flies* volume (1885) takes covert aim at *aesthetic* tiredness:

> No thing is great on this side of the grave,
>> Nor any thing of any stable worth:
>> Whatso is born from earth returns to earth:
> No thing we grasp proves half the thing we crave.   (*CP,* 2:325)

This could almost be mistaken for straightforward Rossettian ruefulness. Phrased as negatively as her favorite borrowing from Ecclesiastes, "And there is nothing new under the sun" (*CP,* 1:72; Eccl. 1:8), and reliant on the term "half," which is her watermark—as in "Half content, half un-content" (*CP,* 2:98) and "glories half unveiled" (*CP,* 2:143)—it seems characteristic and serious. The reader detects, however, such oddities as the expansion of "nothing" to "no thing," the truncation of "whatsoever" to "whatso," and the feebleness of the second line's twice-generalizing "any." As the poem continues, the increasing glibness of rapid-fire gener-alizations climaxes in the eighth line's egregious cliché:

> The tidal wave shrinks to the ebbing wave:
>> Laughter is folly, madness lurks in mirth:
>> Mankind sets off a-dying from the birth:
> Life is a losing game, with what to save?   (*CP,* 2:326)

With this question, the joke is sprung; at the sonnet's turn, the next phrase, "Thus I," retroactively exposes the octave as a self-citation and a mild satire on the speaker's whiningly intoned *contemptus mundi.* What follows are three lines of alliterative high jinks at the expense of her own bias towards gloom:

> Thus I sat mourning like a mournful owl,
>> And like a doleful dragon made ado,
>> Companion of all monsters of the dark.

Though the owl and dragon are genuinely scriptural (Mic. 1:8), Rossetti is responsible for the irreverent plethora of *m*'s and *d*'s. With only a ter-cet left and monsters to dispatch, Rossetti signals the speaker's epiphany with a quick exclamation and brings on the dawn:

> When lo! the light cast off its nightly cowl,
>> And up to heaven flashed a carolling lark,
>> And all creation sang its hymn anew.

The ascending skylark is an obvious makeshift, but it suffices. Rossetti has shared her fun, and after the archaically clunky, doleful "ado" we gladly allow her the bird's carol. It accomplishes the needed transition to the natural canticle that turns the speaker's gloom into exultation or at least a sense that the singing, which has gotten labored and predictable, will now be done *for* her.

The reader's sense of making allowances for this ending is instructive, a reminder that the representation of gained or recovered spiritual happiness is no guarantee of a successful poem. It is an undeniable truth that Rossetti's efforts at saintly rapture are routinely disappointing. For persuasive gladness, none supersedes "A Birthday," so admired by Virginia Woolf, or passes the litmus text of its final lines' exuberance: "the birthday of my life / Is come, my love is come to me" (*CP,* 1:37). *The Face of the Deep* includes one auspicious attempt at imagining eternal bliss, a sonnet beginning with an image of ignited joy and a perfectly worded, nearly palindromic characterization of the fullness of heavenly desire:

> The joy of Saints, like incense turned to fire
>   In golden censers, soars acceptable;
>   And high their heavenly hallelujahs swell
> Desirous still with still-fulfilled desire.   (*CP,* 2:289)

All the meanings of "still" ("ever yet" unsatisfied, "calm" with ecstasy) and the contradictions of desire (to be desire, desire must not be fulfilled) are at work to enrich the lines that follow. Rossetti does not, unfortunately, maintain the force of her "incense" simile or the pleasing idea that human joy is inherently a form of homage. Instead she falls to narrating—"Sweet thrill the harpstrings of the heavenly quire"—and to inventorying the props, costumes, and details of the paradisal milieu:

> All robed in white and all with palm in hand,
>   Crowns too they have of gold and thrones of gold;
>   The street is golden which their feet have trod,
>   Or on a sea of glass and fire they stand:
>   And none of them is young, and none is old,
>   Except as perfect by the Will of God.

There are enough poems in this mode to turn readers away from the religious verse and lend prima facie support to Stevenson's claim that Rossetti's late work adds "little of significance to her achievement." The difficulty with "The joy of Saints" is, in part, its dependence on what McGann faults as a "portentous but obscure" idiom that leaves readers unable to find "any human or worlded equivalents" for its textual conventions. Even those who know the biblical code and might ordinarily find comfort in its familiar images and phrasings detect the problem, viz., that Rossetti is impatient with her poem. Instead of moving with the poem's emotion (the joy that "soars" and "swells"), she moves through a static list, relying on grammatical parataxis to accumulate robe *and* palm, crown *and* throne, glass *and* fire, young *and* old in a hurried substitute for empathy; such compounding does not, in the end, communicate the sweet joy it purports to tell of.[9]

It might be taken as a general rule that when a Rossetti poem seems merely rote or dull, the formal culprit is a discernible forcing of its momentum. "Whitsun Eve" is an especially instructive example of a poem that comes to ruin despite an especially promising beginning. The speaker is one of Rossetti's beguilingly timid souls, one of "the small who fear" or worry that they are "failing now" (*CP,* 2:333; 2:224–25), but who occasionally become resentful (a sign of their smallness) and familiarly accusatory. In this instance, the opening words belong to the Lord (Rev. 3:14), and the speaker, in a mildly emboldened bit of back talk, impugns divinely professed love with an "if/why" question:

> "As many as I love."—Ah, Lord, Who lovest all,
> If thus it is with Thee why sit remote above,
> Beholding from afar, stumbling and marred and small,
> So many Thou dost love?   (*CP,* 2:233)

The poetic rules of encounter prescribe two ways to resolve such a challenge: either the Lord has the last, winning word (in both the endearing and the triumphant sense of that term) or the speaker is moved to recant, prompted by a recollection of the appalling sacrifice made by the God who "died for us" (*CP,* 2:321). Here, however, the speaker crumples instantly, castigates the stumblers "Whom sin and sorrow make their worn reluctant thrall," and proceeds to amplify their unworthiness in three additional lines:

> Who fain would flee away but lack the wings of dove;
> Who long for love and rest; who look to Thee, and call
> To Thee for rest and love.   (*CP,* 2:233)

Somewhere between the stanzas an understanding takes shape that does not make it into the poem. Without it, these guilty admissions on behalf of "so many" seem authorially preconceived. Rossetti *knows* too precisely how she wants this exchange to end and hasn't the patience to discover the speaker's motive for getting there. There is no turn, nothing comparable to the move from paradox to assurance to image in "Joy is but sorrow" or the apostrophic shift that greets "sweetheart Pain." There is nothing unexpected in the poem's own process: what had begun so vigorously, with bold language and a rhythmically witty "stumbling" into the sudden cascade of "stumbling and marred and small" becomes utterly programmed. The syntax goes so slack that phrase boundaries recur exactly at midverse while simple coordination ("sin and sorrow," "love and rest," "look . . . and call," "rest and love") ekes out the dully unmodified iambic rhythm. A possible reason for the flatness of the second stanza is that the poem itself is a "reluctant thrall" to the scriptural source of its opening line and the appended gloss in *The Face of the Deep*. In the text of Rev. 3:19, the expression of divine love is coupled with a warning to the backsliding Christians of Laodicea, "As many as I love, I rebuke and chasten: be zealous therefore, and repent." Rossetti's prose meditation on the passage accepts the injunction to "repent" and provides a remorseful collective echo: "We know that Thou lovest us all, we all being liable to chastening" (*FD,* 141). Then comes her poem and its quietly brazen chiding of the Lord with a portion of his own utterance: "'As many as I love'—Ah, Lord, Who lovest all / If thus it is with Thee why sit remote above?" Unfortunately, the biblical context has already made the response to this question so apparent—the Lord is present (not "remote") in the sufferings that chastise sinners—that it short-circuits the poetic process. At their best, Rossetti's poems are acts of sustained self-surprise; they find out where they are going only when they get there, or, to put it another way, "the clarity" they "arrive at is unforeseeable." The true devotional poem grapples with its truth and refuses to be aesthetically "overburdened by foreseen" endings (*CP,* 2:140). It has texture.[10]

Brazenness: *The Face of the Deep* and the Emancipation of Poetry

Critics have speculated on what prompted Rossetti to undertake a prose study of Revelation and to amass 552 pages of citation, prayerful meditation, and "little bits of verse" as a commentary on the most daunting book in the scriptural canon (*L,* 3 : 346). The impetus, as biographers suggest, might well have been the death of her mother, Frances, the lifelong companion whom Christina did not hesitate to describe as "so dear a saint" (*CGRFL,* 232). In a black-bordered letter to a family friend, the unhappy daughter candidly admits that she has "been grieved before but never so desolate as now" (*L,* 3 : 309). It is not hard to imagine a sorrowful Rossetti turning to the prophecy that describes, in Carolyn Bynum's words, "how time and individual experience are permeated with the eternal" and committing herself to a study of humankind's apocalyptic destiny. Formally, Rossetti's title, *The Face of the Deep: A Devotional Commentary on the Apocalypse,* suggests the influence of Isaac Williams, a contributor to the *Tracts for the Times* and, more germanely, the first author in a series entitled *Devotional Commentary on the Gospel Narrative.* Rossetti respected Williams's devotional poetry and made illustrations in her personal copy of *The Altar* (1849). Her departures from Williams's mode of commentary suggest, however, a distinctive hermeneutic ambition. Palazzo points out that Rossetti's combination of prayers, litanies, and scriptural parallels "to a certain extent replace the quotations from the Church Fathers, which abound in Williams's work," and Robert M. Kachur finds her intending to demonstrate "how she and other 'unlearned' women" might assume the traditionally male privilege of scriptural exegesis. The aim of her commentary, in his view, is "to critique the patriarchal restrictions on women's writing practices within the church itself" and to influence the thinking of Anglican clergymen. This clarification of the gendered division of commentators' labor is helpful, since Rossetti may indeed have felt antagonized by clerical objections to women's interpretive efforts, but as a general explanation it probably loses sight of a deeper concern.[11]

Rossetti's motive for writing, as every page of the book shows, is revulsion from the "taint of cruelty" that suffuses the sacred text and the terror that, as Northrop Frye tells us, "is inseparable" from apocalypse (*FD,* 458). It is not the Anglican male exegete but John of Patmos who stands as Rossetti's adversarial muse and against whose fearsome narrative she raises her protest. When presented with Revelation's image of a vengeful Christ wielding a sickle, Rossetti explains that he comes not to mow but to reap and that "the reaper embraces and draws to his bosom that good grain which he cuts down" (*FD,* 364). Confronted with the horrific punishment of the great whore—"these shall hate the whore, and shall make her desolate and naked, and shall eat her flesh, and burn her with fire" (Rev. 17:16)—Rossetti decries such brutal loathing of evil and makes an eloquent plea against the sin of hating sinners (*FD*, 408). Throughout *The Face of the Deep*, Rossetti sets herself to do the nearly impossible, to meditate as a believer on John's warnings and threats while somehow softening his account of "doom, the Judgment, the opened Books, the lake of fire"; she is to admit the uncertainty of "final perseverance," to remember Christ's words on "the resurrection of damnation," and yet to master the anxiety these instill (*FD*, 15, 75, 100). Her aim as she works her way through John's repetitive text is to achieve, over and over, the equilibrium she identifies as holy fear "without terror" and trust "without misgiving" (*FD*, 10).[12]

When describing Rossetti's method in *The Face of the Deep* it is easiest to begin with what she does not do. First and foremost, her patience with received doctrine prevents her from rejecting passages as "unrecoverable" in the manner of such later writers as theologian Mary Daly or professing such nonstandard beliefs as, say, universal amnesty at the Last Judgment. Her orthodoxy is certified by the title-page motto, "Published under the Direction of the Tract Committee," which means, practically speaking, that an editorial board of Anglican priests vetted the manuscript. Their approval, Lorraine Kooistra assures us, was "no easy matter." Second, despite occasionally mentioning a "commentator" she has "turned to" (*FD*, 195), Rossetti gives no information about John's overall structure, omitting to point out, for example, that the epistolary opening is followed by a series of visions associated with two heavenly books, the one opened (Rev. 6:1), the other ingested (Rev. 10:10). Nor does she offer even a cursory narrative outline: there is nothing comparable to the sketch she once provided for *The Divine Comedy* or her efficient hint that the *Vita nuova* is "composed of alternate prose and verse" in which the reader finds "an elaborate continuous exposition of [Dante's] love for Beatrice, interspersed with ever-renewed tribute of praise from his lowliness to her loftiness" (*P*, 188–89). It would have been appropriate to say that Revelation is insistently repetitive and that, as Bernard McGinn explains, many sections of John's vision reiterate "the same basic message of present persecution, imminent destruction of the wicked and reward of the just." Perhaps such information is obviated by what Rossetti takes to be the like-mindedness of a readership that belongs to her "beloved Anglican Church" (*FD*, 540). Orthodox believers hardly needed to be told the book's contents or reminded of the recent debates about its transmission and the challenge, by Ernest Renan and others, to the identity of John himself. To them the apocalyptic visionary was none other than the Galilean son of Zebedee, the Savior's "beloved Disciple," the author of three New Testament epistles and the Gospel According to John (*FD*, 11). Rossetti assumes, moreover, that her readers have no interest in the kind of speculation she dismisses in her earlier book, *Letter and Spirit*, as irrelevant fretting over "the precise architecture of Noah's Ark," "the astronomy of Joshua's miracle," and "the botany of Jonah's gourd" (*P*, 283). Her tone is less amused in *Face of the Deep* but her attitude is the same: "curious investigation" is an impediment to "meditation" (*FD*, 334, 409).[13]

Rossetti's broadest statement about her project comes more than midway into the book where, in an allusion to her title, she offers a modest, perhaps even a baffled, admission of inexpertness. Because the obscure wording of Rev. 15:15 creates some uncertainty about the speaker, she pauses to explain her hesitation and her procedure:

> But I take this opportunity of calling attention to my ignorance of, sometimes, a very critical point in the text on which I venture to meditate; and if in consequence I misrepresent the person of the speaker or the word spoken, I ask pardon for my involuntary error. Only should I have readers, let me remind them that what I write professes to be a *surface* study of an unfathomable depth: if it incites any to dive deeper than I attain to, it will so far have accomplished a worthy work. My suggestions do not necessarily amount to beliefs; they may be no more than tentative thoughts compatible with acknowledged ignorance. (*FD*, 365)

This is a genuinely humble disclaimer, but one that also permits her, as Colleen Hobbs succinctly puts it, to reserve "her right to observe the obvious." There are knots in the text that Rossetti—untrained in Greek—cannot pretend to unsnarl and so she needs to invoke some version of the modesty topos if she is to continue her study. Similarly, her professed conviction that Revelation announces a "divine mystery" to all, but explains it to none, releases her from the expectation that she "expound prophecy" (*FD*, 401, 195). She avoids, for example, a historical reading of the millennium and spurns chiliastic expectations that stem from the promise that the faithful will have "power over the nations" (Rev. 2:26); she writes bluntly that "this power appears to be punitive, destructive," and that a Christian's proper concern is with "overcoming himself" and not his neighbor (*FD*, 83). Her approach to the violence of John's prophecy is to read it as a warning to become "harmless as doves"; the book, she contends, "shows us destruction lest we destroy ourselves" (*FD*, 195, 15).[14]

In practice, Rossetti's habit is to take "disjointed portions" of the text, a few verses at a time, and to work through them "piece by piece" (*FD*, 174). "Words," she says, are the "wards" of apocalyptic mystery, and she allows individual terms to direct her to related passages throughout Scripture (*FD*, 103). Wholeheartedly accepting what Frank Kermode describes as commentators' typical assumption, i.e., that "the Bible is its own interpreter," she develops her meditations by exploring textual correspondences. Her hunt for glosses is not strictly exegetical and never philological or even aesthetic. She is not tempted by "wormwood" at Rev. 8:11—which she might have traced back to the Psalms or Jeremiah—a fascinating word used by George Herbert in "Repentance" and by Rossetti herself in the purgation scene of "Goblin Market,"

> Her lips began to scorch,
> That juice was wormwood to her tongue,
> She loathed the feast.   (*CP*, 1:24; 493–95)

Instead she pursues simple and generic terms which, because they occur in a wide range of contexts, permit her to liberate the meaning she seeks. She has designs on these words and wants them to help her mute this hectoring Apocalypse. Needless to say, a purposefully segmenting method permits her to lift passages discretely out of context and strip them of their original reference. Her appropriation of Job's aphorism on the inevitability of suffering, "Yet man is born unto trouble, as the sparks fly upward" (Job 5:7), provides a signal example of what can be gained by careful selection and realignment. Rossetti modifies the tenor, making the "sparks" a simile for aspiration toward the divine: "sparks fly upward scaling heaven by fire" (*FD*, 460). Incorporated into her sonnet on "the bottomless pit" at Rev. 20:3, Job's canonical image allows her to express a hope that for those who have set their faces "upward," the threatened "abyss / Is as mere nothing":

> So sparks fly upward scaling heaven by fire,
> Still mount and still attain not, yet draw nigher
> While they have being to their fountain flame.

To saints who mount, the bottomless abyss
  Is as mere nothing: they have set their face
  Onward and upward toward that blessed place
    Where man rejoices with his God. . . .   (*FD,* 460; *CP,*
                                                     2 : 182)

While neither expounding nor disclaiming a doctrine of hell, Rossetti takes biblical fire as "a figure" for meditation and manages, by orthodox means, to soften the threat of damnation (*FD,* 460).[15]

The single most striking aspect of *The Face of the Deep* is that, like the *Vita nuova,* it is a formal hybrid. In an extraordinary feat of devotion and presumption, Rossetti gives her poems a place within the larger verbal structure of commentary and canonical text; the 403 verses of John's 22 chapters share space with 210 lyrics by Rossetti. The brazenness of aligning prophecy and her own poetry, of suggesting an affinity between John's divine prompting and her own aesthetic inspiration, is protectively obscured by the modest diligence of her prose. A brief example from Rev. 3 will show how she cites a verse, then isolates a single clause and works through her sequence of text-prose-poem.

11. Behold, I come quickly: hold that fast which thou hast, that no man take thy crown.

"Behold, I come quickly."—But some man would answer Lord, sayest Thou that Thou comest quickly Who all these eighteen hundred years hast not come? Well may we pray that we may interpret.

Christ's blessed words are truth, sending forth wisdom by unnumbered channels. For He uses many seasons and modes of coming, besides and before that final coming when every eye shall see Him. To some exalted souls He has come ere now in vision and special revelation. To all His brethren down to the poorest and hungriest He comes, or is ready to come, in the Blessed Sacrament of His Body and Blood. To every man who loves Him and keeps His words He comes beyond the world's comprehension and makes His abode with him (*see* St. John xiv. 22, 23).[16] To His beloved He comes in their death whereby they go to Him. In any or in all of these ways we believe and are sure that He kept faith with His faithful Philadelphians.

On the other hand not the creature of time but only the Lord of time and eternity can pronounce on what is or is not *quickly* brought to pass. At eighteen we think a year long, at eighty we think it short: what terminable duration would seem long to us, what such duration would not seem short, if we had already passed out of time into eternity? Wherefore He alone Who saith "quickly" can define quickly.

O Gracious Lord Christ, Who lovest Thine elect with an ever-lasting love, keep us, I pray Thee, peaceful and trustful in our due ignorance until the day break and the shadows flee away.

> Oh knell of a passing time,
> Will it never cease to chime?
> Oh stir of the tedious sea,
> Will it never cease to be?
> Yea, when night and when day,
> Moon and sun pass away.

> Surely the sun burns low,
> The moon makes ready to go,
> Broad ocean ripples to waste,
> Time is running in haste,
> Night is numbered, and day
> Numbered to pass away.   (*FD*, 120–21)

Rossetti's method is to fend off the literalist's complaint about "all these eighteen hundred years" with a literalism of her own. First she glosses the word "come," carefully tracing its uses as these vary in application from external to inward manifestation: Christ comes in vision, in the sacrament, in life and at death to those who love him. She corroborates the verb's semantic richness with an allusion to Christ's own use of it at the Last Supper (John 14:23). Her sentence "He comes beyond the world's comprehension" tactfully conflates an uncomprehending apostle's question with Christ's answer so that readers who consult the gospel—and Rossetti's directive to "*see* St. John" virtually inscribes such readerly activity—will find an inference about the vice of skepticism. For the word "quickly," she provides a rather charming reminder of an eighteen-year-old's or an eighty-year-old's eager misperception of time. It is perhaps relevant to recall that as a young woman, Rossetti's own sense of time's dragging oppressiveness found expression in lines that would appear in *The Germ.* "A Pause of Thought," dated February 14, 1848, is impatiently unresigned to the need for patience:

> And hope deferred made my heart sick in truth:
> But years must pass before a hope of youth
>   Is resigned utterly.   (*CP,* 1:51)

And while still in her teens she wrote a "Song" lamenting the desynchronizing effect of an obscure grief that leaves the singer "old before my time" (*CP,* 1:40). Now, four decades later, youth's misunderstanding of duration provides an analogy for all humanity's time-bound restiveness and its possible abatement. So she prays for trust and adds her poem. To resume her meditation, she isolates the next scriptural clause, "hold that fast which thou hast," then adds more commentary and another poem.

"Oh knell of a passing time" was discussed above, and it is interesting to see how its import differs in its two published contexts. To the reader who comes upon it latterly in Rossetti's collection of poems, the discomfort recorded seems endemic to the human condition, for as James Merrill brilliantly says of poets' abstractions, "when we say 'Time' we mean ourselves." In *Verses,* as time's wearing depredations are lamented, the uncertain origin of the responding "yea" and "Surely" keeps the poem properly open to the tension between exhaustion and the assurance that exhaustion will end. On its prior appearance in *The Face of the Deep,* however, it is precisely this openness that is foreclosed by the glossing commentary. The temporal-eternal polarity established in Rossetti's meditation instructs the reader to fault human restlessness as a failure of trust while the included prayer fends off any sense of ambiguity in the poem's structure: the reiterated question, "Will it never cease?" is pre-interpreted as an expression of "our due ignorance" and the answering "Yea" becomes the Lord's graciously corrective reply. From the divine perspective "time *is* running in haste" and the firm "yea . . . surely" refutes humanly subjective misunderstanding. Such an overdetermined interpretation is welcome to some readers but a problem for those who prefer a poetry that acknowledges without rebuking humankind's temporal discontent. Eventually—and fortunately—when the poems have accomplished their devotional purpose in *The Face of the Deep,* Rossetti liberates them from her prose, entrusting them to readers who develop weak or strong readings according to their own lights. As we shall see,

Rossetti arranges the *Verses* in a way that celebrates her medium and the richness of poems *as* poems.[17]

The Face of the Deep is both a focused and a sprawling project. Rossetti's narrowing of attention to individual verses opens the text to the play of solemnly quirky associations and enables her to decant various worries about contemporary culture. Like many a writer before and after her, she is alarmed about what her contemporaries read. Wordsworth set a famous example in the "Preface" to *Lyrical Ballads* by complaining that "frantic novels," "extravagant stories in verse," and newspaper reports of "extraordinary" incidents have a blunting effect on the "discriminating powers of the mind." Rossetti suspects that the danger extends to the soul as well and suggests that "it becomes a matter of conscience what poems and novels to read, and how much of the current news of the day" (*FD*, 76). While she never mounts a coherently historical—and certainly not a political—interpretation of John's vision, she does comment on what she takes to be "ominous" signs of the times (*FD*, 243). Apocalyptic commentary, as Steven Goldsmith observes in *Unbuilding Jerusalem,* virtually requires the author to complain in more or less "cranky" and antithetical fashion "about the degenerate state" of contemporary affairs.[18]

In keeping, then, with her chosen genre, Rossetti offers scattered remarks on what she vaguely calls modern "women's self-assertion" (*FD*, 409). The utter conventionality of her notion of gender relations has been a cause of regret and resentment as well as protectively sympathetic interpretation by recent critics. Sharon Smulders explains that "for Rossetti, enfranchisement and equality were spiritual rather than temporal objectives," and she virtually assures women who are "subordinate on earth" that they will "profit from the reversal prefigured" in Luke 14:10, i.e., those who sit in "the lowest room" will be summoned to "go up higher." Smulders concludes that "Rossetti's conservatism is curiously revolutionary," though her use of "curiously" admits to the strain in her argument. Diane D'Amico's ampler account begins with the "public stand" Rossetti takes in 1889 when she allows her name to appear among the signatories to "An Appeal against Female Suffrage," published in the journal *Nineteenth Century.* Once again, the Rossettian distinction between social and spiritual subordination, or, in D'Amico's words, the belief that women will be equal with men in "a time and place beyond the world of exile," is said to mitigate what otherwise seems to be a "reactionary" view of women's rights. Such analyses may be thought to concede as much as they contest, and in any case, even the staunchest appreciation of what Hobbs chooses to call Rossetti's "startling revision of gender roles" can do little to make certain of her pronouncements palatable. Rossetti exasperates with the invidiousness of her comparison crediting men with "keener, tougher, more work-worthy gifts" than women and the sourness of her explanation that curiosity is "a feminine weak point inviting temptation, and doubly likely to facilitate a fall when to indulge it woman affects independence" (*FD*, 76, 520). We are left to conclude that a great poet need not be a particularly adventurous social thinker and perhaps ruefully concede that she cannot or need not prefigure us. At the same time, however, Rossetti confronts the reality of biblical misogyny and gamely attempts to take the sting out of the lesson that "we women may elicit" from religious tradition (*FD*, 416). Faced with the legacy of Eve's "lapse," Jezebel's prophetic "pretensions," and the apocalyptic prostitute's "transcendent wickedness," Rossetti still manages to find scrupulously precise biblical authority for women's positive role in the world (*FD*, 310, 76, 416). "Woman" may often figure as the temptress, but this does not presume her to be incapable of good; for "in the Bible," Rossetti explains as she makes a typical move from image to word, "the word *tempt* (or its derivatives) is used in a good or in an evil sense, according to the agent or to the object aimed at" (*FD*, 358).[19]

As a conservative, practicing Anglican, Rossetti is wary of secularism in all its forms, whether manifested as the declining and "chilled" observance of the Sabbath, the degrading of charitable giving to a mere "investment," or the latter-day fascination with mesmerism, hypnotism, and that spiritualism "which is not spirituality" (*FD*, 243, 337). Regarding this last, Rossetti tactfully allows it to go unmentioned that in the 1860s her two brothers attempted to retrieve what F. D. Maurice, in his *Lectures on the Apocalypse,* scorns as "mock messages from the departed." At the time, she responded to Gabriel's report on a seance with typically firm resistance: "To me the whole subject is awful and mysterious: though, in spite of my hopeless inability to conceive a clue to the source of sundry manifestations, I still hope simple imposture may be the missing key:—I hope it, at least, so far as the hope is not uncharitable" (*L*, 1 : 209). The strongest disapproval in *The Face of the Deep* is aimed, not surprisingly, at the indifference of fellow Christians "who stand callous amidst the fears, torments, miseries of others" (*FD*, 418). Parenthetically, we might mention Rossetti's own efforts, in later years, for the relief of indigent women; the famous letter to Swinburne in which she describes herself as "an escaped Governess" is, in fact, an appeal on behalf of an applicant for a pension from the Governesses Benevolent Institution (*L*, 3:231). Rossetti knows, as Auden will later say, that everyone "turns away / Quite leisurely" from another's "disaster," and so she specifically praises those activists who "all but enter within the vortex of evil" to do "rescue work" (*FD*, 418). Activism has its limits, however, and as a woman true to her class, Rossetti cringes whenever political agitation goes beyond peaceful petitioning or the organizing of relief aid. When commenting on the "recent troubles in Ireland" and the "strikes and unions" in England, she condemns the "terrorism resorted to" as a rehearsal "on a minor scale" of the last days' disruptions (*FD*, 349). We might note that in the nineteenth century, the word "terrorism" alludes to the French Revolution, as in "the terrorism of the Jacobins" (*OED*), but it comes to be used for all forms of intimidation, from the "boycotting" practiced during the Irish land agitation of 1880s (*FD*, 349) to the London Dock Strike of 1889, which, while signally important in the history of collective bargaining, involved violence between strikers and strikebreakers. Given this history, Rossetti's use of the word "minor" (rehearsal "on a minor scale") may be significant, for it shows that she is not heavily invested in reactionary class-antagonism or inclined to rant about growing social chaos. It is indicative of her true concern that none of the poems in *Face of the Deep* deal topically with the social evils she mentions. Sensing perhaps that her prose strays too far into mere opinion and finding herself beyond the range of her reticent lyric voice, she closes off such passages without a culminating or strictly relevant poem.[20]

Another look at the text-prose-poem alignments shows that while the times may be distressing, the text of Revelation is, to her, the truly frightening phenomenon. Her piecemeal method aims to localize and her commentary to master the anxiety triggered by "these appalling revelations" (*FD*, 335). Over and again, her glosses work to minimize apocalyptic threats so that her poems can then replace harrowing fear with subtler feelings. It is worth remembering that even a high degree of literary sophistication is not incompatible with dread of the "second death" foretold so insistently in Revelation. Confronted with lurid calls to repent and frequent warnings of damnation, Rossetti is on the alert to extract every bit of consolation and scrap of a hint, however implausible, concerning the extent of divine mercy. Thus she responds to an utterly formulaic adoration passage in which all creation is said to praise God—"every creature which is in heaven, and on the earth, and under the earth, and such as are in the sea" (Rev. 5:13)—as if it were a factual report on the "absolute unanimity amongst all creatures" (*FD*, 189). Since the vision presents all "in company" with each other, she strains for the inference that none are predestined to damnation:

> whoever conscientiously and unflinchingly puts and keeps himself in harmony with this text, must find that for practical purposes even predestination itself is shorn of difficulties and terrors. For here we behold things transitory in company with things permanent uplifting praises; the former utilizing for praise the only time they have; the latter for identical praise anticipating the eternity which awaits them. This is to take our Master at His word when He said: "Take therefore no thought for the morrow: for the morrow shall take thought for the things of itself." (*FD*, 190)

Drawing her last phrase from the Sermon on the Mount (Matt. 6:34), Rossetti attempts to bring together the warnings of the fiery visionary with the reassurances of his loving master. As modern Bible scholars concede, such alignment is the signal challenge John's text poses: his "harsh and demanding" warnings that evildoers will be "condemned to eternal torment" has a far different impact from the exhortation by Jesus to love one's enemies and his own practice of healing and forgiving. After wending her way through the ensuing glosses on Rev. 5:13, Rossetti returns to the thought of "absolute unanimity" among the praise-giving creatures and imagines a chant that includes all creation. Her poem's elegant redundancy as it hymns their hymn is itself a form of joyous excess in a poem about "measureless" joy:

> Voices from above and from beneath,
>   Voices of creation near and far,
>   Voices out of life and out of death,
>   Out of measureless space,
>   Sun, moon, star,
>   In oneness of contentment offering praise.

> Heaven and earth and sea jubilant,
>   Jubilant all things that dwell therein;
> Filled to fullest overflow they chant,
>   Still roll onward, swell,
>   Still begin,
>   Never flagging praise interminable.   (*FD,* 191; *CP,* 2:269)

There is excess, too, in the repetition of "jubilant" and in the happy proliferation of negatives, "Never flagging" and "interminable." There is
pleasure in the contraction of the stanzas to three-syllable lines that iso-
late the "Sun, moon, star" amid cosmic/poetic space and constrain the
unstoppable song so that the reader may *feel* it "still begin." In each stanza
the short verse gauges the following pentameter's expansion so that it
manifests something of the "unflagging" pulsation of the praise it praises.
In celebrating creation's rolling, swelling "chant," Rossetti frees herself
to acknowledge the harmonious "overflow" of feelings into language.
The final stanza, as noted earlier, instructs the reader to eschew apocalyptic fear and participate "today" in the cosmic orison:

> Thou who must fall silent in a while,
>   Chant thy sweetest, gladdest, best, at once;
> Sun thyself today, keep peace and smile;
>   By love upward send
>   Orisons,
>   Accounting love thy lot and love thine end.

The tranquil joy of this "accounting" is, of course, a hard thing to hold
on to; seventeen more chapters of Revelation will strain and severely test
the ability to "keep peace and smile." It has been said that "Knowledge
is a continual process of knowing, Love of loving," and the same should
be said of spiritual hope. Eric Griffiths puts the matter precisely when
he remarks that the "calm" such a poem achieves "is not something
possessed once and for all, but will have to be worked towards again,
patience being an incessant rehearsal of itself."[21]

    At the opening of the seventh seal, in one of Revelation's typically cat-
aclysmic visions, a third of earth's trees and grass are burnt up; a third of
the sea becomes blood, its creatures die and ships sink; a third of all rivers
and fountains are made bitterly poisonous to men. Finally, there is mayhem in the sky: "And the fourth angel sounded, and the third part of the
sun was smitten, and the third part of the moon, and the third part of the

stars; so as the third part of them was darkened, and the day shone not for a third part of it, and the night likewise" (Rev. 8:12). In an attempt to mitigate the ferocity of this cosmos-smashing chapter, Rossetti focuses on the *limited* extent of the sky's damage! With Pauline hints about divine "long-suffering" and urgings to "redeem the time," she assesses the devastation, finds "*two*-thirds left," and takes heart (Col. 1:11; Eph. 5:16; *FD*, 254–55). Accusing herself of having "long dwelt on the threat" and "too long overlooked the promise," she resolves to remain hopeful until absolutely all "brightness is diminished" (*FD*, 254–55). Even as a mathematical allegory, this resolve to ignore partial annihilation is absurd; but as a step in the meditation process it moves far enough away from John's text to allow access to legitimately devotional feelings. In a telling passage cited later in the book, the psalmist admits to quailing dread of God's wrath and pleads, "while I suffer thy terrors I am distracted" (Ps. 88:15; *FD*, 485). This emotional logic is the key to Rossetti's handling of the present passage; extreme fear of the Lord must and does give way to the calmer vigilance of true spirituality. The meditation culminates with the sonnet noted earlier, the beautifully sad lament at the dimming of the sun's "exuberant lustre" and the pallor of a "morning that is scarcely morn" (*CP*, 2:252). The strength of the poem is that its grief is prelude to a "softly protesting" reminder that "light" will shine "full" in the New Jerusalem.

Though the poems in *The Face of the Deep* work resourcefully to contain Revelation's horrifying implications, John's text still enmeshes them in its nightmarish scenarios. In obvious and not-so-obvious ways, the generic mixing has some regrettable consequences. The famous difficulty of the canonical material creates a predisposition to regard the poems as virtual prose and to focus on their contribution, however evasive, to the prophecy's abstractable meaning. As discussed earlier with the example of "Whitsun Eve" (*CP*, 2:233), John's hectoring text sometimes completely overdetermines the direction a poem takes and damages it at the moment of its inception. More typically, the harm occurs at the reading stage when the conjoined Scripture and commentary have a tendency to dispel valuable ambiguities of the kind found in "Oh knell of a passing time" and to overwhelm subtle tonalities (*CP*, 2:274). In context, the fine small courage of "One woe is past," the "meek" rebound after a "blast" of "pain and fear," is almost ludicrously incommensurate with the visitation of Apollyon's locust horde, which is the woe Revelation 9:12 actually enumerates (*FD*, 265).

> And there came out of the smoke locusts upon the earth: and unto them was given power, as the scorpions of the earth have power. And it was commanded them that they should not hurt the grass of the earth, neither any green thing, neither any tree; but only those men which have not the seal of God in their foreheads. And to them it was given that they should not kill them, but that they should be tormented five months: and their torment was as the torment of a scorpion, when he striketh a man. And in those days shall men seek death, and shall not find it; and shall desire to die, and death shall flee from them.   (Rev. 9:3–6)

The idea of a torment so agonizing that its victims yearn for death absolutely precludes stratagems for endurance and Rossetti's poem cannot effectively absorb or displace such ominous cruelty. Comparable damage is inflicted on many of the poems, though it would be a heart-wearying task to spell out the enfeebled readings thus produced. Attention might be called, however, to the way the prose *as prose* casts a lingering pall that prevents full engagement with the medium of poetry per se. The reader who is immersed in John's cryptic formulations and Rossetti's densely packed glosses is repeatedly disconcerted by syntactical strangeness and the nearly physical strain of the book's glaring and frequent disjunctions. Anyone committed to penetrating this challenging text-and-commentary is induced to forget what some readers, distracted by topicality, are already too likely to forget, viz., that poetry does not accomplish its ends by the same means as prose. Its primary concern is not to arrange an argument but to order the flow of emotions as these are felt in the timing of syllables and verses, the pacing of rhymes, and the overall momentum of stanzas. Palpably and irreparably, the congested ongoingness of *The Face of the Deep* makes an onerous imposition on the rhythms of Rossetti's lyrics. James Merrill, author of the epic trilogy *The Changing Light at Sandover,* once described prose as "a mildly nightmarish medium, to which *there is no end . . .* and only at rare and irregular intervals affording that least pause in flight." What Merrill means with his pun is that the pause is poetry's essential feature; ranging from the "least" possible hesitation between paired stresses to the stretch across line breaks. The "pause" is Merrill's metonym for tempo, for the momentum of the poem as a whole including the pace of individual lines and the gradual or sudden halt that confers closure. It is precisely the reader's sensitivity to poetry's emphatic or faint or nearly subliminal pausing that is numbed by the demands of John's long and Rossetti's even longer prose discourse. With the publication of *Verses,* the poems escape the commentary's "nightmarish medium."[22]

In the final pages of *The Face of the Deep,* Rossetti insists that the full meaning of Revelation still eludes her and that, once again, her "understanding breaks down" (*FD,* 547). At the same time, however, it is clear that her "anxious ignorance" has dissipated and that the book's terrors are no longer a persecution (*FD,* 342). Never expecting to decipher the vision's "occult unfulfilled signification" but only to find the "consolatoriness" hidden there, her commentary comes to a calmly prayerful close (*FD,* 309, 237). She has succeeded in finding each and every "loophole of hope" the sacred text allows (*FD,* 260). A little over a year later, and while the commentary is well on its way to multiple reprintings, Rossetti brings out the collected *Verses* of 1893. This, her last book, is a kind of writer's testimonial declaring that though she has published a considerable amount of prose, her commitment, first and last, is to poetry. The reader can be glad of this book in which the best of the poems, now stripped of their prose encumbrances, recover something of the primacy of attention they had for Rossetti when she was writing them. Absorption in the aesthetic, which poets have variously described as absolute, exhilarating, passionate, "the pure case of the human attempt to find in consciousness freedom from consciousness," is what enabled her to endure her long immersion in Revelation. Now that her poems are free to *be* poems, Rossetti clusters them in thematic groups that call attention to their differences *as* poems and to the virtuosity prompted by successive new formal ideas. A profession of faith in her art, the volume asks us to understand that for her the writing of these poems is every bit as dignified and spiritual as the themes they take up.[23]

A brief look at one pair will indicate what is gained when poem adjoins poem. The first, "Our Mothers, lovely women pitiful," originally appears in the comment on the infamous Mother of Harlots at Revelation 17 : 4 – 5. Temporarily overwhelmed by the depiction of sin's own "filthiness," Rossetti mounts a startlingly uncharacteristic diatribe complete with a reference to the blood-sucking horseleech's daughters (Prov. 31 : 10) and verses from Proverbs warning "woman against herself" (*FD,* 400). Unfortunately, this vigorous pastiche allows Rossetti insufficient maneuverability to separate the allegorical Mother and her evil scriptural daughters from women in general. Alarmed at the possibility Palazzo acknowledges, i.e., that Rossetti "seems to be reiterating the very victimisation and blatant misogyny which angers modern feminist theologians," one welcomes as a general proposition Antony Harrison's view that a Rossettian lapse into patriarchal vilification entails an implicit rejection of its misogyny. Citing an example from her *Goblin Market* volume, Harrison finds Rossetti using such material to condemn "materialism, hedonism, and false amatory ideologies" while at the same time displaying traditionally "degraded constructions of woman's nature" and exposing them as crude stereotypes. In this particular section of *The Face of the Deep* Rossetti most certainly balks at the ugliness of what she assembles and, without even attempting a transitional comment, inserts her sonnet "Our Mothers, lovely women pitiful" (*FD,* 401). An elegy to the mothers and sisters whose gracious lives provide an "unforgotten memory" of what can be "learned in life's sufficient school," this lyric counterexample contests, if only obliquely, the tendency of biblical authors to disparage women (*CP,* 2:292). In *Verses,* of course, the Great Whore is nowhere in sight and hostile portrayals of women are not an immediate concern; there the sonnet is followed by another, better elegy, "Safe where I cannot lie yet." In *The Face of the Deep,* this second poem accompanies Revelation 6:7, the opening of the fourth seal (the signal that beckons Death on a pale horse), and a grisly apostrophe hailing "corruption" and "the worm" as "my father . . . my mother, and my sister" (Job 17:14). Such kinship prompts Rossetti to express a humble "trust that some we love rest safely in Paradise," and her poem immediately takes up the word "safe" (*FD,* 205). Though its lovely little quintains are meant to dispel the ghastliness of the biblical material, the attempt, needless to say, is not altogether successful.[24]

Once these poems are moved to *Verses,* not only do they shed their onerous expository burdens, they become linked expressions of affection for the cherished dead. The tenderness of the sonnet becomes visible as it imagines humanly flawed saints encouraging their faltering kinswoman: "Hope as we hoped, despite our slips and scathe, / Fearful in joy and confident in dule" (*CP,* 2:292). The slight oddity of their diction, which owes something to Arthurian romance and medieval balladry, serves to locate their kindly exhortation in a verbal realm suggestive (on the analogy between earlier and higher) of heavenly origin. The following elegy, which is spoken from earth, reciprocates this warm regard, but in an

utterly different style. With all the spareness of bereavement, it longingly
remembers the loved dead:

> Safe where I cannot lie yet,
>   Safe where I hope to lie too,
> Safe from the fume and the fret;
>   You, and you,
> Whom I never forget.   (*CP,* 2:292)

The magical intimacy of these lines is achieved without a single particularizing detail, not even the previous poem's kinship terms. Instead there
are the well-paced pronouns suggesting that the speaker need only shift
her remembering glance to signal the loved addressee. The comma does
it all; separating the words "you, and you," it allows the merest pause for
turning the head or the mind's eye from one "you" to another. The second stanza builds a protective list of sensations manqué, as in "Dream-
Land," only now they portend both safety and the return of sentience
(*CP,* 1:27). Lilting and alliterated, the stanza glides along until slowed by
paired stresses at the word "wait":

> Safe from the frost and the snow,
>   Safe from the storm and the sun,
> Safe where the séeds wáit to grow
>   One by one
> And to come back in blow.

The thought must "wait," as do the seeds, for the completion deferred
until the absolutely last word and the emblematic blooming in eternity.
The vowel sounds of "seeds wait to grow" shift from a high frontal to
low back as the thought goes underground, while the running-on of the
line mimes the pushing growth it describes. This time the unhesitating
pace of "one by one" (without comma) conveys the sense of proliferation: each and every one, one after another after another. The final line
adds a further little acoustic surprise as the word "back" recedes to the
back of the mouth and then brings the "b" forward to shape the awaited
"blow." By its gently solemn playfulness, the lyric corroborates the
speaker's affection for the preceding sonnet's "unforgotten" women. Together the two poems dramatize the reach of love's reminiscence.[25]

Rossetti knows a great deal about loss and frailty and the plain fact that life is often unrewarding. When the irritable English poet Philip Larkin grumbled to his twentieth-century interviewer that "it is very much easier to imagine happiness than to experience it," he quoted Rossetti to illustrate his own discontent, "Life, and the world, and mine own self, are changed / For a dream's sake," testifying to the resonance of "Mirage" and to the impact of its ever-so-mild verb "changed" (*CP*, 1:56). Rossetti takes bitter disappointment as her topic without being embittered and tells of silent hopelessness in an evocative language that lodges itself permanently in the reader's memory. The poem was written at one of Rossetti's creative peaks, between the completion and publication of "Goblin Market," but it has something like the blended honesty and understatement that characterize the best work of her later years. In each of her books, Rossetti writes poignantly of comfortless isolation, imperfect affections, and the affliction that in her early devotional poems goes by the name of weariness. Over the years, she repeatedly summons the courage that is only fitfully adequate to the "gnawing pain" of accumulating sorrows; "Parting after parting" has taught her that patience is not indomitable and consolation only sporadic and fleeting (*CP*, 2:277). Nonetheless, Rossetti knows that poetry recovers the intensity that helps one live and, as McClatchy so beautifully says, that it "raises the pitch and status" of the human cry. Her protracted involvement with John of Patmos's eschatological prophecy, whatever its elusive meanings, plainly stimulates her own tendency to imagine life viewed-from-the-end. His fierce vision of all creation as deathstruck draws her out of whatever dark silence tempts her, and she rallies like the heliotropic flowers in her spring roundel. She is stirred to lament spiritual dullness as the cruelly inflicted "stripes" of divine abandonment and to protest wasting tedium with the matching restlessness of her poem's formal agitation. In a broad range of voices and attitudes she wails clamorously with a "wail of loss," beckons pain with the tenderest of love songs, and makes mock of dolefulness. One of her favorite biblical passages, the protesting verse "Thou hast asked a hard thing," might be taken as her motto, not as a feeble complaint but as a clear-sighted statement of fact and a way of bracing for the effort life requires (2 Kings 2). Faced again and again with the reality of hard things, she responds with a supple resilience that locates the precise moment of courageous rebound from woe, that scrounges for cheer in sensations of "remotest heat," and that finds exhilaration in winter's "keenness." All the while, and with a wonderful tenaciousness, she refuses to give up on the chance of joy and allows gladness to ripple through her poems with speeding rhythm and flamboyant language. Most important, she has the true artist's talent for self-forgetfulness amid a paradoxically liberating absorption in the individual poem. *Verses* attests by its scrupulous and exquisite variations on lyric form that the hard things *are* hard and that art gives repeated and time-resistant access to a necessary harmony, courage, and clarity. Rossetti's last book is a crucial endorsement of poetry as a way of life.[26]

Notes

INTRODUCTION

1. Philip Larkin, "The Trees," in *Collected Poems,* ed. Anthony Thwaite (London: Faber, 1988), 166.

2. Gosse is cited in Mary Arseneau's introduction to *The Culture of Christina Rossetti: Female Poetics and Victorian Contexts,* ed. Mary Arseneau, Antony H. Harrison, and Lorraine Janzen Kooistra (Athens: Ohio Univ. Press, 1999), xviii. For "when . . . flagged," see Marya Zaturenska, *Christina Rossetti: A Portrait with Background* (1949; New York: Macmillan, 1970), 274. Sandra M. Gilbert and Susan Gubar, *The Madwoman in the Attic: The Woman Writer and the Nineteenth-Century Literary Imagination* (New Haven, Conn.: Yale Univ. Press, 1979), 558.

3. Heather Dubrow, *Echoes of Desire: English Petrarchism and Its Counterdiscourses* (Ithaca, N.Y.: Cornell Univ. Press, 1995), 3, 8. In her overall view of Petrarchism, Dubrow diverges from those who narrowly identify "the Petrarchan lover with the subservient and often unsuccessful candidate for patronage" or who encapsulate "Petrarchism as a successful assertion of male power and the concomitant erasure of the female" (10).

4. Lawrence Lipking, *Abandoned Women and Poetic Tradition* (Chicago: Univ. of Chicago Press, 1988), 82, 83, 86–87, 81. Lipking traces the evolution in these translations of Sappho's representation as a suicidal poet.

5. Stephen Booth, *Precious Nonsense: The Gettysburg Address, Ben Jonson's Epitaphs on His Children, and Twelfth Night* (Berkeley: Univ. of California Press, 1998); see the analysis of "Little Boy Blue" (4–9), "monumentally clumsy" and "Home on the Range" (6), "pertinence . . . antelope" (7), and "process . . . implies" (9).

6. For "ringing melody . . . heart," see Henry Buxton Forman, "Criticisms on Contemporaries," qtd. in Lona Mosk Packer, *Christina Rossetti* (Berkeley: Univ. of California Press, 1963), 259–60. Lorraine Janzen Kooistra, *Christina Rossetti and Illustration: A Publishing History* (Athens: Ohio Univ. Press, 2002), 83 and 283 n. 16; also *LDGR,* 2:586. Virginia Woolf, "I Am Christina Rossetti," in *The Second Common Reader* (New York: Harcourt, 1932), 265.

7. Packer, *Christina Rossetti,* 114–15. Jan Marsh, *Christina Rossetti: A Writer's Life* (New York: Viking, 1995), 207. For "love . . . saviour," see Kathleen Jones, *Learning Not to Be First: The Life of Christina Rossetti* (Gloucestershire: Windrush Press, 1991), 81.

Allison Chapman, *The Afterlife of Christina Rossetti* (New York: St. Martin's Press, 2000), 72, and William Michael Rossetti, *PW,* 481.

8. Thomas Bewick, *A History of British Birds,* 2 vols. (London: Longman, 1847), 1:140. "The Gardener's Daughter," *The Poems of Tennyson,* ed. Christopher Ricks (London: Longman, 1969), 513. The *Oxford English Dictionary* entry for *halcyon* cites Philemon Holland's 1601 translation of Pliny: "They lay and sit about mid-winter . . . and the time whiles they are broodie, is called the halcyon daies: for during that season the sea is calm and navigable, especially in the coast of Sicilie."

9. Catherine Belsey, *Desire: Love Stories in Western Culture* (Oxford: Blackwell, 1994).

10. *Gerard Manley Hopkins: Selected Letters,* ed. Catherine Phillips (Oxford: Clarendon, 1990), 26.

11. For "the foundation . . . happiness," see Belsey, *Desire,* 3. Michael Schmidt, *Lives of the Poets* (New York: Knopf, 1999), 479. Belsey, *Desire,* 15.

12. Jeff Nunokawa, *Tame Passions of Wilde: The Styles of Manageable Desire* (Princeton, N.J.: Princeton Univ. Press, 2003), 29. The passage cited refers to Oscar Wilde's career, a trajectory Nunokawa reconstructs as an "exodus story." Robert Hass, *Twentieth Century Pleasures: Prose on Poetry* (New York: Ecco, 1984), 16, 58.

ONE   Questions of Desire in *Goblin Market and Other Poems*

1. Jerome J. McGann, "Christina Rossetti's Poems: A New Edition and a Revaluation," *Victorian Studies* 23, no. 2 (1980): 239; Antony H. Harrison, *Victorian Poetry* 32, nos. 3–4 (1994): 204; Arseneau, *Culture of Christina Rossetti,* xxiii. Kooistra, *Christina Rossetti and Illustration,* 247.

2. See Kooistra's discussion of illustrated editions and children's editions (*Christina Rossetti and Illustration,* 206, 207) and her illuminating account of Rossetti's inclusion in school textbooks (195–212). The anthologists' comments are by Jerome Hamilton Buckley, ed., *Poetry of the Victorian Period,* 3rd ed. (Glenview, Ill.: Scott, Foresman, 1965), v, and Cecil Y. Lang, ed., *The Pre-Raphaelites and Their Circle,* 2nd ed. (Chicago: Univ. of Chicago Press, 1975), 505. Gilbert and Gubar, *Madwoman in the Attic,* 564–75. The scholarly studies alluded to are Deborah Ann Thompson, "Anorexia as a Lived Trope: Christina Rossetti's 'Goblin Market,'" *Mosaic* 24, nos. 3–4 (1991): 89–106; Mary Wilson Carpenter, "'Eat me, drink me, love me': The Consumable Female Body in Christina Rossetti's *Goblin Market,*" *Victorian Poetry* 29, no. 4 (1991): 415–34; Diane D'Amico, *Christina Rossetti: Faith, Gender, and Time* (Baton Rouge: Louisiana State Univ. Press, 1999), 68–83, 95, 104–8; Richard Menke, "The Political Economy of Fruit," in *Culture of Christina Rossetti,* 105–36; and Herbert F. Tucker, "Rossetti's Goblin Marketing: Sweet to Tongue and Sound to Eye," *Representations* 82 (2003): 117–33. On the illustrations by Craft and Bolton, see Kooistra, *Christina Rossetti and Illustration,* 241–44 and plates 13, 14.

3. Adam Phillips provides an account of infant pleasure in *The Beast in the Nursery* (New York: Pantheon, 1998), 56. On "mouth-joy," see Donald Hall, "How to Peel a Poem," *Harpers* (Sept. 1999), where he explains, while commenting on a poem by Thomas Hardy, that "we read poems with our mouths, not with our eyes, not with our ears, not with our intelligences. And this is a poem with enormous mouth-joy" (47).

4. For another use, with an alternative spelling as "balked desire," see Rossetti's undated "A Ballad of Boding" (*CP,* 2:79). While it is certain that Dante Gabriel Rossetti gave "Goblin Market" its title, his role in its revision must be inferred from Christina's note, dated Dec. 7, 1893, acknowledging "the general indebtedness of my first and second volumes to [Gabriel's] suggestive wit and revising hand" (*CP,* 1:234). Germaine Greer, *Slip-Shod Sibyls: Recognition, Rejection and the Woman Poet* (London: Penguin, 1995), ascribes all the "Goblin Market" emendations to Gabriel; while admiring these as "genuine revisions," Greer nonetheless objects to what she describes as Gabriel's "masterful attitude to the work of another" (382). It is not at all clear, however, how much Gabriel was involved in Christina's first book; documentary evidence credits him with two titles, "Cousin Kate" (*CP,* 1:239) and "At Home" (*LDGR,* 2:394), and a single line change in "House to Home" (*CP,* 1:263; 13). His role in preparing *The Prince's Progress* for publication is taken up in chapter 2.

5. Cora Kaplan, "The Indefinite Disclosed: Christina Rossetti and Emily Dickinson," in *Women Writing and Writing about Women,* ed. Mary Jacobus (London: Croom Helm, 1979), 67.

6. Ruskin's letter is dated "towards 20 January 1861" in *Ruskin: Rossetti: Preraphaelitism: Papers from 1854 to 1862,* ed. William Michael Rossetti (London: Allen, 1899), 258–59. For Coleridge's prefatory comment, see Coleridge, *Poetical Works,* ed. J. C. C. Mays (Princeton, N.J.: Princeton Univ. Press, 2001), 483. On ballad rhythm, see Derek Attridge, *The Rhythms of English Poetry* (New York: Longman 1982), 84–96.

7. U. C. Knoepflmacher, *Ventures into Childland: Victorians, Fairy Tales, and Femininity* (Chicago: Univ. of Chicago Press, 1998), 319–20; Knoepflmacher speculates that Rossetti's poem "affronted Ruskin in his self-appointed role as preserver of the desexualized femininity he associated with childhood" (320). Kooistra, *Christina Rossetti and Illustration,* discusses renderings of the kissing scene, noting that George Gershinowitz's watercolor "She kissed and kissed her with a hungry mouth," in a fine-art edition of *Goblin Market* (Boston: David R. Godine, 1981), was intended for "both adult and child" audiences (210 and plate 8).

8. For "insistent body," see Phillips, *Beast in the Nursery,* xiv. Isobel Armstrong, *Victorian Poetry: Poetry, Poetics and Politics* (London: Routledge, 1993), 350–51. Eric S. Robertson, *English Poetesses: A Series of Critical Biographies, with Illustrative Extracts* (London, 1883), 341. In 1883, when Robertson wrote that the transformation scene ends with Laura sinking into a "delicious dream," Rossetti, to whom he had sent preliminary copy, told him emphatically to "*see* original text!" (*L,* 3:157). Upon publication, Robertson removed the adjective and, evidently, revised his opinion of the poem.

9. See Kooistra, *Christina Rossetti and Illustration,* on "moral . . . sameness" (69), "historical particularity" (14), "transmission . . . place" (15), "dialogic" structure (68), and the frontispiece and title-page illustrations (66–75).

10. Matthew Campbell, *Rhythm and Will in Victorian Poetry* (New York: Cambridge Univ. Press, 1999), describes Rossetti's final litany as a "virtuoso exercise," noting that her multiple similes are actively "seeking for a means to describe the vigorous complexity" of a body that is "surrendering its agency"; he speculates that a sustained epic simile would have slowed Laura's "toppling" (56–57).

11. This line appears in "Lord Thomas and Fair Ellinor" just as the young lord informs the "Fair Ellinor, / That should have been his bride" of his impending marriage to another woman. See Thomas Percy, ed., *Reliques of Ancient English Poetry,* 3 vols. (Edinburgh, 1858), 3:67; 15–16.

12. On strains of desire, see Jeff Nunokawa's introduction to *Tame Passions of Wilde.* C. H. Sisson's characterization is from *Christina Rossetti: Selected Poems* (Manchester: Carcanet, 1984), 9; both Sisson and poet-editor Elizabeth Jennings in *A Choice of Christina Rossetti's Verse* (London: Faber, 1970) include the five poems under discussion.

13. William Wordsworth, "Preface to *Lyrical Ballads*" (1800), in *Lyrical Ballads, and Other Poems, 1797–1800,* ed. James Butler and Karen Green (Ithaca, N.Y.: Cornell Univ. Press, 1992), 756. "Remember," as scored by André Previn in his "String Quartet (With Soprano)," was premiered in New York City at Carnegie Hall on May 4, 2003, by Barbara Bonney and the Emerson String Quartet ("Quartets Inspired by a Poem and a Story," *New York Times,* May 8, 2003, Arts Section: E5).

14. Mill, "Thoughts on Poetry and Its Varieties," *Autobiography and Literary Essays by John Stuart Mill,* ed. John M. Robson and Jack Stillinger (Toronto: Univ. of Toronto Press, 1981), 348, 350 n., 351. Northrop Frye, *Anatomy of Criticism: Four Essays* (1957; Princeton, N.J.: Princeton Univ. Press, 1971), 366.

15. Herbert F. Tucker, in his influential essay "Dramatic Monologue and the Overhearing of Lyric," in *Lyric Poetry: Beyond New Criticism,* ed. Chaviva Hošek and Patricia Parker (Ithaca, N.Y.: Cornell Univ. Press, 1985), discusses the "voices of history and feeling" as he explores the "plot of lyricism resisted" in Browning's "My Last Duchess" and "Fra Lippo Lippi" (230, 231). For discussion of the space, silence, and meaning occasioned by a line break, see Jonathan Culler's chapter "Poetics of the Lyric," in *Structuralist Poetics: Structuralism, Linguistics, and the Study of Literature* (Ithaca, N.Y.: Cornell Univ. Press, 1975), 161–88, and Christopher Ricks's subtle essay titled "William Wordsworth 1: 'A Pure Organic Pleasure from the Lines,'" in *The Force of Poetry* (1984; Oxford: Clarendon, 2001), 89–116.

16. Florence Emily Hardy, *The Life of Thomas Hardy 1840–1928* (1962; repr., Hamden, Conn.: Archon Books, 1970), 209–10. Wordsworth, *Lyrical Ballads,* 755 n. Yeats, "In a Drawing Room," in *The Variorum Edition of the Poems of W. B. Yeats,* ed. Peter Allt and Russell K. Alspach (New York: Macmillan, 1977), 686.

17. On "musical expression," see William Michael Rossetti (*CGRFL,* 133). Louisa May Alcott's "Behind the Mask," adapted as *The Night Governess* by writer/composer Polly Pen, premiered at McCarter Theatre, Princeton University, May 2–21, 2000.

18. James William Johnson, "Lyric," *Princeton Encyclopedia of Poetry and Poetics,* ed. Alex Preminger, enl. ed. (Princeton, N.J.: Princeton Univ. Press, 1974). McGann, "Christina Rossetti's Poems," 239. Susan Conley provides an especially sensitive treatment of the amended "Echo" in "Rossetti's Cold Women: Irony and Liminal Fantasy in the Death Lyrics," in *Culture of Christina Rossetti,* noting the excision of a stanza on Hades and observing the technique whereby the speaker's "prolonged agony is captured in the present participles used as successive adjectives ('thirsting longing')"; in "the division at lines 10–11 of the pentameter line, slowing it down";

and in "the heavy finality of 'no more' and its double rhyme with 'slow door'" (279). Robert Pinsky, "A Man Goes into a Bar, See, and Recites: 'The Quality of Mercy Is Not Strained,'" *The New York Times Book Review,* Sept. 18, 1994, 16.

19. Comments on "A Triad" are drawn from several sources: "rage . . . existence," from Greer, *Slip-Shod Sibyls,* 372; "critique . . . illusion," from Marsh, *Christina Rossetti,* 185; "redolently feminine," from Margaret Reynolds, "Speaking Unlikeness: The Double Text in Christina Rossetti's 'After Death' and 'Remember,'" in *Culture of Christina Rossetti,* 5.

20. On the "generic . . . silence," see Jennifer A. Wagner-Lawlor, "The Pragmatics of Silence, and the Figuration of the Reader in Browning's Dramatic Monologues," *Victorian Poetry* 35, no. 3 (1997): 292.

21. Dubrow, *Echoes of Desire,* 86; Dubrow gives the example of Spenser's *Amoretti* 43, in which "the poet laments that his speech will only renew the lady's anger" (83).

22. For "a kind . . . kinship," see Janet Galligani Casey, "The Potential of Sisterhood: Christina Rossetti's 'Goblin Market,'" *Victorian Poetry* 29, no. 1 (1991): 70. For "protecting . . . unity," see Helena Michie, "'There Is No Friend Like a Sister': Sisterhood as Sexual Difference," *ELH* 56, no. 2 (1989): 404. Joseph Bristow, "'No Friend Like a Sister'?: Christina Rossetti's Female Kin," *Victorian Poetry* 33, no. 2 (1995): 272.

23. Bristow, "'No Friend Like a Sister,'" 273. Regarding Allingham's ballad collection, Gabriel mentions in 1854 that he and Elizabeth Siddal "are going to illustrate the Old Scottish Ballads which Allingham is editing for Routledge" (*LDGR,* 1:200). Dolores Rosenblum, *Christina Rossetti: The Poetry of Endurance* (Carbondale: Southern Illinois Univ. Press, 1986), 158–59.

24. Percy, *Reliques of Ancient English Poetry,* 3:105–7. Anne Carson, *Eros the Bittersweet* (1986; repr., Normal, Ill.: Dalkey, 1998), 117–22. Carson's brilliant study of Greek writing about love opens with Sappho's fragment 130, noting that the poem "is not recording the history of a love affair but the instant of desire" (4). Drawing on texts from Aeschylus through Xenophon, Carson examines the temporalities of love, both the inaugural, instantaneous "now" and the historied "then" of love's "linear enactments" (5).

25. For a vivid reading of the "The Convent Threshold," see John Schad, *Victorians in Theory: From Derrida to Browning* (Manchester: Manchester Univ. Press, 1999); Schad responds to the novice's bloodied bed linen at line 117 with a series of acute questions: "Is this the guilt of menstruation . . . of a 'scarlet' woman . . . of incest?" and he speculates, "If incest, this poem foretells a tale of guilt: the tale of Freudian psychoanalysis. Like Freud's early case-studies, the poem links the scene of incest to both the work of the unconscious . . . and such classic symptoms of hysteria as insomnia . . . and sobbing" (11).

26. Sharon Smulders, *Christina Rossetti Revisited* (New York: Twayne, 1996), 44.

27. For the "bony bird," see "The Gay Goss-Hawk," in *Sir Walter Scott's Minstrelsy of the Scottish Border,* ed. T. F. Henderson, 3 vols. (1902; Detroit: Singing Tree, 1968), 3:192.

28. Helena Michie, "The Battle for Sisterhood: Christina Rossetti's Strategies for Control in Her Sister Poems," *Journal of Pre-Raphaelite Studies* 3, no. 2 (1983): 38; see

also Rosenblum, *Christina Rossetti,* for the claim that "the rejected woman is always authentic" (161). Smulders, *Christina Rossetti Revisited,* 46. William Morris, *The Defence of Guenevere, and Other Poems,* ed. Margaret A. Lourie (New York: Garland, 1981), 149. Barbara Herrnstein Smith, *Poetic Closure: A Study of How Poems End* (Chicago: Univ. of Chicago Press, 1968), 34.

29. An intermediate sixteen-stanza version of "Maude Clare" appeared in *Once a Week* in 1859 and was, as Antony H. Harrison notes, Rossetti's first publishing success, preceding Macmillan's interest in her work by two years (*L,* 1:xxiii). For Harrison's account of the revisions, see *Christina Rossetti in Context* (Chapel Hill: Univ. of North Carolina Press, 1988), 4–8, 12. For "houses and lands" in "Lord Thomas and Fair Ellinor," see Percy, *Reliques of Ancient English Poetry,* 3:66; 9.

30. Dubrow, *Echoes of Desire,* 8.

31. Armstrong, *Victorian Poetry,* 352.

32. For "the risks . . . art," see Gilbert and Gubar, *Madwoman in the Attic,* 573; for "claim . . . poetry," see Catherine Maxwell, "Tasting the 'Fruit Forbidden': Gender, Intertextuality, and Christina Rossetti's 'Goblin Market,'" in *Culture of Christina Rossetti,* 83. McGann, "Christina Rossetti's Poems," 252.

33. Louise Glück, *Proofs and Theories: Essays on Poetry* (Hopewell, N.J.: Ecco, 1994), 25.

34. See W. David Shaw, *Victorians and Mystery: Crises of Representation* (Ithaca, N.Y.: Cornell Univ. Press, 1990), 262.

35. For the hypersensitivity of Tennyson's line, see James Richardson, *Vanishing Lives: Style and Self in Tennyson, D. G. Rossetti, Swinburne, and Yeats* (Charlottesville: Univ. Press of Virginia, 1988), 40. Arthur Hallam's essay "On Some of the Characteristics of Modern Poetry" is readily available in *The Broadview Anthology of Victorian Poetry and Poetic Theory,* ed. Thomas J. Collins and Vivienne J. Rundle (Peterborough, Ontario: Broadview, 1999); it characterizes Keats, Shelley, and Tennyson as "Poets of Sensation" (1192, 1195). For "the impression . . . senses," see W. B. Yeats, "Art and Ideas" (qtd. in Harold Bloom, *The Ringers in the Tower: Studies in Romantic Tradition* [Chicago: Univ. of Chicago Press, 1971], 145).

36. For "crystal . . . openness," see Armstrong, *Victorian Poetry,* 352. For "Poetry . . . starts," see Ricks, "William Wordsworth," 107. *The Poems of A. E. Housman,* ed. Archie Burnett (Oxford: Clarendon, 1997), 379. On "ascensus," see Richard Howard, *Alone with America: Essays on the Art of Poetry in the United States since 1950* (New York: Atheneum, 1969), 296. On "reasonable opacity," see Dan Pagis, "Toward a Theory of the Literary Riddle," in *Untying the Knot: On Riddles and Other Enigmatic Modes,* ed. Galit Hasan-Rokem and David Shulman (New York: Oxford Univ. Press, 1996), 91. Shaw, *Victorians and Mystery,* makes the interesting suggestion that the replies are "laconic" and "only as satisfactory as the pilgrim's questions. Better and fuller answers must await better questions" (268).

37. For more on the bounds of teasing and riddling, see Pagis, "Toward a Theory of the Literary Riddle," 92. On the "sign" of "individuality," see McGann, "Christina Rossetti's Poems," 246, 247. Iona and Peter Opie, eds., *The Oxford Nursery Rhyme Book* (New York: Oxford Univ. Press, 1955), include "There was a girl in our town" in a cluster of riddles under the heading "Hidden Names" (155).

38. On "nonimporting pattern . . . coherence," see Booth, *Precious Nonsense,* 6; Booth uses both "nonsense" and "non-sense" to talk about "kinds of coherence and incoherence in works of art" and to consider the ways that poetry, as an acoustic art, "participates in systems in which coherence is . . . literal," i.e., of the letter (8).

39. Armstrong, *Victorian Poetry,* 359.

TWO   Influence and Restraint

1. Felicia Hemans is described by McGann and Riess as "the most published English poet of the nineteenth century" (*Landon,* 20) and Paula R. Feldman verifies her handsome earnings in "The Poet and the Profits: Felicia Hemans and the Literary Marketplace," in *Women's Poetry, Late Romantic to Late Victorian: Gender and Genre, 1830–1900,* ed. Isobel Armstrong and Virginia Blain (New York: St. Martins Press, 1999), 71–101. John Arthur Roebuck wrote a lengthy critique of Landon for the *Westminster Review;* see *Landon,* 303–25. Both women are rapidly becoming better known: Angela Leighton's *Victorian Women Poets: Writing Against the Heart* (Charlottesville: Univ. Press of Virginia, 1992) opened a rich vein of inquiry, scholarly selections of both poets are readily available, and biographical research continues apace. Cynthia Lawford, for example, provides important new information on Landon's long-term relationship with her mentor-editor, William Jerden, and the hitherto unremarked fact that she bore him three children; see "Diary," *London Review of Books,* Sept. 21, 2000, 36–37. For the quip on names, see McGann, "Christina Rossetti's Poems," 251.

2. "Prefatory Notice," in William Michael Rossetti, ed., *The Poetical Works of Mrs. Felicia Hemans* (1878; New York: Crowell, 1890), 24; Hemans's modern editor, Susan Wolfson, reprints the later of William Rossetti's two prefaces, remarking that it was "often republished as an authoritative biography and critical assessment" of Hemans's work (*Hemans,* 603–9, 603). For "one . . . age," see Edmund Gosse, *Critical Kit-Kats* (London: Heinemann, 1896), 138.

3. Tricia Lootens, "Hemans and Home: Victorianism, Feminine 'Internal Enemies,' and the Domestication of National Identity," *PMLA* (1994): 243.

4. Ellen Moers, *Literary Women* (New York: Oxford Univ. Press, 1985), 176. Susan J. Wolfson, "'Domestic Affections' and 'the spear of Minerva': Felicia Hemans and the Dilemma of Gender," in *Re-Visioning Romanticism: British Women Writers, 1776–1837,* ed. Carol Shiner Wilson and Joel Haefner (Philadelphia: Univ. of Pennsylvania Press, 1994), 160. Leighton, *Victorian Women Poets,* 31.

5. Concerning *Aurora Leigh,* see Linda H. Peterson, "Rewriting 'A History of the Lyre': Letitia Landon, Elizabeth Barrett Browning and the (Re)Construction of the Nineteenth-Century Woman Poet," in Armstrong and Blain, *Women's Poetry;* Peterson astutely notes that while "the marriage ending of *Aurora Leigh* has been controversial among contemporary feminist critics, primarily for seeming to succumb to the conventions of the marriage plot, it looks different in its historical and generic contexts" (128).

6. Landon's "Stanzas on the Death of Mrs. Hemans," which first appeared in the *New Monthly Magazine* 44 (1835), was included by Frederic Rowton in his section "Mrs. Laetitia Elizabeth Maclean (Miss Landon)," in *The Female Poets of Great Britain*

(1853; Detroit: Wayne State Univ. Press, 1981), 442; Wolfson lists additional reprintings (*Hemans* 571). Barrett's "Stanzas Addressed to Miss Landon, and Suggested by Her 'Stanzas on the Death of Mrs Hemans'" first appeared in the *New Monthly Magazine* 45 (1835) signed only as "B" (*Landon* 363). For the list of "Immortals," see *The P.R.B. Journal: William Michael Rossetti's Diary of the Pre-Raphaelite Brotherhood, 1848–1853,* ed. William E. Fredeman (Oxford: Clarendon, 1975), 107.

7. The golden violet of Landon's title would come to mind many years later when Christina, writing to William, suggests the flower for Gabriel's grave: "I think . . . that a golden violet was (was it not?) a Provençal prize for poetry. Perhaps, tho', you would think this arrogant: *I* surmise that no one besides ourselves might scent the allusion" (*L,* 3:209). Glennis Stephenson, "Letitia Landon and the Victorian Improvisatrice: The Construction of L.E.L.," *Victorian Poetry* 30, no. 1 (1992): 8. Rosenblum, *Christina Rossetti,* 10. Rowton, *Female Poets,* 428; Rowton found Landon's song in *The Golden Violet* (145). For "fulfills . . . stroke" and "orders of cogency," see Debra Fried, "Rhyme Puns," in *On Puns: The Foundation of Letters,* ed. Jonathan Culler (Oxford: Blackwell, 1988), 84, 98.

8. For "constraining . . . edification," see Leighton, *Victorian Women Poets,* 18; for "the mercy of passion," see Armstrong, *Victorian Poetry,* 328.

9. Leighton, *Victorian Women Poets,* 76.

10. Greer provides an account of Landon's brief marriage to George Maclean, noting that the couple married on June 7, 1838, and arrived in August at his post in Cape Coast Africa, where Landon was found dead on October 15, 1838. According to the coroner, Landon died "of an overdose of prussic acid, incautiously administered by her own hand" (*Slip-Shod Sybils,* 354). *Elizabeth Barrett to Miss Mitford: The Unpublished Letters of Elizabeth Barrett Barrett to Mary Russell Mitford,* ed. Betty Miller (London: Murray, 1954), 77–78. Leighton provides a sterner reading of Elizabeth Barrett's response to Landon's work in *Victorian Women Poets,* 71–75.

11. Laman Blanchard, *Life and Literary Remains of L.E.L.,* 2 vols. (London: Henry Colburn, 1841), encouraged the belief that Landon was childless; and certainly Rossetti assumed this to be the case. For Cynthia Lawford's recent findings to the contrary, see note 1. On the "gaiety and cheerfulness" of Landon's social manner, see Rowton, *Female Poets,* 427; additionally, William Howitt reports in *Homes and Haunts of the Most Eminent British Poets,* 3rd ed. (London, Routledge, 1857), that Landon's "manner and conversation were not only the very reverse of the tone and sentiment of her poems, but she seemed to say things for the sake of astonishing you with the very contrast" (438).

12. For the "tantalizing initials," see Stephenson, "Letitia Landon," 2. Confusion persists about the epigraph by E. B. Browning which appears on page 136 of the first edition of *The Prince's Progress;* it has been mistakenly supposed that Gabriel excised it from this edition with the effect of erasing the poem's ties to a female precursor (Chapman, *Afterlife of Christina Rossetti,* 75).

13. Although direct influence is not the issue here, the "Description of Spring, Wherein Each Thing Renews Save Only the Lover," by Henry Howard, Earl of Surrey, anticipates Rossetti's "L.E.L."; seasonal details fill the sonnet's first twelve lines

and defer mention of the lover's sorrow until the final pun: "among these pleasant things / Each care decays, and yet my sorrow springs" (*The Renaissance in England,* ed. Hyder E. Rollins and Herschel Baker [Boston: Heath, 1954], 195).

14. On Gabriel Rossetti's "absolute . . . judgments," see Jerome McGann, *Dante Gabriel Rossetti and the Game That Must Be Lost* (New Haven, Conn.: Yale Univ. Press, 2000), 2.

15. Greer, *Slip-Shod Sibyls,* 272.

16. Joan Rees, "Christina Rossetti: Poet," *Critical Quarterly* 26, no. 3 (1984): 70. For discussion of the beloved who "stays inaccessible," see Carson, *Eros the Bittersweet,* 27.

17. For Gabriel Rossetti's debt to Keats's elegiac sensibility, see Richardson, *Vanishing Lives,* 100–101. The reviewer's phrases, "fury . . . madness" and "confused . . . battle," are from John Roebuck's *Westminster Review* article "The Poetry of L.E.L." (*Landon,* 312).

18. Chapman, *Afterlife of Christina Rossetti,* 74, 68, 80; Greer, *Slip-Shod Sibyls,* 382.

19. For riddling images of unwelcome "transformation," see Richard Bauman, "'I'll Give You Three Guesses': The Dynamics of Genre in the Riddle Tale," in Hasan-Rokem and Shulman, *Untying the Knot,* 73.

20. Of the four poems in "the squad," Rossetti keeps two for *The Prince's Progress,* "After This the Judgment" (*CP,* 1:184) and "Martyr's Song" (*CP,* 1:182). The remaining two appear in the 1875 edition under new titles, "Twilight Night," part 1 (*CP,* 1:212), and "By the Waters of Babylon. B.C. 570" (*CP,* 1:218).

21. "A Royal Princess" first appeared in *Poems: An Offering to Lancashire. Printed and Published for the Art Exhibition for the Relief of Distress in the Cotton Districts* (London: Emily Faithfull, 1863), 2–10.

22. On "Casabianca," see Lootens, "Hemans and Home," 241.

23. Virginia Blain, ed., *Victorian Women Poets: A New Annotated Anthology* (Harlow, UK: Longman, 2001), 21.

24. David G. Riede, *Dante Gabriel Rossetti and the Limits of Victorian Vision* (Ithaca, N.Y.: Cornell Univ. Press, 1983), provides a brief discussion of Gabriel's nervous collapse in June 1872, and what Riede tactfully calls the "the symptoms following the breakdown" (186–87); biographers agree that Rossetti did not fully recover.

25. Wolfson, "'Domestic Affections,'" 147. Procter, "A Woman's Answer," in *Victorian Women Poets: An Anthology,* ed. Angela Leighton and Margaret Reynolds (Cambridge, Mass.: Blackwell, 1995), 318.

26. On Helen of Troy, see John J. Winkler, "Double Consciousness in Sappho's Lyrics" in *The Lesbian and Gay Studies Reader,* ed. Henry Abelove, Michèle Aine Barale, David M. Halperin (New York: Routledge, 1993), 579. "A Fight over the Body of Homer" is the manuscript title of "The Lowest Room" (*CP,* 1:301). Rosenblum, *Christina Rossetti,* 164.

27. On the timing of *Aurora Leigh,* see Marsh, *Christina Rossetti,* 184; for Gabriel's early admiration of Barrett Browing's poem, which he called "an astounding work, surely," see *LDGR,* 1:309.

28. Oswald Doughty, *A Victorian Romantic: Dante Gabriel Rossetti* (London: Muller, 1949), explains that in mid-October 1875, "the cumulative effects of a long spell of

solitary toil, of loneliness, over-work, restlessness, the demands of a landlord insisting upon an inspection of the dilapidation of the house during Gabriel's tenancy, and increasing debts now culminating in what Rossetti referred to as 'a bloody writ,' combined to persuade him to set off with George Hake for Bognor where he . . . spent the next nine months, experiencing there, said Watts, 'the most secluded life he ever led before or afterwards, suffering most of the time from ill-health'" (573).

29. George Hake is described by William as Gabriel's "secretary" (*CGRFL,* 88). For "insufficiently . . . enough" and discussion of belittlement, see Phillips, *Beast in the Nursery,* 137.

30. For "essential qualities . . . rest," see Rees, "Christina Rossetti," 60.

31. For discussion of the ideal riddle's "soluble" qualities, see Pagis, "Toward a Theory of the Literary Riddle," 84. Rossetti's phrase, "inning and outing," is in Mackenzie Bell, *Christina Rossetti: A Biographical and Critical Study* (1898; New York: Haskell, 1971), 131.

32. The omission of "By the Sea" from *The Prince's Progress* was occasioned by its appearance in *A Round of Days Described in Original Poems by Some of Our Most Celebrated Poets* (1866); it was selected again for *Picture Posies: Poems Chiefly by Living Authors* (1874) before inclusion in Rossetti's own volume of 1875 (*CP,* 1:297). Within Rossetti's lifetime, the poem was reprinted by Elizabeth Amelia Sharp in *Sea-Music: An Anthology of Poems and Passages Descriptive of the Sea* (London: Scott, 1887), 228.

33. Shaw, *Victorians and Mystery,* 267.

THREE   The Nonsense and Wisdom of *Sing-Song: A Nursery Rhyme Book*

1. Title references are to Sandra M. Gilbert's chapter "The Aesthetics of Renunciation" in *Madwoman in the Attic,* Rosenblum's *Christina Rossetti: The Poetry of Endurance,* and Eric Griffiths's "The Disappointment of Christina G. Rossetti," *Essays in Criticism* 47, no. 2 (1997): 107–42; Griffiths contends that Rossetti "is not only at times a disappointing poet but also, more thoroughly, a poet of disappointment" (108). My own title offers a characterization as well: "Christina Rossetti and the Poetry of Reticence," *Philological Quarterly* 65, no. 4 (1986): 495. Armstrong, "Christina Rossetti—Diary of a Feminist Reading," in *Victorian Women Poets,* ed. Tess Cosslett (London: Longman, 1996), 158. *Sing a Song of Popcorn: Every Child's Book of Poems,* ed. Beatrice Schenk de Regniers, Eva Moore, Mary Michaels White, and Jan Carr (New York: Scholastic, 1988), includes "Who has seen the wind?" "The Caterpillar" (which is Rossetti's "Brown and furry"), "Hurt no living thing," and "What is pink?" from *Sing-Song,* while *A Child's Anthology of Poetry,* ed. Elizabeth Hauge Sword with Victoria Flournoy McCarthy (Hopewell, N.J.: Ecco, 1995), includes "The Caterpillar" and "Who has seen the wind?" as well as "Precious Stones" (which is Rossetti's "An emerald is as green as grass"), "What is pink?" and, from the *Goblin Market* volume, the sonnet "Remember" (*CP,* 1:37). Elizabeth Danson, "And When the Weeds Begin to Grow / It's Like a Garden Full of Snow," *Fourth Genre: Explorations in Nonfiction* 3, no. 2 (Fall 2001): 95. "A Christmas Carol" is thought to have lingered in the mind of A. E. Housman; see *The Poems of A. E. Housman,* ed. Archie Burnett

(Oxford: Clarendon, 1997), 186, 500. Thomas Burnett Swann, *Wonder and Whimsy: The Fantastic World of Christina Rossetti* (Francestown, N. H.: M. Jones, 1960).

2. Fried, "Rhyme Puns," 99.

3. For "Barber, barber" see *NRNT,* 121, and the commentary on this jingle in Opie, *Oxford Dictionary of Nursery Rhymes,* 78. On rhyme, see Arden Reed's "The Mariner Rimed," in *Romanticism and Language,* ed. Arden Reed (Ithaca, N.Y.: Cornell Univ. Press, 1984), 168, where Reed notes Barbara Johnson's translation of Derrida's defini-tion, "rhyme—which is the general law of textual effects—is the folding-together of an identity and a difference," in *Dissemination* (Chicago: Univ. of Chicago Press, 1981), 277. For riddle theory, see Hasan-Rokem and Shulman's introduction, *Unty-ing the Knot,* 5. The category of "animal poems" is used in Barbara Garlitz, "Christina Rossetti's *Sing-Song* and Nineteenth-Century Children's Poetry," *PMLA* 70 (June 1955): 540; Archer Taylor, *English Riddles from Oral Tradition* (New York: Octagon, 1977), includes hundreds of examples under the categories "Comparisons to an An-imal" and comparisons "to Several Animals."

4. The addendum is from Smulders, *Christina Rossetti Revisited,* 79.

5. William S. Baring-Gould and Ceil Baring-Gould, eds., *The Annotated Mother Goose, Nursery Rhymes Old and New* (New York: Potter, 1962), 204, 203; the Baring-Goulds' reference is to Richard Inwards, *Weather Lore. The Poetical Works of Gerard Manley Hopkins,* ed. Norman H. Mackenzie (Oxford: Clarendon, 1990), 117. For the Ice-landic riddle, see Andrew Welsh, *Roots of Lyric: Primitive Poetry and Modern Poetics* (Princeton, N.J.: Princeton Univ. Press, 1978), 29; I am indebted throughout this discussion of *Sing-Song* to Welsh's excellent chapter "Riddle" and, beyond that, to Northrop Frye's treatment of babble, riddle, and doodle as elements of lyric in *Anatomy of Criticism,* 275–80. Wordsworth's phrase comes as part of his answer to the trio of questions—"What is a Poet? To whom does he address himself? And what language is to be expected from him?"—added to the "Preface" in 1802 (*Lyrical Ballads,* 751.)

6. Roderick McGillis, "Simple Surfaces: Christina Rossetti's Work for Children," in *The Achievement of Christina Rossetti,* ed. David A. Kent (Ithaca, N.Y.: Cornell Univ. Press, 1987), 221–22, 222.

7. For "animate . . . world," see Shlomith Cohen, "Connecting through Riddles, or the Riddle of Connecting," in *Untying the Knot,* 299. On "beauty . . . passivity," see Claudette Sartiliot, *Herbarium Verbarium: The Discourse of Flowers* (Lincoln: Univ. of Nebraska Press, 1993), 4. On the logical form of metaphor, see A. K. Ramanujan, "Why an Allama Poem Is Not a Riddle: An Anthological Essay," in *The Collected Essays of A. K. Ramanujan,* ed. Vinay Dharwadker (New York: Oxford Univ. Press, 1999), 309–23; citing authors as various as Allama Prabhu and Oscar Wilde, Ramanujan develops a comparative account of metaphor, oxymoron, and paradox.

8. For "fundamental paradoxes," see Ralph A. Bellas, *Christina Rossetti* (Boston: Twayne, 1977), 89. Fried, "Rhyme Puns," remarks that a "pun's virtues" are "extravagance, surprise, excess, a big build-up to a little explosion" (83).

9. On dipody, see Derek Attridge, *Rhythms of English Poetry;* Attridge describes dipodic rhythm as "the tendency for rhythmic beats to alternate between stronger and

weaker" (114) and provides an example with two scansions: "The first scansion implies a relatively slow, emphatic reading, with a beat for every stressed syllable . . . the second . . . implies a faster reading with half as many beats" (115).

10. See Lucy Rollin, *Cradle and All: A Cultural and Psychoanalytic Reading of Nursery Rhymes* (Jackson: Univ. Press of Mississippi, 1992), for "Birds . . . language" by Lévi-Strauss (26–27) and Rollin's "size . . . survive" (27).

11. Welsh, *Roots of Lyric,* 30.

12. Wordsworth, "The Old Cumberland Beggar" (line 85), in *Lyrical Ballads,* 231. Louise Bogan, "Variation on a Sentence," *The Blue Estuaries: Poems 1923–1968* (New York: Ecco, 1977), 99. For "emerges . . . questioned" and the alignment of dreaming and questioning, see Susan J. Wolfson, *The Questioning Presence: Wordsworth, Keats, and the Interrogative Mode in Romantic Poetry* (Ithaca, N.Y.: Cornell Univ. Press 1986), 20–21, 28.

13. Marina Warner, *No Go the Bogeyman: Scaring, Lulling, and Making Mock* (New York: Farrar, Straus, 1998), 192.

14. On "shaming," see Rollin, *Cradle and All,* 105. "Cross Patch" is annotated by the Opies as "Lines to conciliate a sulky child, also common as a taunt" (*Oxford Dictionary of Nursery Rhymes,* 161). See Jane Taylor, *Rhymes for the Nursery,* 7th ed. (London: Darton, 1812) for "The Quarrelsome Dogs," addressed to "little children" (80), and "Romping" (56–57).

15. On "the pie incident," see Opie, *Oxford Dictionary of Nursery Rhymes,* 278. For "Do as you're bid," see Rollin, who cites the full quatrain,

> Come when you're called,
> Do as you're bid,
> Shut the door after you,
> Never be chid,

and notes that it was first aimed at servants (*Cradle and All,* 24); Halliwell includes both "Come when you're called" and the variant, "Speak when you're spoken to" (*NRNT,* 32). According to Jan Marsh, Gabriele Rossetti referred to Christina as an "angelic little demon" and one (along with Gabriel) of the "two storms" (*Christina Rossetti,* 5).

16. Smulders, *Christina Rossetti Revisited,* 108. For details on the death of William and Lucy's child Michael, see the diary Christina kept for her mother, Frances (*CGRFL,* 228); Rossetti's elegy for this nephew, "Michael F. M. Rossetti. Born April 22nd, 1881; Died January 24th, 1883," appeared in the *Athenaeum* (*CP,* 3:48, 377). For "tinged . . . indefinitely," see Lila Hanft, "The Politics of Maternal Ambivalence in Christina Rossetti's *Sing-Song,*" *Victorian Literature and Culture* 19 (1991): 224; Hanft regards the "infanticidal wishes in *Sing-Song*" as Rossetti's way of legitimizing feelings that resist the Victorian "idealization of maternity" and the "conflation of female identity with reproductive function" (225, 227). For the phrase "controlled . . . hate," see Nicholas Tucker, "Lullabies and Child Care: A Historical Perspective," in *Opening Texts: Psychoanalysis and the Culture of the Child,* ed. Joseph H. Smith and William Kerrigan (Baltimore, Md.: Johns Hopkins Univ. Press, 1985), 21. Warner's remarks in *No Go the Bogeyman* may be located as follows: "songs . . . risks" (196), the "blessing . . .

curse," "Break a leg," "the traditional . . . wolf," "lullabies . . . perils" (201), "cast . . . death" (194).

17. For Gilbert's "cryptic . . . vanished," see *Inventions of Farewell: A Book of Elegies* (New York: Norton, 2001), 123. "A Child's Grave," in Jane Taylor, *Hymns for Infant Minds* (New York: Carter, 1850), 110–112; 17–28. Booth, *Precious Nonsense,* 74.

18. Phillips, *Beast in the Nursery,* 44. Gilbert includes "Why did baby die" in *Inventions of Farewell,* 265.

19. "Fiddle, faddle, feedle" is from "An Owl in an Oak," in Opie, *Oxford Dictionary of Nursery Rhymes,* 401. For "assertions . . . chaotic," see Booth, *Precious Nonsense,* 3–4; Booth discusses the nursery rhyme "Little Boy Blue" as prelude to his meticulous demonstration that culturally valued texts are "to a significant degree composed of nonsense, demonstrable nonsense," while at the same time making full sense (4). U. C. Knoepflmacher, *Ventures into Childland,* 349. See also John Davies, *Everyman's Book of Nonsense* (London: Dent, 1981), for the clustering of Rossetti's "When fishes set umbrellas up" with "The peacock has a score of eyes" under the single new title "Fishy Tale" (189).

20. For "robust . . . vivisection," see William Flesch, "The Conjuror's Trick, or How to Rhyme," *Literary Imagination* 3, no. 2 (2001): 186. Frye, *Anatomy of Criticism,* 80.

21. For "initiation . . . language," see Rollin, *Cradle and All,* 16; see also Deborah Thacker, "Disdain or Ignorance? Literary Theory and the Absence of Children's Literature," *The Lion and the Unicorn* 24, no. 1 (2000); Thacker calls for further conceptualizing of the "child's apprenticeship to language" (8). Warner, *No Go the Bogeyman,* 229. McGillis, "Simple Surfaces," 219.

22. "An Essay on Criticism" (lines 371–73), in *Alexander Pope,* ed. Pat Rogers (Oxford: Oxford Univ. Press, 1993), 29. For "Rooted . . . effort," see James Richardson, *Vanishing Lives,* 67, and the precise account of poetic speed, pacing, and flow at 65–69. On "self-arrested stress," see Attridge, *Rhythms of English Poetry,* 66. Kathryn Burlinson, "'Frogs and Fat Toads': Christina Rossetti and the Significance of the Nonhuman," in *Culture of Christina Rossetti,* 178. For "Ding, Dong, Bell," see Opie, *Oxford Dictionary of Nursery Rhymes,* 174.

23. The animal sounds are culled from "A Farmyard Song," in Opie, *Oxford Nursery Rhyme Book,* 182; from "My Cock Lilly-Cock," in *NRNT,* 333; and from the memory of "Old Macdonald Had a Farm." See Phillips on "noisy silence" and "life without words" (*Beast in the Nursery,* 42, 43). For "the act . . . subject," see Glück, *Proofs and Theories,* 25.

24. Welsh, *Roots of Lyric,* 123. McGillis, "Simple Surfaces," 224.

25. Words lacking "a perfect rhyme" include "chimney," "circle," "desert," "monarch," "virtue," and "wisdom"; see also *The Complete Rhyming Dictionary Revised,* ed. Clement Wood, rev. Ronald J. Bogus (New York: Dell, 1991), for a list of iambs and monosyllables "which appear to be rhymeless" (117–18). Griffiths, "Disappointment of Christina Rossetti," 110.

26. On "drawing out" pronunciation, see Attridge, *Rhythms of English Poetry,* 97.

27. William Carlos Williams, "Spring and All," in *Imaginations,* ed. Webster Schott (New York: New Directions, 1970), 115.

FOUR   **Ambitious Triangles**

1. "In an Artist's Studio" and William's note first appear in the posthumous *New Poems by Christina Rossetti,* ed. William Michael Rossetti (New York: Macmillan, 1896), 114, 383; they are later included in *PW,* 330, 480. The comment "feeds . . . addiction" is by Leighton, *Victorian Women Poets: An Anthology,* 354; "deanimation . . . re-animation" is by Elisabeth Bronfen, *Over Her Dead Body: Death, Femininity and the Aesthetic* (New York: Routledge, 1992), 174. Rosenblum provides an important early discussion of "In an Artist's Studio"; glancing at *Vampyre,* by the Rossettis' maternal uncle John Polidori, she remarks, "This beautiful woman vampirized by art is a version of the woman dead before death. The difference is that she lives, however weakly, detached from her image, and that the speaker has the capacity to see the woman unmasked" (*Christina Rossetti,* 135). For details of the 1869 exhumation and retrieval of Dante Gabriel Rossetti's manuscript poems from Elizabeth Siddal's coffin, see McGann, *Dante Gabriel Rossetti and the Game,* 62–64. Smulders, *Christina Rossetti Revisited,* 127. Chapman, *Afterlife of Christina Rossetti,* 96. For metaphorical use of the verb "fed," see the first sonnet of Petrarch's *Canzoniere:* "Voi ch' ascoltate in rime sparse il suono / di quei sospiri ond' io nudriva 'l core," which Musa translates as "O you who hear within these scattered verses / the sound of sighs with which I fed my heart" (*C* 1).

2. For "clear-eyedness . . . entrapments," see Valentine Cunningham, *The Victorians: An Anthology of Poetry and Poetics* (Malden, Mass.: Blackwell, 2000), 662. Edmund Gosse, in a review for the *Examiner* (Dec. 18, 1875) later reprinted in *Critical Kit-Kats,* praises "After Death," "On the Wing," and "Venus's Looking-Glass"; regrets that Rossetti omitted "A Triad" from her 1875 collection; and, in the comparative manner of Victorian critics, measures her work against Gabriel's: "In 'The World,' where she may be held to come closest to her brother as a sonneteer, she seems to me to surpass him" (155–56). Samuel Waddington's *English Sonnets by Living Writers* (London: Bell, 1881) includes "If Only," "Rest," "The World," "Autumn Violets," "After Communion," "On the Wing," and "After Death." In her letter telling Gabriel this news, Rossetti refers to "On the Wing" by its 1866 title, "A Dream" (*L,* 2:226). Often reprinted, "Remember" is the final poem in *The Collins Book of Love Poems,* ed. Amanda McCardie (London: Collins, 1990), 180. It appears with several other of Rossetti's pieces in Sword and McCarthy's *Child's Anthology* (236) and Gilbert's *Inventions of Farewell* (411).

3. The publication history of *The House of Life* is succinctly summarized by Cecil Y. Lang: "[The sonnets] range in date of composition from 1848 to 1881, in date of publication from 1863 to 1881. Some of them (sixteen) were first published as a group in the *Fortnightly Review,* March, 1869; a larger group (fifty) was first published in book form in *Poems,* 1870, under the title 'Sonnets and Songs, towards a work to be called "The House of Life"' . . . . [And the] final version, called 'The House of Life; A Sonnet-Sequence,' appeared in *Ballads and Sonnets,* 1881" (*Pre-Raphaelites and Their Circle,* 503). On Tennyson's response to Gabriel's translation, see Doughty, *Victorian Romantic,* 108. Christina Rossetti's knowledge of Dante and Petrarch was more than a casual result of her Italian heritage; she knew the translations by her friend Charles

Bagot Cayley, both his *Dante's Divine Comedy* (1851–55), a terza rima version, and *The Sonnets and Stanzas of Petrarch* (1879), which is the first complete translation of Petrarch's poems by "a single hand" (William Whitla, "Questioning the Convention: Christina Rossetti's Sonnet Sequence 'Monna Innominata,'" in Kent, *Achievement of Christina Rossetti,* 97). Rossetti also attended lectures on *The Divine Comedy* at the University of London over a three-year period beginning in 1878 (Marsh, *Christina Rossetti,* 457, 471). Alison Milbank, *Dante and the Victorians* (Manchester: Manchester Univ. Press, 1998), discusses Charles Cayley's and Christina Rossetti's poems in Italian (137–40).

4. *Dante Gabriel Rossetti: The Early Italian Poets,* ed. Sally Purcell (Berkeley: Univ. of California Press, 1981), 124. Hereafter, *Early Italian Poets.*

5. Unless otherwise specified, Christina Rossetti's comments on Dante are from *P,* 184–86.

6. Regarding Beatrice, both Rossettis take Dante's dismay on seeing her at a wedding to be a hint at her otherwise unmentioned marriage; in a footnote to his *Vita nuova* translation, Gabriel claims that it is "difficult not to connect Dante's agony at this wedding-feast, with our knowledge that in her twenty-first year Beatrice was wedded to Simone de' Bardi" (*Early Italian Poets,* 167).

7. For a brief summary of Dante's life, including chronology and family details Christina did not know, see Guiseppe Mazzotta, "Life of Dante," in *The Cambridge Companion to Dante,* ed. Rachel Jacoff (Cambridge: Cambridge Univ. Press, 1993), 1–13; Mazzotta notes that Dante married Gemma Donati in 1285 (five years before the death of Beatrice), that the couple had four children, and that Dante's last years in Ravenna were spent surrounded by his children "and most likely his wife" (10–12).

8. Gabriele Rossetti, in his *Disquisitions on the Antipapal Spirit,* trans. Caroline Ward, 2 vols. (London, 1834), contends that Dante's *Commedia* is written in the "secret language" of antipapal allegory (1:164), that Satan represents the corrupted "Latin Church" (1:72), and that "the imaginary Beatrice" (1:161) embodies "the qualities of true Pope and true Emperor" (1:164). See Mary Arseneau, "'May My Great Love Avail Me': Christina Rossetti and Dante," in *Culture of Christina Rossetti,* for helpful commentary on Gabriele's "long-held opinion that Beatrice had 'no objective existence at all'" (24).

9. John Hollander, *The Work of Poetry* (New York: Columbia Univ. Press, 1997), 104. For "image . . . poet," see Dubrow, *Echoes of Desire,* 24; Dubrow refutes those who overemphasize "the potency of the Petrarchan poet" with her own nuanced commentary on "the seesaw between power and powerlessness which defines the Petrarchan voice" (24, 25). See also Lynn Keller, "Measured Feet 'in Gender-Bender Shoes': The Politics of Form in Marilyn Hacker's *Love, Death, and the Changing of the Seasons,*" in *Feminist Measures: Soundings in Poetry and Theory,* ed. Lynn Keller and Christanne Miller (Ann Arbor: Univ. of Michigan Press, 1994), 260–86; Keller provides an overview of the theoretical rejection of the sonnet genre and successfully discredits the contention "that formalist verse necessarily embodies a particular (patriarchal) ideology" (260). See Adrienne Rich, "When We Dead Awaken: Writing

as Re-vision" (1971), reprinted with a new introduction in *Claims for Poetry,* ed. Donald Hall (Ann Arbor: Univ. of Michigan Press, 1982), 351.

10. Arnaut Daniel's reply to Dante in *Purg.* 26.148 is the only passage in the *Commedia* that is not in Italian. In the *Canzoniere,* Petrarch ends each stanza of poem 70 by quoting a precursor, one of whom is Arnaut Daniel.

11. On "genuine . . . soul," see Mary Robinson, *Sappho and Phaon: In a Series of Legitimate Sonnets,* ed. Terence Allan Hoagwood and Rebecca Jackson (Delmar, N.Y.: Scholar's Facsimiles, 1995), 25. Margaret Reynolds, "'I lived for art, I lived for love': The Woman Poet Sings Sappho's Last Song," in *Victorian Women Poets: A Critical Reader,* ed. Angela Leighton (Oxford: Blackwell, 1996), 298; for more on the "legitimate sonnet," see McGann, "Mary Robinson and the Myth of Sappho," *Modern Language Quarterly* 56, no. 1 (1995): 64–65. See "Laura to Petrarch," and "artificial . . . passion," in Robinson, *Sappho and Phaon,* 119, 25.

12. Dubrow, *Echoes of Desire,* 25. Regarding *Monna Innominata,* Antony H. Harrison provides a full account of its fourteen-sonnet structure, or what he terms a "macrosonnet"; while his influential reading is too detailed to rehearse here, his summary may be cited: "On its most basic level it begins with an exclusive focus on *eros* and the desire for physical union with the beloved. But the speaker's desire for earthly love gives way to spiritual aspirations. . . . In the speaker's vision of heaven, *eros* is transmuted into *agapē*" (*Christina Rossetti in Context,* 153–54, 167). Some critics suggest that the speaker of *Monna Innominata* renounces the beloved because of religious commitments, while others, including Joan Rees, see religious aspiration as a constant value and consoling recourse when the lovers are inexplicably separated (Rees, *The Poetry of Dante Gabriel Rossetti: Modes of Self-Expression* [Cambridge: Cambridge Univ. Press, 1981], 155).

13. Rees specifies some of the "reminiscences of Mrs. Browning" discernible in *The House of Life,* including such "similar episodes" as "the receipt of letters from the beloved" and the tendency of both poets to "give weight to their sonnets by rich and sonorous language and especially by resonant last lines" (*Poetry of Dante Gabriel Rossetti,* 161). For Dorothy Mermin's comparison, see *Elizabeth Barrett Browning: The Origins of a New Poetry* (Chicago: Univ. of Chicago Press, 1989), 140. For Buchanan's reference to Mrs. Browning, see "The Fleshly School of Poetry: Mr. D. G. Rossetti," in *Broadview Anthology of Victorian Poetry,* 1335. Marjorie Stone, "'Monna Innominata' and 'Sonnets from the Portuguese': Sonnet Traditions and Spiritual Trajectories," in *Culture of Christina Rossetti,* also considers Christina Rossetti's "response to all three poetical precursors . . . to have been shaped by her ambivalent reaction to Dante Gabriel Rossetti's 'The House of Life'" (46).

14. Dubrow, *Echoes of Desire,* 11–12, 21. Translations of Petrarch, unless otherwise indicated, are from Musa's bilingual edition of *The Canzoniere.*

15. For "abstractable" versus "inherent," see McGann, *Dante Gabriel Rossetti and the Game;* in discussing Gabriel Rossetti's paintings, McGann questions whether "the 'idea' of artistic work" is "an inherent practice or an abstractable conception" (20) and distinguishes the discursive from "the artistic process" (25). For Hopkins's remarks on style, see *Gerard Manley Hopkins: Selected Letters,* ed. Phillips, 26, 27, 26–27.

For "coexist . . . agitation," see Richard Poirier, *The Renewal of Literature: Emersonian Reflections* (New Haven, Conn.: Yale Univ. Press, 1988), 29, qtd. in Susan J. Wolfson, *Formal Charges: The Shaping of Poetry in British Romanticism* (Stanford, Calif.: Stanford Univ. Press, 1997), 46.

16. For "the book . . . memory," see D. G. Rossetti, *Early Italian Poets,* 151. In summarizing the chronology of Dante's remembrances in the *Vita nuova,* McGann observes that "its key date [falls] in June 1290, the month of Beatrice Portinari's death. The story it tells begins in 1274, when Dante first sees Beatrice (he is nine years old, she is eight). For nine years—according to the *Vita Nuova's* retrospective prose account—he haunts her presence, trying to see her whenever he can. Then in 1283 she gives him her famous 'salutation.' This event throws him wholly under the domination of love" (*Dante Gabriel Rossetti and the Game,* 40).

17. Tricia A. Lootens, *Lost Saints: Silence, Gender, and Victorian Literary Canonization* (Charlottesville: Univ. Press of Virginia, 1996), 118, 120; see also Lootens's persuasively unembarrassed account of Barrett Browning's sequence (116–21). For "consummated . . . desire," see Dubrow, *Echoes of Desire,* 64. Richardson, *Vanishing Lives,* 107, 108.

18. In citing the epigraphs to *Monna Innominata,* I give the translations made by William Michael Rossetti for his notes to the poem (*PW,* 462–63). For the context of *Purg.* 8.3, see *The Divine Comedy,* trans. John Ciardi (New York: Norton, 1977), 226: as night falls in ante-Purgatory, Dante the pilgrim compares his unsettled mood to that of sailors who hear evening bells from land on their first day out and think of home and friends. I am indebted to William Whitla for the precise location of Rossetti's citations of Dante and Petrarch ("Questioning the Convention," 98–100). Hardy, "The Self-Unseeing," in *The Complete Poems of Thomas Hardy,* ed. James Gibson (New York: Macmillan, 1976), 166.

19. For "singular . . . X's," see Hollander, *Work of Poetry,* 104. The phrase "snows of yester-year" is Gabriel Rossetti's translation of "les neiges d'antan" from François Villon's "Ballade des dames du temps jadis," in "The Ballad of Dead Ladies," *The Works of Dante Gabriel Rossetti,* ed. William M. Rossetti (London, 1911), 541–42.

20. The "implicit narrative" of *The House of Life* concerns, in McGann's unraveling, "a young man, an artist, and two (at least two) idealized women. The young man's love for one of the women succeeds to his love for the second. The first woman dies—it is not entirely clear whether her death occurs before or after his second love—and the events radically intensify the man's erotic yearning for perfect love. This new desire is haunted by feelings of guilt and remorse, and dominated by ambiguous images of death and otherworlds" (*Dante Gabriel Rossetti and the Game,* 39). Richardson, *Vanishing Lives,* 115.

21. Casella sings Dante's canzone at *Purg.* 2.112, and Statius hails Virgil at *Purg.* 21.133–34.

22. For "shade . . . rivalry," see Mary B. Moore, *Desiring Voices: Women Sonneteers and Petrarchism* (Carbondale: Southern Illinois Univ. Press, 2000), 181. Mermin, *Elizabeth Barrett Browning,* 6.

23. Lootens, *Lost Saints,* 121. Gabriel Rossetti's "remarkable self-confidence" is cited by McGann as a factor in his "intellectual leadership among a group of extraordinary

artists" (*Dante Gabriel Rossetti and the Game*, 2–3). For reservations about "masculine assumptions" apparent in Rossetti's "The Portrait" (*HL* 10), see Marjorie Stone, "'Monna Innominata,'" in *Culture of Christina Rossetti*, 61.

24. On what "some say" about lovers, see the conclusion of "Jessie Cameron" (*CP*, 1:118) as discussed on pp. 110–11 of this volume. See Griffiths, "Disappointment of Christina Rossetti," for "exultant . . . lack" (112), "communicate . . . character" (109), "real distress" (112), and "suffering voice" (113).

25. In the translation "relating the casualties of our life," William Michael Rossetti's choice of "casualties" is a bit odd; Whitla offers Charles Cayley's rendering, "counting the chances that our life befall" ("Questioning the Convention," 100).

26. For "natural . . . preserve," see Griffiths, "Disappointment of Christina Rossetti," 114.

27. See Thomas Wyatt's "My Lute Awake," John Keats's "La Belle Dame Sans Merci," and "simply . . . so," in Smith, *Poetic Closure*, 63.

28. Roland Greene, *Post-Petrarchism: Origins and Innovations of the Western Lyric Sequence* (Princeton, N.J.: Princeton Univ. Press, 1991), 49. For "art . . . memory," see Rees, *Poetry of Dante Gabriel Rossetti*, 160. Lionel Stevenson, *The Pre-Raphaelite Poets* (New York: Norton, 1974), 118. Bellas, *Christina Rossetti*, 75.

29. Rees, *Poetry of Dante Gabriel Rossetti*, 156.

30. Griffiths, "Disappointment of Christina Rossetti," 133. Kathleen Blake, *Love and the Woman Question in Victorian Literature: The Art of Self-Postponement* (Sussex, UK: Harvester, 1983), 18. See Elizabeth Amelia Sharp, *Women's Voices: An Anthology of the Most Characteristic Poems by English, Scotch, and Irish Women* (New York: White, [188-?]), for "essentially . . . poems" (vii), "Women . . . apologetically" (ix), "gradually . . . away" (ix), "lack . . . experience" (ix); Sharp's fine selection includes Rossetti's "Dream-Land," "A Birthday," "Confluents," "Echo," "The Hour and the Ghost," "Rest," "Loves Lies Bleeding," "The World," *Later Life* 6, and *Later Life* 26.

31. For details of Rossetti's trip to Italy from May 22 to June 6, 1865, see Harrison's introduction to the *Letters*, 1:xxxiv; and also Marsh, *Christina Rossetti*, 335–37.

FIVE   Rossetti's Finale

1. Virginia Woolf, "I Am Christina Rossetti," 263, 262. For "five hundred a year," see the conclusion to *A Room of One's Own* (1929; Harmondsworth, UK: Penguin, 1945). According to D'Amico, *Christina Rossetti*, Rossetti's *Verses* (1893) continued to be published into the twentieth century and "by 1912, twenty-one thousand copies . . . had been printed" (148).

2. Lynda Palazzo, *Christina Rossetti's Feminist Theology* (New York: Palgrave, 2002), 94. Arthur Symons's 1887 review of "Miss Rossetti's Poetry" is excerpted in Edna Kotin Charles, *Christina Rossetti: Critical Perspectives, 1862–1982* (London: Associated University Presses, 1985), 41; see Charles for others' comments on "Good Friday" (63) and "Who Shall Deliver Me?" (29). For Gabriel Rossetti's "Songs of the Art Catholic," see *Dante Gabriel Rossetti: His Family Letters,* ed. William Michael Rossetti (London, 1895), 113. The religious poems in *The Germ* include William Michael Rossetti's "Jesus Wept" as well as, among Dante Gabriel Rossetti's sonnets for pictures, "A Virgin and Child, by Hans Memmeling" and "A Marriage of St. Katharine, by the same"; see *The*

Germ: The Literary Magazine of the Pre-Raphaelites, pref. Andrea Rose (Oxford: Ashmolean Museum, 1984), 179, 180. For "Virtue," see *George Herbert,* ed. Louis L. Martz (Oxford: Oxford Univ. Press, 1994), 73. David A. Kent, "'By thought, word, and deed': George Herbert and Christina Rossetti," in *Achievement of Christina Rossetti,* notes that Rossetti owned "William Pickering's edition of Herbert's complete writings (the first such edition)," the first volume of which is signed and "dated December 5, 1848, her eighteenth birthday" (255). In her fourteenth year, Rossetti had written "Charity," which, as indicated by Maria Rossetti's manuscript note, was also "imitated from that beautiful little poem 'Virtue' by George Herbert" (*CP,* 3:101, 399).

3. The facts of Gabriel Rossetti's death are as follows: After what William Michael Rossetti describes as "an attack of partial paralysis" on December 11, 1881, Gabriel moved to Birchington-on-Sea and was joined by Frances and Christina in early March; he died there on Easter Sunday April 9 and was buried April 14, 1882, in Birchington Churchyard (*CGRFL,* 103, 223); see the diary that Christina kept for her mother at this time (*CGRFL,* 222–26), her letters from Birchington (*L,* 3:15–35), and also Jan Marsh, *Dante Gabriel Rossetti: Painter and Poet* (London: Weidenfeld, 1999), 525–27.

4. For Gabriel's "prohibition of burial at Highgate where Lizzie was buried," see Doughty, *Victorian Romantic,* 583, 669, and Marsh, *Christina Rossetti,* 494. The painlessness of Gabriel's death is emphasized in Christina's diary entry for April 9, 1882: "The instant cause of death assigned by Dr. Harris was that the uraemic poison touched the brain, and he afterwards assured us that there was no pain" (*CGRFL,* 225); for the implausibility of such an assurance, see Sherwin B. Nuland, *How We Die: Reflections on Life's Final Chapter* (New York: Knopf, 1994), 140–43. On Gabriel's a-religious views, see McGann, *Dante Gabriel Rossetti and the Game,* 91; see Marsh, *Christina Rossetti,* for the view that "To Christina . . . it was grievous that Gabriel died unbelieving" (494). Booth, *Precious Nonsense,* 90.

5. Mary Howitt, who in 1854 had been almost the first to publish Rossetti's work, reacts in 1879 to one of the recent lyrics as if it were uttering "a cry out of my own heart—to be delivered from *Self.* It was the whole cry of an earnest soul embodied in a few words; a wonderful little outburst of prayer" (*L,* 1:79 n. 7). Howitt does not give the title, though possibly, as an extraordinarily busy author, editor, and translator (of Hans Christian Andersen, among others), she may have been struck by "Who Shall Deliver Me?" with its lament about life's "turmoil, tedium, gad-about" (*CP,* 1:227). For "Tuning of my breast," see "The Temper," *George Herbert,* 44. "Orisons" is the only noun Rossetti ever allows to appropriate a full line (*CP,* 2:269). In the *Pageant* volume, "What's in a Name?" notes the brevity of the word "spring" and suggests, in a single verse, that the actual season may "Superabound" (*CP,* 2:110). See pp. 127 and 129 (chapter 3 of this volume) for discussion of "Gratuitous" in "My God, wilt Thou accept and will not we" (*CP,* 2:210) and "Everywhere!" in the nursery rhyme "Wrens and robins in the hedge" (*CP,* 2:24).

6. For "secure pieties," see Hass, *Twentieth Century Pleasures,* 20. Fried, "Rhyme Puns," 83.

7. For Dr. Johnson, see Ricks, *Force of Poetry,* 278.

8. For "absolute . . . process," see Hass, *Twentieth Century Pleasures,* 16.

9. Woolf, "I Am Christina Rossetti," 265. Stevenson, *The Pre-Raphaelite Poets,* 117. McGann, in Kent, *Achievement of Christina Rossetti,* 8.

10. For "clarity . . . unforeseeable," see *Recitative: Prose by James Merrill,* ed. J. D. McClatchy (San Francisco: North Point Press, 1986), 8.

11. Carolyn Walker Bynum, *Last Things: Death and the Apocalypse in the Middle Ages,* ed. Carolyn Walker Bynum and Paul Freedmen (Philadelphia: Univ. of Pennsylvania Press, 2000), 4. Kent and Stanwood summarize biographers' estimates (ranging from two and a half to seven years) for how long Rossetti worked on *The Face of the Deep,* published in 1892 (*P,* 331). Little is known of the book's composition except that within a few months of Frances Rossetti's death on April 8, 1886, Christina mentions in a letter to Theodore Watts that she has begun "reading and thinking over part of the New Testament, writing down what I can as I go along. I work at prose and help myself forward with little bits of verse" (*L,* 3:346). She provides no information about her project's evolution, the order of her poems' composition, or the process of fitting them to the prose text, i.e., whether the poems were already available to be gathered into the commentary or written specifically for individual glosses or both. For Rossetti's illustration in Isaac Williams's *The Altar,* see the page reproduced in Mary F. Sandars, *The Life of Christina Rossetti* (London: Hutchinson, 1906), 211. Palazzo, *Christina Rossetti's Feminist Theology,* 122. Robert M. Kachur, "Repositioning the Female Christian Reader: Christina Rossetti as Tractarian Hermeneut in *The Face of the Deep,*" *Victorian Poetry* 35, no. 2 (1997): 205, 207.

12. Northrop Frye, *Words with Power: Being a Second Study of "The Bible and Literature"* (New York: Viking, 1990), 113. For a thoroughgoing account of John's admonitions, see Adela Yarbro Collins, "The Book of Revelation," in *The Origins of Apocalypticism,* ed. John J. Collins, vol. 1 of *The Encyclopedia of Apocalypticism,* ed. Bernard McGinn and Stephen J. Stein, 3 vols. (New York: Continuum, 1998); John's threats and promises were meant, in Collins's view, to encourage the Christian religious minority "to avoid compromise with the corrupt and idolatrous culture of the hellenized and romanized cities of Asia Minor, no matter what the cost" and may have contributed "to the survival of a Christian perspective that could not simply take its place as one ancient cult among many" (412).

13. For discussion of Daly's *Gyn-Ecology: The Metaethics of Radical Feminism,* see Palazzo, *Christina Rossetti's Feminist Theology,* 131. Kooistra, *Christina Rossetti and Illustration,* 144. Bernard McGinn, "Revelation" in *The Literary Guide to the Bible,* ed. Robert Alter and Frank Kermode (Cambridge: Harvard Univ. Press, 1987), 525; McGinn provides a brief "history of the ways in which Revelation has been read," along with a reminder that current scholarship does not identify the author of Revelation as the gospel writer or the disciple but as "an itinerant Christian prophet of Asia Minor who wrote in the last decade of the first century" (527–40, 524).

14. Colleen Hobbs, "A View from 'The Lowest Place': Christina Rossetti's Devotional Prose," *Victorian Poetry* 32, nos. 3–4 (1994): 416. Hobbs finds analogues for Rossetti's disclaimer in the writings of fourteenth-century women mystics and cites Elizabeth Alvilda Petroff, *Medieval Women's Visionary Literature* (New York: Oxford Univ. Press,

1986), for the observation, "Women writers assert that they have not studied how to express themselves; they are ignorant of rhetoric; they have not read any of their ideas in books" (Petroff, 27, qtd. in Hobbs, 426). Regarding expectations about the millennium, Adela Yarbro Collins, "Book of Revelation," summarizes the divergent views, noting that "the official eschatological teaching of the major denominations . . . is rooted in Augustine . . . and does not include an earthly reign of Christ between the second coming and the final state," but fundamentalist teaching regards Revelation as a literal forecast of the end times when resurrected martyrs will reign with Christ on earth (411).

15. Frank Kermode, "The Canon," in Alter and Kermode, *Literary Guide to the Bible*, 605.

16. Rossetti's parenthesis directs the reader to John's narrative of the Passover supper and Jude's quizzing of Jesus about his promise to manifest himself to those who keep his commandments: "Judas saith unto him, not Iscariot, Lord, how is it that thou wilt manifest thyself unto us, and not unto the world? Jesus answered and said unto him, If a man love me, he will keep my words: and my Father will love him, and we will come unto him, and make our abode with him" (John 14:22–23).

17. Merrill, *Recitative*, 102.

18. Wordsworth, "Preface to *Lyrical Ballads*" (1800), in *Lyrical Ballads*, 746–47. On "cranky apocalypses," see Steven Goldsmith, *Unbuilding Jerusalem: Apocalypse and Romantic Representation* (Ithaca, N.Y.: Cornell Univ. Press, 1993), 4; Goldsmith objects to any "aesthetic" or other version of apocalypse that "makes obsolete and thus displaces the need for political apocalypse" (7).

19. Sharon Smulders, "Women's Enfranchisement in Christina Rossetti's Poetry," *Texas Studies in Literature and Language* 34, no. 4 (1992): 578, 583. D'Amico, *Christina Rossetti*, 130, 138, 134. Hobbs, "A View from 'The Lowest Place,'" 411. In commenting on the word "tempt," Rossetti surely has in mind the divine injunction to sacrifice Isaac: "And it came to pass after these things, that God did tempt Abraham" (Gen. 22:1).

20. Frederick Denison Maurice, *Lectures on the Apocalypse* (London: Macmillan, 1885), 314.

21. For "harsh . . . torment," see Adela Yarbro Collins, "Book of Revelation," 412. For "Knowledge . . . loving," see McGann, *Dante Gabriel Rossetti and the Game*, 37. Griffiths, "Disappointment of Christina Rossetti," 126.

22. Merrill, *Recitative*, xiii.

23. For "pure . . . consciousness," see Hass, *Twentieth Century Pleasures*, 169.

24. Palazzo, *Christina Rossetti's Feminist Theology*, 127. Antony H. Harrison, *Victorian Poets and the Politics of Culture: Discourse and Ideology* (Charlottesville: Univ. Press of Virginia, 1998), 129.

25. For Rossetti's other uses of "scathe," see the discussion of "L.E.L." on p. 84 of this volume. For "dule," see the ballad "Edward, Edward," in which Edward's mother suspects that he grieves "Sum other dule" besides the loss of his horse (Percy, *Reliques of Ancient English Poetry*, 1:46).

26. Larkin, *Required Writing: Miscellaneous Pieces 1955–1982* (New York: Farrar, 1982), 56. See J. D. McClatchy's introduction to Merrill, *Recitative*, viii.

Index

"Rest" (Rossetti), 156, 252n2, 256n30
Revelation. *See* Apocalypse of John
Reynolds, Margaret, 163, 243n19
Rhymes for the Nursery (Taylor), 13
Rich, Adrienne, 162
Richardson, James, 146, 170, 174–75, 244n35
Riede, David G., 247n24
Robertson, Eric, 24, 241n8
Robinson, Mary, 4, 163–64
"Rock-a-Bye-Baby" (cradle song), 140
rocking songs, 135, 140
Roebuck, John Arthur, 245n1
Rollin, Lucy, 13, 129–30, 136, 250n10
Rollins, Hyder E., 3
"Romping" (Taylor), 137, 250n14
Rosenblum, Dolores, 43, 72, 100, 252n1
Rossetti, Christina: ambition of, 2, 9, 13; annual income from poetry, 198; celebrity as occasion of humor for, 78; fearing fall into silence, 203–4; and her mother's death, 219; on paradoxes of Christianity, 127; patience of style of, 1–2, 11; in relief of indigent women, 228; and Dante Gabriel Rossetti's death, 200–201, 257nn3-4; on Elizabeth Siddal, 154, 155; on spiritualism, 227; as "storm" as a child, 138, 250n15; on terrorism, 228; on women's rights, 226–27
—characteristics of poetry of: aesthetic economy of, 12; affirming-while-denying in, 30; on Beatrice, 158–59; the bittersweet as characteristic of, 29–38; case against Dante and Petrarch, 156–68; collegial working practice of, 12; consulting Dante Gabriel Rossetti, 85–106; "death lyrics" of, 30; departures from available myths of love, 13; on desire as central to poetry, 11; Hemans influencing, 64, 67–69, 93, 96–97; Herbert influencing, 257n2; knowledge of Dante and Petrarch, 252n3; Landon influencing, 1, 12, 64–65, 71–76; lifelong interest in the sonnet, 156; one-word characterizations of, 117; "perfection" of, 2, 66–67; poems as acts of sustained self-surprise, 218; and

the poetry of others, 1–2; pseudonym used by, 77; repetition in, 36, 98, 151, 157, 183, 230; reticence sustaining her as a poet, 57; as returning again and again to promise of happiness, 11; revival of interest in, 15; Dante Gabriel Rossetti consulting, 90; and Sappho, 4; sensory deprivation in, 191; simplicity of, 108; as soft-voiced, 39; and the sonnet tradition, 154–97; as stanzaic poet, 149; unanswerable questions in, 20; understatement of, 106, 113, 124; watchfulness underlying images of, 213; wordlessness as concern of, 12, 14, 17, 52, 204
—works of: "Advent," 199; "After Communion," 252n2; "After Death," 121, 156, 243n19, 252n2; "Amor Mundi," 214; "An Apple-Gathering," 5; "As violets so be I recluse and sweet," 212; "Autumn Violets," 74, 252n2; "Baby cry—," 135–36; "A baby's cradle with no baby in it," 140–41; "A Ballad of Boding," 241n4; "Birchington Churchyard," 200, 201–3, 206–7; "Brown and furry," 248n1; "'A Bruised Reed Shall He Not Break,'" 54–55, 105; "Charity," 257n2; "A cold wind stirs the blackthorn," 210–11; *The Complete Poems,* 15; "Confluents," 256n30; "The Convent Threshold," 11, 46–47, 48, 73; "Cousin Kate," 241n4; "Dante: The Poet Illustrated Out of the Poem," 158; "Dead in the cold, a song-singing thrush," 139; "A diamond or a coal?," 131; "Eight o'-clock," 136; "An emerald is as green as grass," 132; "Enrica, 1865," 75; essays on Dante and Petrarch, 13; "Fata Morgana," 45, 69, 88; "Freaks of Fashion," 143; "From House to Home," 241n4; "The Ghost's Petition," 91–92, 109; "Good Friday," 199; "Good Lord, to-day," 205–6; "Hop-o'-my-thumb and little Jack Horner," 137–38; "Hopping frog, hop here and be seen," 145–47; "The Hour and the Ghost," 256n30;

sonnets (*continued*)
252n2, 256n30. See also *Later Life;
Monna Innominata;* "Remember"
Sonnets from the Portuguese (Elizabeth Barrett Browning): firsts recorded in, 169,
170; inequality of lovers in, 176, 177;
lover-readers in, 181; *Monna Innominata*
and, 13, 71, 105–6, 161, 163, 165, 167,
172–74; and Dante Gabriel Rossetti's
The House of Life, 166, 254n13; self-
deprecation in, 177–79; on time apart,
185; "too so-and-so-all-overish" quality of, 167
"Sound Sleep" (Rossetti), 72–73
spiritualism, 227
sprung rhythm, 121
Statius, 176
Stephenson, Glennis, 72
Stevenson, Lionel, 188, 216
Stone, Marjorie, 254n13
"Stratton Water" (Dante Gabriel Rossetti), 91
style: relevance of, 3; Rossetti all but
boasting about, 107; in Rossetti's love
poetry, 167; Rossetti's patience of style,
1–2, 11
"Sweet Death" (Rossetti), 199–200
"Swift and sure the swallow" (Rossetti),
133
Swinburne, Algernon, 4, 204, 228
"Switzer's Wife, The" (Hemans), 98
Sword, Elizabeth Hauge, 248n1

Taylor, Jane, 13, 137–38, 140–41
"Tears, Idle Tears" (Tennyson), 37, 38
Tennyson, Alfred, Lord: "Break, Break,
Break," 37; English Idyls, 6; "Enoch
Arden," 34; on feeling of ghostliness,
202; Hopkins on, 167; *Idylls of the King,*
88; "The Lady of Shalott," 35, 46;
"The Lotos-Eaters," 34, 37; "Mariana,"
30; and Rossetti's "Echo," 37, 38; and
Rossetti's "May," 56; and Dante Gabriel
Rossetti's translations of Dante, 157;
"Tears, Idle Tears," 37, 38
terrorism, 228

"Testimony, A" (Rossetti), 199
Thacker, Deborah, 251n21
"There is but one May in the year" (Ros-
setti), 152–53
"There is one that has a head without an
eye" (Rossetti), 123
"There remaineth therefore a rest" (Ros-
setti), 89
"Thorn, The" (Wordsworth), 110
"Thou who must fall silent in a while"
(Rossetti), 205, 230
Time Flies (Rossetti), 199, 204, 215
"Time lengthening, in the lengthening
seemeth long" (Rossetti), 209
"Traveller at the Source of the Nile, The"
(Hemans), 67
"Triad, A" (Rossetti), 40, 73, 126, 252n2
Tucker, Herbert F., 33, 242n15
"Tune me, O Lord, unto one harmony"
(Rossetti), 204–5
"Twilight Calm" (Rossetti), 37
"Twist me a crown of wind-flowers"
(Rossetti), 134

understatement, 106, 113, 124, 174
"Under the Rose" (Rossetti), 93, 95–97
"Unexpected Pleasure, An" (anonymous),
9–10
Unpublished Poems (Rossetti): "Charity,"
257n2; "In an Artist's Studio," 154–56,
175; "Lord Thomas and Fair Margaret"
44–45; "Seeking Rest," 89; "There
remaineth therefore a rest," 89
"Up-hill" (Rossetti), 5, 57–59, 199

"Vaudois' Wife, The" (Hemans), 67
Venetian Bracelet, The (Landon), 12, 65,
71, 73
"Venus's Looking-Glass" (Rossetti),
252n2
Verses (Rossetti [1847]), 85
Verses (Rossetti [1893]), 198–218; "As violets so be I recluse and sweet," 212;
"Birchington Churchyard," 200, 201–
3, 206–7; botanical heat- and light-
seeking in, 153; "A Cold wind stirs the

Victor Shea and William Whitla, Editors/*Essays and Reviews: The 1860 Text and Its Reading*

Marlene Tromp/*The Private Rod: Marital Violence, Sensation, and the Law in Victorian Britain*

Dorice Williams Elliott/*The Angel out of the House: Philanthropy and Gender in Nineteenth-Century England*

Richard Maxwell, Editor/*The Victorian Illustrated Book*

Vineta Colby/*Vernon Lee: A Literary Biography*

E. Warwick Slinn/*Victorian Poetry as Cultural Critique: The Politics of Performative Language*

Simon Joyce/*Capital Offenses: Geographies of Class and Crime in Victorian London*

Caroline Levine/*The Serious Pleasures of Suspense: Victorian Realism and Narrative Doubts*

Emily Davies/*Emily Davies: Collected Letters, 1861–1875*
Edited by Ann B. Murphy and Deirdre Raftery

Joseph Bizup/*Manufacturing Culture: Vindications of Early Victorian Industry*

Lynn M. Voskuil/*Acting Naturally: Victorian Theatricality and Authenticity*

Sally Mitchell/*Frances Power Cobbe: Victorian Feminist, Journalist, Reformer*

Constance W. Hassett/*Christina Rossetti: The Patience of Style*